Based on a collective biography of nearly 700 participants in the Great Migration, this book approaches the social history of seventeenth-century New England in a new way. Unlike previous studies that have examined towns and their inhabitants, *New England's Generation* follows seven shiploads of emigrants through the course of their lives in Old and New England. This approach offers the most comprehensive view ever of the patterns and functions of migration within the new settlements, furnishes new insights into the formation of American Puritan society and culture, and captures the dynamism of life within the first generation of New England settlers.

NEW ENGLAND'S GENERATION

New England's generation

The Great Migration and the formation of society and culture in the seventeenth century

VIRGINIA DEJOHN ANDERSON

CAMBRIDGE
UNIVERSITY PRESS

CAMBRIDGE UNIVERSITY PRESS
Cambridge, New York, Melbourne, Madrid, Cape Town, Singapore, São Paulo, Delhi

Cambridge University Press
32 Avenue of the Americas, New York, NY 10013-2473, USA

www.cambridge.org
Information on this title: www.cambridge.org/9780521447645

An earlier version of Chapter 1 appeared as "Migrants and Motives:
Religion and the Settlement of New England, 1630-1640,"
New England Quarterly, LVIII (1985), 339-83.

First published 1991
First paperback edition 1993
8th printing 2008

Printed in the United States of America

A catalog record for this publication is available from the British Library.

ISBN 978-0-521-40506-5 hardback
ISBN 978-0-521-44764-5 paperback

FOR
MY MOTHER AND FATHER
MY SISTERS AND BROTHERS

Contents

Acknowledgments

The idea for this project germinated over a decade ago when I made a transatlantic migration of my own, albeit one from west to east. In 1976, the Marshall Aid Commemorative Commission granted me a scholarship for two years' study in England. It was during this sojourn in the land that New Englanders left that I began to wonder why they had done so and how their lives had been changed by their decision to cross the ocean.

Several institutions have offered generous financial support over the years. The Department of History at Harvard University supplied the funds for computer processing. In 1983, I became the fortunate recipient of a Whiting Fellowship, which allowed me to take a year off from teaching and complete the dissertation upon which this book is based. In 1990, the Eugene M. Kayden Advisory Committee at the University of Colorado selected this book for its Annual Faculty Manuscript Award, providing funds to subvene the costs of publication.

Much of my research was carried out at the New England Historic Genealogical Society. I would like to thank its director, Ralph Crandall, for his valuable assistance in showing me how best to use the Society's rich collections.

Scholars at several universities have been exceedingly generous of their time, reading various parts of the manuscript and supplying thoughtful suggestions. The late Stephen Botein offered particularly incisive advice as I began to revise the dissertation. Daniel Vickers read much of the manuscript and provided greatly needed help with an intractable chapter. To Jeffrey Adler, Steven Epstein, Henry Gemery, Philip Gura, Ruth Helm, Karen Kupperman, Gloria Main, Jackson Turner Main, and the anonymous reviewers of the manuscript, I also owe many thanks. To Richard Brown, I owe a debt of much longer duration. For nearly two decades, he has offered sound advice and steady encouragement as I sought to fulfill a goal I

Acknowledgments

first set for myself during his undergraduate lectures at the University of Connecticut.

During my years of graduate study at Harvard, I was also fortunate to find both an adviser and a group of friends whose enthusiasm, wit, and moral support contributed mightily to my education in general and to this particular project. From the time of its initial formulation as a dissertation topic, this book has benefited from the keen criticism of Bernard Bailyn. Without his patient direction and the example of his own scholarship and intellectual vitality, this would surely have been a different – and no doubt a less satisfactory – book. In addition, Mina Carson, Barbara DeWolfe, Christopher Jedrey, Jennifer Laurendeau, and Helena Wall all demonstrated admirable forbearance during countless discussions about migrating colonists and unruly computers, for which I shall always be grateful.

Frank Smith, Louise Calabro Gruendel, and the staff of Cambridge University Press deserve many thanks for the care and expeditiousness with which they guided this book through production. I would also like to express my gratitude to Marie DeJohn for her work on the cover design.

This book is dedicated to my parents and siblings, the family in which I grew up and to which I owe more than I can say. But I owe a debt of even greater magnitude to the family with whom I now live. Samuel has given his mother a new appreciation of the powerful ties that bind one generation to the next. And I reserve my deepest gratitude for Fred Anderson – for sharing in the making of this book and, most of all, for sharing his life with me.

Introduction

Seventeenth-century America was nothing if not a collection of societies in flux. In different places at different times, utopian schemes for settlement disintegrated upon contact with New World conditions, virulent diseases wreaked havoc upon native and European populations, harsh systems of bound labor appeared, ethnic and religious tensions spawned repeated conflict, and various groups of Europeans and Indians fought devastating wars against each other. Within this panorama of turmoil, however, New England stood apart as a region of unusual stability. No one could have predicted the eventual shape of society in Virginia, or Maryland, or Pennsylvania from either the plans of their leaders or the initial contours of development in those colonies. But in New England as nowhere else, society evolved according to patterns established in the earliest years of settlement. Only there did the framework of social and cultural institutions created by the very first generation of settlers prove to be remarkably durable. Town-based settlement, the predominance of freehold family farms, comparative economic equality, and a profoundly religious culture – these elements describe seventeenth- and eighteenth-century (and even early-nineteenth-century) New England with almost equal accuracy. Certainly up to the time of the Revolution, no inhabitant of any other region of colonial America could discern in its history anything like New England's pattern of cultural continuity.[1]

To argue thus for New England's long-run stability is not to say that its society was untouched by change. Like the rest of colonial America, New England experienced enormous demographic and geographical expansion. Over time, its economy

[1] For one sensitive exploration of this issue, see Timothy H. Breen and Stephen Foster, "The Puritans' Greatest Achievement: A Study of Social Cohesion in Seventeenth-Century Massachusetts," *Journal of American History*, LX (1973), 5–22.

1

became increasingly commercialized. Its colonists fought deadly wars with indigenous peoples. The Dominion crisis at the end of the seventeenth century ushered in a period of rapid political and institutional change. And although the strength of the settlers' spiritual commitment scarcely diminished over time, the specific nature of their beliefs and the context within which they were expressed gradually altered. Thus a century after its founding, this society, created to promote godly worship, found itself assailed by religious revivalists who intended to restore the pure Christianity they feared had been lost among the descendants of the founders.[2]

But if change was not absent from New England's early history, it never dominated the region's development, as in other colonial societies. Structural alterations were limited and primarily affected political institutions; such changes as the issuing of new charters, it should be noted, were largely imposed from outside rather than generated from within. The modest character of material opportunities in New England prevented the economy from becoming the engine of conflict and social division it became elsewhere in North America. Most important, the region's powerful religious ideology helped to contain potentially disruptive events as they arose.[3] It was, perhaps, because change was so effectively circumscribed within manageable boundaries that New Englanders tended to dwell so obsessively upon the relatively minor problems that worked their way out of the few cracks in their impressively solid cultural foundation.

[2] The persistence of a strong religious tradition in New England is the theme of two recent books: Harry S. Stout, *The New England Soul: Preaching and Religious Culture in Colonial New England* (New York, 1986), and Patricia U. Bonomi, *Under the Cope of Heaven: Religion, Society, and Politics in Colonial America* (New York, 1986). Bonomi argues for the importance of religion in other colonial regions as well.

[3] The cohesive influence of religion was stronger in the seventeenth than in the eighteenth century. In eighteenth-century Connecticut, as Richard Bushman has shown, issues of religion affected political disputes during the Awakening; see *From Puritan to Yankee: Character and the Social Order in Connecticut, 1690–1765* (Cambridge, Mass., 1967). (Compare his account of the Bay Colony in the same period, *King and People in Provincial Massachusetts* [Chapel Hill, N.C., 1985]).

Introduction

Historians have long recognized the essentially stable character of colonial New England society; only recently, however, have we come to appreciate how anomalous New England was within the British colonial world.[4] Much of our knowledge about the contrast between New England and the rest of British America comes from an improved understanding of the ways in which other regions were settled. A flood of scholarship dealing with the southern and middle colonies has revealed the importance of examining the character of immigrant populations (including analysis of age, gender, and racial and ethnic composition), the structure and duration of population movements, and the role of commercial interests in the process of settlement as critical factors in explaining subsequent patterns of social development.[5] We have come to realize that, in these other colonial regions, the processes of settlement themselves launched the evolution of distinctive societies.

New England, no less than other parts of British America, owed much of its social character to its experience of settlement, but the connection has been less fully explored for that region than for other colonies. This book began in my attempt to investigate the extent to which New England's curious cultural and social evolution could be traced to its equally unusual process of settlement. New Englanders were the only colonists in British America self-conscious enough to locate the origins of their society in a "Great Migration," and I hoped to discover why they should have made such a portentous claim, and why this founding event should have come to occupy so prominent a place in the region's cultural heritage. Since the magnitude of

[4] The contrast between New England and the rest of British America informs the argument of Jack Greene, *Pursuits of Happiness: The Social Development of Early Modern British Colonies and the Formation of American Culture* (Chapel Hill, N.C., 1988).

[5] The literature on these subjects is vast and is deftly synthesized in Greene, *Pursuits of Happiness*. On immigration to the colonies just before the Revolution, see also Bernard Bailyn, *Voyagers to the West: A Passage in the Peopling of America on the Eve of the Revolution* (New York, 1986), and for a more general view, see his *The Peopling of British North America: An Introduction* (New York, 1986).

3

the migration that peopled the New England colonies was so slight in comparison to the vastly larger flows of English men and women to other colonial regions, it was clear from the beginning that the movement's claim to greatness had to rest more on symbolic than on objective grounds. But it seemed no less significant (and indeed, all the more interesting) for that fact. Eventually I became convinced that somehow the distinctive New England sense of identity was related to, and perhaps somehow also fostered by, its origins in the Great Migration. But how? And what was the relationship between the discoverable facts of the Great Migration and the symbolic character it assumed in the region's foundation story? How had the lives of the settlers been changed by their translation from English men and women into New Englanders? These were the questions with which I began the project; and, insofar as I have been able to answer them, this book is my response.

In order to study the processes of New England settlement, I selected a research strategy that allowed me to recapture the dynamics of population movement without sacrificing the rich detail of individual lives. This book is essentially a collective biography of 693 English emigrants who participated in the Great Migration. The subjects for study were drawn from evidence that specifically related to their emigration, that is, from passenger lists for seven ships that sailed during the 1630s.[6]

[6] The ship lists were obtained from the following sources. The *Hercules* (sailed from Sandwich in 1635) and another Sandwich ship that sailed in 1637: Eben Putnam, "Two Early Passenger Lists, 1635–1637," *New England Historical and Genealogical Register,* LXXV (1921), 217–27, with corrections by Elizabeth French Bartlett in *NEHGR,* LXXIX (1925), 107–9; a ship from Weymouth, 1635: William S. Appleton, "More Passengers for New-England," *NEHGR,* XXV (1871), 13–15; this is reprinted in John Demos, ed., *Remarkable Providences 1600–1750* (New York, 1972), 39–41; the *James* of Southampton, 1635: Louise Brownell Clarke, *The Greenes of Rhode Island, with Historical Records of English Ancestry, 1534–1902* (New York, 1903), 768–9; the *Rose* and the *Mary Anne,* both of Great Yarmouth, 1637: Charles Boardman Jewson, ed., *Transcripts of Three Registers of Passengers from Great Yarmouth to Holland and New England,* Norfolk Record Society, *Publications,* XXV (1954), 21–3, 29–30; the *Confidence* of Southampton, 1638: Henry Stevens, "Passengers for New En-

Introduction

These seven lists are, so far as I can tell, the only complete published passenger rosters that preserve all the information on the original documents; they are not hypothetical lists reconstructed by genealogists or local historians.[7] Each supplied enough information to permit accurate tracing of specific individuals in New England records. Much of our knowledge of the migration is derived from evidence from the Winthrop Fleet of 1630, but the ships included here sailed later in that decade, when most New Englanders actually arrived: Three of the seven vessels sailed in 1635, three in 1637, and one in 1638.[8] The ships' ports of departure – Sandwich, Weymouth, Southampton, and Great Yarmouth – also reflect what we know of the variety of the settlers' English origins.[9]

gland, 1638," *NEHGR*, II (1848), 108–10, with corrections by H. G. Somerby in *NEHGR*, V (1851), 440. In my choice of a research strategy, I followed the method used so effectively by T. H. Breen and Stephen Foster in their suggestive article, "Moving to the New World: The Character of Early Massachusetts Immigration," *William and Mary Quarterly*, 3rd ser., XXX (1973), 189–220. Breen and Foster also analyzed the two Yarmouth ships and the Sandwich ship from 1637.

[7] Summarized versions of all but the *Confidence* list are in John Camden Hotten, ed., *The Original Lists of Persons of Quality . . . and Others Who Went from Great Britain to the American Plantations, 1600–1700* (London, 1874), xix–xxi, 283–6, 289–95. Incomplete versions of all but the Weymouth list are in Samuel G. Drake, *Result of Some Researches among the British Archives for Information Relative to the Founders of New England: Made in the Years 1858, 1859, and 1860* (Boston, 1860), 44–50, 55–9, 82–5. All of the lists are printed in Charles Edward Banks, *The Planters of the Commonwealth* (Boston, 1930), 114–17, 125–8, 135–9, 181–90, 195–8. Banks usually reordered the lists, often omitting certain information, such as servant status or birthplace, mixing up family or household groups, or adding persons whom he thought belonged to a particular ship, although the names were not listed.

[8] According to John Winthrop's record of arriving vessels, the three busiest years of the migration were 1634, 1635, and 1638; see his *The History of New England from 1630 to 1649*, ed. James Savage, 2 vols. (Boston, 1825), I, passim.

[9] Winthrop's account of ship arrivals likewise indicates that most vessels left from a variety of ports in southern England; his history records ships sailing from London, Southampton, Bristol, Barnstaple, Weymouth, Ipswich, Great Yarmouth, Gravesend, and Sandwich; see *History of New England*, ed. Savage, I, passim.

Once I had collected the names from the seven lists, I followed individual emigrants through the rich genealogical and local historical materials available for seventeenth-century New England and then analyzed the data by computer.[10] This aggregative, quantified data provided the basis for identifying certain modal types of experience among the settlers and, in turn, furnished a meaningful context within which the more detailed stories of individuals and families could be explored. In the chapters that follow, the narrative sketches in the broad outlines of that context, and case studies focus on people whose representativeness has been established by the aggregative analysis. Technical information concerning method and quantification is located in the footnotes and the Appendix, to which readers specifically interested in the presentation of evidence can refer.

The use of representative cases to communicate the character of collective experience raises the larger issue of the degree to which the emigrants studied here are representative of the entire body of New England settlers. Because the 693 emigrants were not chosen randomly from a universe of all participants, but rather comprised the complete set of cases included on the seven ship lists, no claim can be made for perfect representation. Moreover, the survival of information on the migrants in genealogical accounts and local records is simply too irregular to be subjected to the most rigorous quantitative analysis. But if

[10] An invaluable research tool was Clarence Torrey's "New England Marriages Prior to 1700," a bound copy of a manuscript in twelve volumes located at the New England Historic Genealogical Society in Boston (and recently made available on microfilm). This is essentially an index of New England couples, organized by husband's surname, who married in New England before 1700; it also includes couples who married in England and participated in the Great Migration. Next to each couple's name is the date of the marriage, if known, followed by a series of annotations indicating references to the couple in genealogies and local histories. Using Torrey's index eliminated the need to search through a number of genealogies of families with the same surname to find the one containing the emigrant in question. I ultimately consulted over 200 genealogies and local histories in compiling data on the 693 emigrants and was able to find at least some additional information for 83.4 percent of them (578 of 693).

it is difficult to assess the extent to which the group represents the totality of experiences among all participants in the Great Migration, certain evidence suggests that they were at least not *un*representative. Perhaps the best indication is that much of the analysis of demographic patterns and levels of wealth included here corresponds quite closely to data obtained by social historians examining other groups of settlers.[11] In addition, the geographic dispersal of these colonists roughly matches what we know of settlement patterns as a whole for the period; that is, most settlers remained in the Bay Colony or Plymouth, and far fewer traveled to Connecticut, New Haven, Rhode Island, or New Hampshire.[12] And since these colonists, unlike those

[11] Richard Archer's recent analysis of the early New England population provides a useful context within which to evaluate the demographic evidence presented here. Archer has constructed a profile of 22,164 colonists who either migrated to New England before 1650 or were born there between 1620 and 1649. Many of the statistics derived from his much larger sample – such as the age structure of the emigrant population, frequency of geographic mobility among New England's first generation, and rates of remigration back to England – match (sometimes almost identically) the figures presented in this book. See Richard Archer, "New England Mosaic: A Demographic Analysis for the Seventeenth Century," *WMQ*, 3rd ser., XLVII (1990), 477–502. The New England Historic Genealogical Society is currently sponsoring a research project on the Great Migration aimed at gathering as much information as possible on all known emigrants to New England during the 1630s. The completion of this project, which lies well in the future, will also provide valuable perspective on the representativeness of the group of settlers examined here.

[12] One important exception is that Connecticut is probably underrepresented here. Jackson Turner Main has noted that early Connecticut settlers differed in age and family structure from emigrants to Massachusetts. The settlement patterns outlined in this study thus would not have appeared in precisely the same form in Connecticut, although within a few decades the two societies came to resemble each other more closely. See his *Society and Economy in Colonial Connecticut* (Princeton, N.J., 1985), 4–10. Two stylistic points should also be made. Throughout the text, I refer to "New England" as a generic term, much as contemporaries did, although the narrative principally concerns Massachusetts and Plymouth Colony, where nearly 90 percent of these emigrants settled. Second, to avoid repetition, I simply refer throughout the text to "the emigrants," omitting the obvious qualification that I mean the conclusions to pertain only to "the emigrants in this study."

examined in most other treatments of early New England social history, were selected on the basis of their appearance on ship registers rather than their residence in a particular community, their stories may in fact reflect more comprehensively the general experience of the colonial population; at the very least, their patterns of migration within New England are described in greater detail than has previously been possible.

This book, then, offers both a study of individuals and an examination of their collective participation in the Great Migration. It could not have been written without recourse to the unusually rich literature on early New England society and culture that generations of scholars have produced. It does, however, differ from almost all previous work in its prosopographical method and in the questions it seeks to answer. I have not attempted to explore the relationship between the Puritans' experience and the origins of American culture, nor have I tried to describe exhaustively any single aspect of early New England life. The intensive examination of the individual lives of people who were nothing if not ordinary has necessarily precluded the extensive analysis of such formal topics as politics, economics, religion, or family life. Instead, these appear in the narrative only as they emerged in the lives of the emigrants: people whose lives were not made up of topical categories, but rather of attendance when necessary to public matters and attendance at all times to the work, worship, marriage, reproduction, and death that made up daily life.

Following a roughly chronological framework, the narrative explores particularly critical phases in the emigrants' lives. Chapters 1 and 2 focus on the experience of emigration itself, describing the settlers' lives before they set foot in New England. Addressing in the first chapter the question of the emigrants' motivation, I argue that religious factors predominated in making the difficult decision to leave England. This did not mean that economic factors were of no concern to the emigrants, for no matter how steadfast their faith, they could scarcely have afforded to be indifferent to the need to earn their daily bread. Leaders of the migration, seeking to reassure their anxious followers, succeeded in convincing them that such secular concerns, far from threatening their religious purpose, actually harmonized with spiritual goals. So long as prospective settlers aimed to achieve not riches but competency – a modest prosperity that would sustain a family's economic independence – their souls would not be endangered.

Chapter 2 describes the settlers' preparations for departure and the events of the voyage – the singular experience that distinguished New England's first generation from all others to come. The tasks of disengaging themselves from the social, economic, and familial ties that bound them to England and then embarking on a transatlantic voyage (which for most settlers was their first time at sea) created common bonds among people who often had not known one another; indeed, in a real sense these shipboard associations constituted the first "New England communities." Like the towns the emigrants would eventually form on land, these seaborne communities served both practical and spiritual ends. Unlike the later bonds linking townsfolk, however, those forged among shipmates would for the most part prove only temporary. Once safely ashore, the emigrants scattered as they went about settling the new land.

Chapters 3 and 4 investigate, in turn, two of the most pressing challenges that confronted the new colonists: finding a home and making a living in a place quite unlike the England they had left behind. The Great Migration *to* New England, it appears, was followed by a "Great Reshuffling" *within* the region as colonists dispersed and recombined in the dozens of communities they founded within the first decade or two of settlement. Most settlers spent their first few years on the move, settling only when they found a town they liked well enough to make it their permanent home. This distinctive pattern of short-term mobility succeeded by a remarkable persistence grew from the region's equally distinctive system of land distribution, which bestowed enough benefits on town founders to guarantee that latecomers to established communities would find it advantageous to move on and found new towns for themselves. The pursuit of individual advantage, however, never overwhelmed the religious impulse that had inspired the emigration from England. For the most part, settlers steeped in the communal imperatives of their Puritan faith circumscribed their behavior in order to maintain a workable balance between their search for economic security and their commitment to the larger community of which they were members.

Achieving economic security for their families, even within the modest definition sanctioned by Puritan ideals, proved to be no easy task. Chapter 4 explores the ways in which colonists changed occupations and adapted their work lives to suit conditions in a strange new world where land was plentiful but labor and capital were scarce – a place, in other words, utterly unlike the England they had left. Success, as often as not, depended less on English background or previous social status than on versatility and luck: Settlers willing either to abandon their old crafts or to combine such work with farming might do quite well, and in a land hungry for labor, families with several sons enjoyed an advantage over their less prolific neighbors. For most settlers, however, doing well in New England meant no more than achieving a modest prosperity. Nevertheless, this marked one instance, rare in seventeenth-century America, when actual experience matched the aspirations of the colonists. In the end, most New Englanders obtained the competencies with which, their leaders had assured them, God would bless a faithful people.

How such modest achievements as these could ever have been elevated to quasi-mythical status as a – indeed, *the* – Great Migration is the subject of the final chapter. In it I argue that the migration's unique character created a set of conditions that, given the social experience and cultural predispositions of early New Englanders, invited precisely such an interpretation. Because it was brief in duration and made up largely of middling families sharing a common world view, the Great Migration resembled a single event more than a process, and in that it was unlike the much more extended migrations that peopled other parts of British America. The coherence of New England's founding was then magnified by the prolonged survival, as a distinct cohort, of the founders themselves. Alone among New World colonists, New Englanders could identify a single generation of founders responsible for creating virtually everything distinctive and enduring about their society. And only New Englanders shared a religious tradition powerful enough to imbue the founders' efforts with a transcendent significance and to enjoin the commemoration of the founding by successive generations as a duty of both filial and spiritual piety. New England's founding myth had no rivals in early America, and it certainly did not fit the particular histories of other regions. But New Englanders never asserted that their migration's claim to greatness rested on numerical magnitude. In the end, it was their singular interpretation of the movement's meaning, rooted in the experience of a single generation and amplified by a dutiful posterity, that made New England's migration great.

Note: I have made limited alterations to the texts of seventeenth-century sources so that they might correspond more closely to modern usage. I have substituted "i" for "j," "v" for "u," "f" for "ff," and "th" for "y" and have expanded abbreviations. Otherwise, spelling and punctuation are reproduced exactly from the original texts.

1

Decision

Even as they boarded the ship *Hercules* in the spring of 1635, Nathaniel and Lydia Tilden could not have expected to live long in New England. At a time when few English men and women lived past the age of sixty, Nathaniel was nearly fifty-two and Lydia had recently turned forty-seven. Their family bore eloquent witness to the unpredictability of life: Of the dozen children Lydia had borne, five already lay in their graves. The remaining three sons and four daughters would accompany their parents westward across the Atlantic.

The Tildens were leaving the town of Tenterden, located in England's southeasternmost county of Kent. The small community of scarcely 500 inhabitants had been the home of three generations of the family. Although many of his neighbors made their livings through the manufacture of broadcloth, Nathaniel was a prosperous farmer. As the years passed, he achieved considerable local prominence; in 1622, for instance, he was chosen mayor of his town. Yet just over a decade later, Tilden and his family decided to abandon their settled life in Tenterden. Nathaniel rented out his house and lands, gathered his family and seven servants, and began a thirty-mile journey to the port of Sandwich, where the New England-bound *Hercules* lay at anchor.[1]

---

[1] Information on the Tilden family is from Walter Goodwin Davis, *The Ancestry of Joseph Neal 1769–c.1835 of Litchfield, Maine* (Portland, Me. 1945), 53–9. Nathaniel's will, which mentions his rented Tenterden house and lands, is printed in *Mayflower Descendant*, III (1901), 220–2. During the first half of the seventeenth century, the expectation of life at age 30 for English men was 29.8 years; for women it was 29.6 years; see E. A. Wrigley and R. S. Schofield. *The Population History of England, 1541–1871: A Reconstruction* (London, 1981), 250. For expectation of life at birth, see ibid., 252; Peter Laslett, *Family Life and Illicit Love in Earlier Generations* (Cambridge, 1977), 182; and E. A. Wrigley, *Population and History* (New York, 1969), 87. For a discussion of Tenterden, see C. W. Chalklin, *Seventeenth-Century Kent: A Social and Economic History* (London, 1965), 32, 117, 121.

In that same spring of 1635, John and Anthony Emery also decided to sail to the New World. The brothers were relatively young men – John was thirty-five and Anthony thirty-three – but they were already well settled in the small market town of Romsey, Hampshire, where they had been born. Both men were carpenters; having finished their apprenticeships a decade or so earlier, they had probably established a modest trade in Romsey and the surrounding area. The brothers had begun to establish families as well. John and his wife, Alice, were the parents of three children, and Anthony and his wife, Frances, had a son and a daughter.

By early April, the Emerys had disposed of most of their English property, retaining only the clothing, tools, and household goods they could conveniently carry with them. They probably converted the remainder of their possessions into cash, to pay for their passages and help them get started in the New World. As the young men traveled with their families to the nearby port of Southampton to board the *James*, their anxiety about the upcoming voyage may have been tempered with the knowledge that, once they arrived in New England, they would easily find work. Massachusetts settlers had repeatedly implored their English friends to encourage carpenters to emigrate, for their skills were sorely needed. Whether or not they knew it before they sailed, John and Anthony Emery would find a warm welcome at their destination.[2]

Late in March 1637, Anne Nickerson made ready to leave the second most populous city in England. Norwich was the only home she had ever known. Twenty-eight years earlier, her

[2] Information on the Emery brothers is from Elizabeth B. Sumner, *Ancestry and Descendants of James Hensman Coltman and Betsey Tobey* (Los Angeles, 1957), 66–7. John Emery's 1683 will and inventory mention "carpenter turner and joyners tools," which he probably brought with him on the voyage, but mention no real estate in England; probate docket no. 8976, copy in bound volume no. 302, pp. 100–2, Essex County Registry of Deeds and Probate Court, Salem, Mass. For recruitment of carpenters, see, for instance, the letter from Thomas Gostlin to John Winthrop, Jr., in *Winthrop Papers*, 5 vols. (Boston, 1929–47), III, 124–5.

parents had carried her beneath the Anglo-Saxon tower of the church of St. Mary at Coslany, near their home in the northern part of the city, to be baptized. It was perhaps in that same church that Anne had married William Nickerson around the year 1627. She and her husband remained in the city, and over the next decade, Anne bore two daughters and two sons. But in 1637 the Nickersons decided to emigrate and arranged for passage on the *Rose*, bound for Massachusetts. As Anne packed up her family's goods that spring, with two-year-old Robert clamoring for her attention, she could at least take comfort in the knowledge that she was not alone in such activity. In a nearby dwelling, her parents, Nicholas and Bridget Busby, and her sister and brothers, were also preparing to depart. Only her recently married sister Catherine would remain behind.[3]

Both Anne's father and husband were weavers in a city renowned for its textile industry. Nicholas Busby had recently served as city *jurat*, examining Norwich-produced cloth and ensuring that civic standards of manufacture were maintained. There was no reason to doubt that, in time, William Nickerson, whose own career as a freeman worsted weaver was well under way, would have followed in his father-in-law's footsteps and achieved similar recognition.[4] Yet both men intended to remove to a land where their hard-earned skills would be in little demand. As the two families made their way to the port of Great Yarmouth, Anne must have wondered about the wisdom of their actions. How well would her aging parents stand the voyage? How would William manage to feed and house his growing family in Massachusetts?

---

[3] Anna C. Kingsbury, *A Historical Sketch of Nicholas Busby the Emigrant* (n.p., 1924), 5–8, 17–19. Norwich's population at this time was about 15,000; John Patten, *English Towns 1500–1700* (Folkestone, Eng., 1978), 251.

[4] William L. Sachse, ed., *Minutes of the Norwich Court of Mayoralty*, Norfolk Record Society, *Publications*, XV (1942), 68; Winifred M. Rising and Percy Millican, compilers, *An Index of Indentures of Norwich Apprentices Enrolled with the Norwich Assembly Henry VII–George II*, Norfolk Record Society, *Publications*, XXIX (1959), 121.

Even as the Nickerson and Busby families arrived in Great Yarmouth, several residents of that port were also preparing to travel to New England. One prospective colonist was a twenty-nine-year-old shoemaker, William Gault. Unlike the bulk of New England emigrants, who traveled in family groups, Gault would make the trip on his own. For although he had passed the age at which most Englishmen of his time married, Gault had not yet found himself a wife. Nevertheless, the young shoemaker had resolved to sail to Massachusetts, where he, like the Emery brothers, would find a ready demand for his craft. In one other sense, too, New England would not prove a disappointment. Within a few years of his arrival in Salem, Gault would marry at last and start a family.[5]

The Great Migration resulted from thousands of similar individual and family decisions to cross the Atlantic and begin a new life in the New England wilderness. Between 1630 and 1640, over 13,000 men, women, and children boarded the crowded ships that would carry them to Massachusetts's shores. Yet the New England emigrants formed only a tiny current in the much larger stream of English folk who abandoned their homes in the seventeenth century for permanent settlement in other lands. By the 1670s, an estimated 200,000 had been, in the words of one contemporary, "wasted" in the repopulation of Ireland. Nearly 250,000 ventured to colonize the beautiful but deadly islands of the Caribbean, and over 100,000 sought to wrest a profit from the mosquito-infested regions of the southern mainland. Simply in terms of numbers, then, any one of these migrations could lay a better claim

---

[5] The information about Gault is scanty – as it is for many of the single emigrants. See the data from the ship list itself in Charles Boardman Jewson, ed., *Transcript of Three Registers of Passengers from Great Yarmouth to Holland and New England*, Norfolk Record Society, *Publications*, XXV (1954), 30 (hereafter, Jewson, ed., *Transcript of Three Registers*); Sidney Perley, *The History of Salem, Massachusetts*, 3 vols. (Salem, Mass., 1924), II, 30. For the age at marriage for Englishmen in this period, see Peter Laslett, *The World We Have Lost*, 2nd ed. (London, 1971), 85, where he finds that the median age at marriage for a sample of 1,000 men was about 25.5 years.

to greatness than could the relatively insignificant trickle of passengers bound for New England.[6]

But those who christened the movement never intended to commemorate its size. The name was invented not by the founders of New England but by their descendants, who wished to celebrate the religious mission of their forefathers. Their ancestors, they believed, had fled to the New World for conscience's sake. Harassed in England for their Puritan beliefs, they realized that their only chance for peace lay in moving to a place beyond the reach of Anglican officials. They chose New England as their destination, a wilderness home where God's saving remnant could re-create the pure church of apostolic times. Though small in size, this migration was great in purpose.

For years, historians have disagreed about the precise causes of the exodus to New England. Some have taken the emigrants at their word and emphasized spiritual motives; others have insisted that a desire for economic improvement lay at the heart of the migration – much as it did in the migrations to the Chesapeake and the West Indies.[7] Still other scholars have argued more recently that a combination of religious, economic, social, and political factors informed individual decisions to move, and that these tangled strands defy unraveling.[8]

[6] Henry A. Gemery, "Emigration from the British Isles to the New World, 1630–1700: Inferences from Colonial Populations," *Research in Economic History*, V (1980), 180, 197–8, 212. Comment about Ireland is from Reynal's *The True English Interest* (1674), quoted in Wrigley and Schofield, *Population History of England*, 224.

[7] For interpretations stressing religious motivation, see Nellis M. Crouse, "Causes of the Great Migration, 1630–1640," *New England Quarterly*, V (1932), 3–36; Samuel Eliot Morison, *Builders of the Bay Colony* (Boston, 1930; rev. ed., 1958), 379–86; Allen French, *Charles I and the Puritan Upheaval: A Study of the Causes of the Great Migration* (Boston, 1955). For arguments emphasizing economic factors, see James Truslow Adams, *The Founding of New England* (Boston, 1921), 121–2; Charles E. Banks, "Religious 'Persecution' as a Factor in Emigration to New England, 1630–1640," Massachusetts Historical Society, *Proceedings*, LXIII (1930), 138–51 (which is followed by a rebuttal by S. E. Morison on pp. 151–4).

[8] N. C. P. Tyack, "Migration from East Anglia to New England Before 1660" (Ph.D. diss., University of London, 1951); T. H. Breen and Stephen Foster, "Moving to the New World: The Character of Early Massachusetts Immigra-

Nevertheless, the Great Migration, taken as a whole, displayed certain distinctive characteristics that provide clues to understanding its origins. First of all, this migration, unlike other English colonization movements of the period, was exceedingly brief. Emigration to the Chesapeake continued for more than a century, but the movement to New England lasted scarcely a decade. It began rather abruptly with the sailing of the Winthrop Fleet in 1630 and ended just as suddenly a dozen years later, shortly before the outbreak of the English Civil War. The disruptions of that conflict alone cannot account for the end of the Great Migration, for the total outflow of English emigrants to the New World was as high during the decade of the 1640s as it had been during the 1630s.[9] But for some reason, very few of these later emigrants chose to make New England their destination.

The opening and closing dates of the Great Migration coincided with the height of the Puritan crisis in England. When Charles I dissolved Parliament in 1629, he deprived the Puritan gentry of any way to protest royal policies through legitimate political channels. Eleven years later, compelled by financial hardship and war with Scotland, the king reopened Parliament and unleashed a pent-up flood of opposition. But this was an opposition tinged with hope; with Charles ensnared in fiscal and political difficulties, the Puritan gentry (and other dissidents) might reasonably have expected to exert greater control

tion," *William and Mary Quarterly*, 3rd ser., XXX (1973), 203; David Grayson Allen, *In English Ways: The Movement of Societies and the Transferal of English Local Law and Custom to Massachusetts Bay in the Seventeenth Century* (Chapel Hill, N.C., 1981), 163–204; David Cressy, *Coming Over: Migration and Communication between England and New England in the Seventeenth Century* (Cambridge, 1987), ch. 3. In a recent article, Tyack argues that religion may well have encouraged the emigration of "humbler folk"; see his "The Humbler Puritans of East Anglia and the New England Movement: Evidence from the Court Records of the 1630s," *New England Historical and Genealogical Register*, CXXXVIII (1984), 79–106.

[9] Gemery, "Emigration from the British Isles to the New World," *Research in Economic History*, V (1980), table A.6., 216. Two years before the Winthrop Fleet sailed, the Massachusetts Bay Company dispatched a small contingent of settlers, who settled at Salem.

over the course of events. The end of the migration to New England thus coincided with the resurgence of Puritan political power in England. Why travel 3,000 miles to create a new society when one could now remake the world at home?[10]

The simultaneous timing of the Great Migration and the English political crisis could not simply have been the product of coincidence, and most accounts of the migration that argue for the movement's religious origins emphasize the participation of Puritans, particularly the Puritan gentry who helped to finance colonization efforts (but who were conspicuously reluctant to emigrate themselves) and the hundreds of ministers who did sail to the New World.[11] The contributions of these individuals obviously helped the movement to succeed, but their efforts would have been in vain had not thousands of ordinary settlers also agreed to move to New England. Any examination of the causes of the Great Migration must address the motives not only of the leaders but also of the followers. And in the case of New England, the composition of the emigrant population sharply differed from that of other emigrant groups moving to destinations elsewhere in British America. It was not, as in the Chesapeake, primarily made up of single young men eager to better their lot, but rather of family groups who might seem unlikely candidates for emigration. The first step toward understanding the Great Migration, then, is an exploration of precisely who these unusual emigrants were, for from that knowledge it becomes possible to discern their reasons for moving to New England.

I

No population of migrants ever precisely replicates the larger population of its original society because migration is by its

---

[10] For a general discussion of the events of the decade preceding the English Civil War, see Conrad Russell, *The Crisis of Parliaments: English History 1509–1660* (Oxford, 1971), 299–341.

[11] Over 200 clergymen traveled to New England before 1660; see Harry S. Stout, "University Men in New England, 1620–1660: A Demographic Analysis," *Journal of Interdisciplinary History*, IV (1974), 377.

nature a selective process. Indeed, most of the people who left the British Isles for the New World in the seventeenth century were radically *unlike* the British population in composition: They were, among other things, overwhelmingly young, male, and unmarried. Thus the single most striking fact that an examination of the Great Migration discloses is how comparatively ordinary the migrants looked – how much *like* the nonmigrating English population. There were of course differences, important ones, between those who left for New England and those who stayed behind. But the fact remains – and its significance can scarcely be overstated – that participants in the Great Migration more closely resembled the English population as a whole than did any other group of emigrants leaving for any other part of the New World.

The young, single males who constituted the bulk of England's emigrants to America in the seventeenth century went overwhelmingly to the tobacco and sugar plantations of the South. Groups of emigrants to the Chesapeake in the seventeenth century, for instance, consistently included a majority of people in their twenties.[12] But among the New England settlers, young adults were far less predominant: Just a quarter of the emigrants were in their twenties when they boarded ship in the 1630s.[13] In fact, the age structure of New England's emi-

[12] James Horn, "Servant Emigration to the Chesapeake in the Seventeenth Century," in Thad W. Tate and David L. Ammerman, eds., *The Chesapeake in the Seventeenth Century: Essays on Anglo-American Society and Politics* (New York, 1979), 61–2; Edmund S. Morgan, *American Slavery, American Freedom: The Ordeal of Colonial Virginia* (New York, 1975), 408. See also Richard S. Dunn, *Sugar and Slaves: The Rise of the Planter Class in the English West Indies, 1624–1713* (Chapel Hill, N.C., 1972), 53.

[13] See Table 1 in the Appendix. All the aggregate information is derived from a computer-aided analysis of 693 emigrants, using the Statistical Package for the Social Sciences. Although some information was available for nearly every emigrant, the mix of types of information varied for each individual. Therefore, depending upon the variables employed, the totals vary in different tables. The coverage for some major variables is as follows: sex, 97.9 percent (679/693); age at migration, 59.6 percent (413/693); English town or parish of residence, 85.1 percent (590/693); occupation (for adult males), 77.7 percent (139/179).

grant population closely resembled that of the home country, with both infancy and old age represented. The *Rose* of Great Yarmouth, for instance, carried one-year-old Thomas Baker as well as Katherine Rabey, a widow of sixty-eight, and this span of ages was by no means unique. In 1632 the Reverend Thomas Welde reported that he traveled with "very aged" passengers, "twelve persons being all able to make well nigh one thousand years," and several others among his shipmates were infants.[14]

The age structure of the emigrant population, though remarkably similar to that of England, was of course not identical to it. The principal differences between the two – essentially a relative dearth of older people and a relative abundance of youth among the settlers – stemmed from the peculiar demands of migration.[15] The hardships accompanying a transatlantic voyage and wilderness settlement evidently daunted prospective emigrants of advanced years. These same conditions, however, provided less discouragement to young adults, who clearly believed that the potential benefits of migration outweighed the risks. Yet even with these qualifications in mind, the fact remains that New England, more than any other seventeenth-century English settlement, attracted people of all ages, and in so doing retained a comparatively normal, multigenerational population structure even in its earliest years.

Similarly, the relative proportions of men and women in the New England emigrant group resembled those of England's or any other normal population – and sharply contrasted with the proportions in other English colonies. If, as one historian has noted, "women were scarcer than corn or liquor in Virginia,"

[14] See Table 2 in the Appendix. Thomas Welde to his Former Parishioners at Tarling, June–July 1632, in Everett Emerson, ed., *Letters from New England: The Massachusetts Bay Colony, 1629–1638*, The Commonwealth Series (Amherst, Mass., 1976), 95.

[15] Only about 1 percent of the emigrants were aged sixty or more, whereas just over 8 percent of England's population belonged to that age category in 1636. The proportion of colonists aged fifteen to twenty-four (26.2 percent), however, outweighed the proportion of English people in that same category (17.7 percent). See Table 2 in the Appendix. Note that in the other age ranges, the percentages of colonists and English folk are almost identical.

they were more abundant than bibles in New England. In the second decade of Chesapeake settlement, there were four or five men for each woman; by the end of the seventeenth century, there were still about three men for every two women.[16] Nearly half of the New England emigrants, however, were female, and this preservation of normal patterns assured the young men of New England greater success than their southern counterparts in finding wives.[17]

The comparatively normal age structure and sex ratio stemmed from the important fact that the Great Migration was primarily a transplantation of families. Nearly nine out of ten emigrants traveled in family groups of one sort or another, and three out of four came in nuclear family units – that is, groups composed of husbands and wives, with or without children.[18] When solitary spouses migrated with their children, they generally intended either to meet a partner already in New England or to wait for his or her arrival on a later ship. Grandparents infrequently booked passage on the emigrant ships, but a few hardy elders made the trip, usually in the company of their children or grandchildren. In 1637, for instance, Margaret Neave sailed to Massachusetts with her granddaughter Rachel Dixson, who was probably an orphan. In the following year, Alice Stephens joined her sons William and John and their families on the voyage. These instances of vertically extended families, including members of three generations, were less common than cases in which emigrant family structure extended horizontally, within a single generation. For example, several groups of brothers, such as the Stephenses and the

[16] Morgan, *American Slavery, American Freedom*, 111, n. 16, 336. See also Russell R. Menard, "Immigrants and Their Increase: The Process of Population Growth in Early Colonial Maryland," in Aubrey C. Land, Lois Green Carr, and Edward C. Papenfuse, eds., *Law, Society, and Politics in Early Maryland* (Baltimore, 1977), 96.

[17] See Table 3 in the Appendix. The ratio varied somewhat among individual ships. The *Rose* was the only vessel carrying a majority of women (sex ratio = 84), whereas the *James*, with nearly two men for every woman, had the most unbalanced ratio (184).

[18] See Table 4 in the Appendix.

Emerys, made the trip together. And when the three Goodenow brothers decided to leave the West Country, they did not depart before convincing their unmarried sister Ursula to come with them.

For most New England settlers, therefore, transatlantic migration did not lead to permanent separation from close relatives. A few unscrupulous men and women apparently sailed in order to flee unhappy marriages, but this was scarcely common. Instead, most nuclear family units arrived in New England intact.[19] When close kin were left behind, they usually joined their families within a year or so. Samuel Lincoln, for instance, who traveled aboard the *Rose* in 1637, joined his brother Thomas, who had sailed four years earlier. Another brother, Stephen, arrived in 1638 with his family and his mother. Edward Johnson, who first crossed the ocean with the Winthrop Fleet in 1630, returned to England in 1637 to fetch his wife and seven children. And for Thomas Starr, who left Sandwich in 1637, migration brought a reunion with his older brother Comfort, a passenger on the *Hercules* two years earlier. Migration made some disruption of kin ties unavoidable, but it was by no means the rule.

Thus the bulk of the emigrants, like the bulk of English folk, continued to live in families – but the families bound for New England were of a special kind. The ships carried mature couples, generally in their thirties, who had been married for about a decade. Given their ages, such couples were likely to have established themselves within their communities. Their families were, on average, slightly larger than those of other English people; emigrant couples with children usually had

---

[19] In about 80 percent of the cases for which there is information (61 of 77), nuclear families moving to New England brought all of their members along. Only eight families – about 10 percent – are known for certain to have left members behind in England. Seventeenth-century court records are interspersed with orders for husbands and wives to rejoin their spouses either in England or New England; see, for instance, George Francis Dow, ed., *Records and Files of the Quarterly Courts of Essex County, Massachusetts*, 8 vols. (Salem, Mass., 1911–21), I, 123–4, 137, 159, 160, 166, 208, 228, 229, 231, 244, 245, 274, 275, 306, 360.

three or more. The typical emigrant family was therefore *complete* – composed of husband, wife, and children – but not yet *completed*. These were families-in-progress, with parents who were at most halfway through their reproductive years and whose continued fertility would make possible New England's remarkable rate of population growth. And these children, both English and American born, proved to be essential sources of labor in a primitive colonial economy.[20]

This same need for labor also encouraged a comparatively large number of emigrants to sail to New England as individuals – comparatively large, that is, relative to the numbers of bachelors and spinsters in the English population but nowhere near the proportion of young, single individuals in England's other New World colonies. At a time when only about 5 percent of English households included one member, 38 percent of the emigrant households apparently consisted of a single individual. Most of these solitary emigrants had never been married and were male (men outnumbered women by ten to one) and young, generally in their twenties.[21] The range of skills they brought with them was wide: Their numbers included shoemakers, a carpenter, butcher, tanner, hempdresser, weaver, cutler, fuller, physician, tailor, mercer, and skinner;

[20] The average age of emigrant husbands was 37.4 years ($N = 81$); for their wives the average was 33.8 ($N = 55$). Ninety out of 99 emigrant families traveled with children. The average number was 3.08, compared to an average of 2.76 for a sample of 100 English communities in this period. See Table 5 in the Appendix and Peter Laslett, "Mean Household Size in England since the Sixteenth Century," in Peter Laslett and Richard Wall, eds., *Household and Family in Past Time: Comparative Studies in the Size and Structure of the Domestic Group over the Last Three Centuries in England, France, Serbia, Japan and Colonial North America, with Further Materials from Western Europe* (Cambridge, 1972), 148.
[21] See Table 4 in the Appendix, which shows that sixty-three people traveled as "solitaries," comprising 38 percent of emigrant households although only 11 percent of the total number of passengers. Not all of these people, of course, would live on their own in New England, but rather would lodge with families. Servants are not included in this category but with the household with which they traveled. The percentage of English one-person households is based on table 4.8 in Laslett, "Mean household size," in Laslett and Wall, eds., *Household and Family in Past Time*, 146.

only half a dozen were unskilled (but also valuable) laborers. Few would remain solitary for long in New England, as ties of marriage soon linked them to family networks in their towns. Within a few years of his arrival in 1635, for instance, Henry Ewell, a young shoemaker from Sandwich in Kent, joined the church in Scituate and married the daughter of a prominent local family. William Paddy, a London skinner, managed to obtain land, find a wife, and get elected to Plymouth's first general court of deputies within four years of his voyage.[22]

But transforming wilderness into farmland demanded more labor than growing families and a sizable group of single workmen could supply. Thus more than half of the emigrant families (and at least a few single emigrants) brought servants to New England. In so doing, they perhaps heeded the advice of one early observer of the region who noted that "men of good estates may do well there, always provided that they go well accommodated with servants." These servants (most of whom were male) formed an integral part – just over 17 percent – of the colonizing population and were, in fact, proportionally more numerous during this initial period of settlement than they had been in England or would be later in New England. Their presence contributed heavily to New England's early success by substantially increasing the ratio of producers to consumers in the newly settled towns.[23]

[22] For Henry Ewell, see James Savage, *A Genealogical Dictionary of the First Settlers of New England, Showing Three Generations of Those Who Came before May, 1692, . . .* , 4 vols. (Boston, 1860–2), II, 132; C. F. Swift, *Genealogical Notes of Barnstable Families, Being a Reprint of the Amos Otis Papers, Originally Published in the Barnstable Patriot*, 2 vols. (Barnstable, Mass., 1888), I, 359. For William Paddy, see Savage, *Genealogical Dictionary*, III, 328–9; Charles Henry Pope, *The Pioneers of Massachusetts, A Descriptive List, Drawn from Records of Colonies, Towns, and Churches, and Other Contemporaneous Documents* (Boston, 1900), 338.

[23] William Wood, *New England's Prospect*, ed. Alden T. Vaughan, The Commonwealth Series (Amherst, Mass., 1977), 70. See Table 4 in the Appendix and Laslett, "Mean Household Size," in Laslett and Wall, eds., *Household and Family in Past Time*, 152. Ann Kussmaul, in examining the prevalence of servants in husbandry – not domestic servants – found that they comprised 1 to 13 percent of the population in a sample of six seventeenth-

Decision

Household heads, however, evidently realized the dangers of having too much of a good thing. Servants, after all, had to have their passages paid for and had to be fed, clothed, and housed. In *New England's Prospect*, William Wood warned would-be emigrants to be selective in engaging additional laborers. "It is not the multiplicity of many bad servants (which presently eats a man out of house and harbor, as lamentable experience hath made manifest)," he wrote, "but the industry of the faithful and diligent laborer that enricheth the careful master; so that he that hath many dronish servants shall soon be poor and he that hath an industrious family shall as soon be rich." Most families attempted to strike a balance between their need for labor and their supply of resources by transporting only a few servants. Nearly half of the families brought just one and another quarter of them brought only two.[24]

In these industrious families with their diligent servants lay key ingredients of New England's future success. If the emigrant population did not precisely replicate that of the mother country, it nevertheless ensured that New Englanders would produce a

century parishes; see her *Servants in Husbandry in Early Modern England* (Cambridge, 1981), 12. Peter Laslett calculated that in Clayworth in 1676, servants were present in 31 percent of the households and comprised 16.7 percent of the population; see *Family Life and Illicit Love*, 90. Since the vast majority of New England servants were male (80 of 114), Kussmaul's figures may provide the more relevant comparison here, indicating that servants in early New England may have been up to twice as common as in England. In addition, Wrigley and Schofield calculated the "dependency ratio" for England over five-year intervals for the period from 1541 to 1871. This ratio measures the number of persons aged zero to fourteen years and over sixty years – presumably those too young or too old to provide much productive labor – as a proportion of every 1,000 persons in the general population. In England in 1636, the dependency ratio was 674 per 1,000; among the New England emigrants studied here, the comparable figure was a considerably lower 475 per 1,000. Wrigley and Schofield, *Population History of England*, 528. For a discussion of the decline of servant labor and the growing reliance on family labor in early New England, see Daniel Vickers, "Working the Fields in a Developing Economy: Essex County, Massachusetts, 1630–1675," in Stephen Innes, ed., *Work and Labor in Early America* (Chapel Hill, N.C., 1988), 49–69.

[24] Wood, *New England's Prospect*, ed. Vaughan, 70–1.

close facsimile of English society. In particular, the predominance of families preserved traditional patterns of patriarchal authority and kinship ties that contributed to social stability. The relatively youthful age structure and even sex ratio promised rapid population growth as emigrant families continued to have children and new families were steadily being formed. Compared to that of England, moreover, this was a labor-maximizing population, with its relative abundance of young workers and servants setting their hands to building a new society in the wilderness – a society in which they too would be full members as they married and started families of their own. But if New England's was the most normal of emigrant populations in the seventeenth century in terms of its demographic structure, the reasons for its transplantation were anything but the ordinary reasons for which English people chose to leave their homes. A look at the English origins of these colonists reveals more clues to the nature of the Great Migration and its causes.

II

The demographic profile of the New England settlers indicates that they were no ordinary migrants, and an examination of their transatlantic exodus demonstrates that it was no ordinary migration. We now know that in this period England's population was extremely mobile, but the Great Migration was not simply an extension of this internal movement. The difference was not merely the greater distance of the ocean passage; instead it stemmed from the character and motivation of the people involved in each case. Within England, migrants tended to be young, poor, and bound for the cities in search of a better life. The New England emigrants, as we have seen, were not, on the whole, particularly young; nor were they particularly poor, and, far from seeking their fortunes in the cities, they moved to what they typically called "a howling wilderness." Their distinctive experience grew from special circumstances that uprooted what otherwise would probably have been a rather stable group of people. The emigrants' reasons for moving across the ocean, in other words, differed from those that compelled other English men and women to move within their homeland.

Dominating all discussions of England's internal migration is the assumption that the search for economic improvement spurred people to take to the roads. In the late sixteenth and early seventeenth centuries, rapid population growth, periodic agricultural depression, and difficulties in England's preeminent industry of textile manufacture disrupted many lives and caused real hardship. Migration offered an obvious escape from unfavorable local conditions, and countless people availed themselves of this option. Since most sought their fortunes in the diversified economies of urban areas, the net effect was an enormous surge of people out of the countryside and into towns and cities. London absorbed the bulk of these migrants; by 1650 an estimated 8,000 people were flocking to the capital each year from all over the country. Provincial centers such as Norwich, Canterbury, and Bristol likewise attracted newcomers from their own hinterlands.[25]

Most of these English migrants were young and poor –

[25] For a general discussion of the English economy in this period, see Keith Wrightson, *English Society 1580–1680* (London, 1982), and B. E. Supple, *Commercial Crisis and Change in England 1600–1642: A Study in the Instability of a Mercantile Economy* (Cambridge, 1959). Specialized regional studies include Peter Clark, *English Provincial Society from the Reformation to the Revolution: Religion, Politics, and Society in Kent, 1500–1640* (Hassocks, Sussex, 1977); G. D. Ramsay, *The Wiltshire Woollen Industry in the Sixteenth and Seventeenth Centuries*, 2nd ed. (London, 1965); K. J. Allison, "The Norfolk Worsted Industry in the Sixteenth and Seventeenth Centuries," *Yorkshire Bulletin of Economic and Social Research*, XII (1960), 73–83, and XIII (1961), 61–77. Studies of internal migration include John H. C. Patten, "Patterns of Migration and Movement of Labour to Three Pre-Industrial East Anglian Towns," *Journal of Historical Geography*, II (1976), 111–29; John Patten, *Rural–Urban Migration in Pre-Industrial England* (Oxford University, School of Geography, *Research Papers*, No. 6, 1973); Peter Clark, "The migrant in Kentish towns, 1580–1640," in Peter Clark and Paul Slack, eds., *Crisis and Order in English Towns, 1500–1700* (London, 1972), 117–63; Peter Spufford, "Population Mobility in Pre-Industrial England," *Genealogists' Magazine*, XVII (1973–4), 420–9, 475–80, 537–43; E. A. Wrigley, "A Simple Model of London's Importance in Changing English Society and Economy, 1650–1760," *Past and Present*, XXXVII (1967), esp. 45–9.

although their poverty was often a function of their youth rather than an indication of permanent economic marginality. These movers, generally between the ages of fifteen and twenty-five or so, sought positions as servants or apprentices; most doubtless hoped to end their years of mobility by settling down as farmers or craftsmen. There was, of course, also an underclass of permanently poor folk who wandered from place to place in search of a bare subsistence and whose presence disturbed an increasing number of their more fortunate countrymen. But theirs was not the common experience; instead, mobility generally accompanied adolescence and ceased with marriage and family formation.[26]

It was precisely at the time of life when most English people ended their youthful years of migration, however, that the prospective New England settlers left their homes. Nearing middle age and encumbered with family responsibilities, they undertook the longest and undoubtedly the most hazardous journey of their lives. In so doing, a very large proportion left the sorts of places that were ordinarily the *destinations* of migrants – urban areas. Indeed, the social and economic backgrounds of the would-be colonists suggest that they had much more to lose than to gain from migration.

Prior to their departure for New England, most settlers lived in one of two types of places: urban areas or wood-pasture agricultural communities. The urban origins of the emigrants are particularly striking: At a time when only about one out of five English people was a town dweller, at least one out of three emigrants lived in a community with 3,000 or more inhabitants. Nearly 150 prospective settlers came from three large towns alone – Norwich, Canterbury, and Salisbury. If the definition of "urban" is broadened to include market towns, a majority of the emigrants – about six out of ten – may be considered urban dwellers. Most market towns, of course, were substantially smaller than provincial capitals such as Norwich or Canterbury;

---

[26] Spufford, "Population Mobility," *Genealogists' Magazine*, XVII (1973–4), 422–4, 537; Clark, "The Migrant in Kentish Towns," in Clark and Slack, eds., *Crisis and Order*, 138–45, 150–3.

nevertheless, these communities served as centers of commercial activity and often of the social life of their surrounding areas, and thus offered their inhabitants a more complex setting for their daily lives.[27]

Because urban residence prevailed far more among the prospective emigrants than among the English population at large, the future New Englanders had considerably more experience than the typical English man or woman with the relatively cosmopolitan atmosphere of these larger and more populous settlements. In such places, the emigrants encountered, and sometimes participated in, complex systems of borough government. They lived among more diverse local populations that often included sizable groups of continental refugees. They frequently dwelled in close proximity to centers of civil and ecclesiastical administration. Perhaps most important, they regularly participated in diversified market economies. Large towns typically contained a wide spectrum of occupational activities and often – as in the cases of Norwich and Canterbury, with their textile industries – supported manufacturing as well as commercial endeavors. Both as producers and as consumers, the emigrants contributed daily to local economies of considerable complexity and sophistication.[28]

[27] Out of 590 emigrants with known English residences, 200 (33.9 percent) came from the seven towns of Norwich (83), Canterbury (35), Salisbury (29), Great Yarmouth (27), Maidstone (15), Dover (8), and London (3). Each of these towns had more than 3,000 inhabitants; population figures are from John Patten, *English Towns 1500–1700* (Folkestone, Kent, 1978), 106, 111–12, 251; C. W. Chalklin, *Seventeenth-Century Kent: A Social and Economic History* (London, 1965), 30–1; Wrigley, "A Simple Model," *Past and Present*, XXXVII (1967), 44. For market towns, see Alan Everitt, "The Marketing of Agricultural Produce," in Joan Thirsk, ed., *The Agrarian History of England and Wales*, IV, 1500–1640 (Cambridge, 1967), 470–5, 488–90. A total of 364 emigrants (61.7 percent of 590 with known residence) lived in communities identified by Everitt as market towns. Although the number of Londoners in this group of emigrants is quite small, many more did move to New England.

[28] For some prospective colonists, urban residence indicated earlier mobility in accordance with the general patterns of English internal migration. Edmund Hawes, for instance, moved from Warwickshire to London to be trained as a cutler and Michael Metcalf made a shorter move from an outlying village to Norwich when he became a weaver's apprentice. See

Many emigrants thus had lived in comparatively open communities: places where population turnover, commercial activity, cultural diversity, and often religious dissent combined to loosen the ties of traditional authority normally associated with life in England's rural villages.[29] It is therefore especially significant that even those prospective colonists who lived in the countryside generally came from relatively open settlements located in wood-pasture areas. These areas specialized in the raising of livestock on cultivated meadows; because pastures often were separated by hedges and stands of trees, such regions appeared thickly wooded in comparison with open-field areas elsewhere in the country. Whether in East Anglia, the Kentish Weald, or the West Country, wood-pasture communities shared distinctive patterns of economic and social organization that fostered individual autonomy. Manorial institutions were particularly weak and therefore exercised little control over farming practices, land distribution, or inheritance. Much of the land was enclosed to form family farms that tended to be dispersed across the countryside rather than gathered into nucleated villages. The emphasis on cattle and pig raising necessitated regular access to markets, both for the sale of meat and dairy products and for the purchase of foodstuffs for domestic consumption. In addition, the specialized tasks of the livestock farmer left slack time, particularly in winter, which encouraged such nonagricultural byemployments as wool combing or flax weaving. Wood-pasture areas thus supported "communit[ies] of individualists," afford-

James W. Hawes, "The English Ancestors of Edmond Hawes of Yarmouth, Mass.," *Library of Cape Cod History and Genealogy*, No. 92 (1912), 1–12; Isaac Stevens Metcalf, *Metcalf Genealogy* (Cleveland, 1898), 8. Information on the emigrants' history of migration within England is too scanty to permit generalization, although it is interesting to note that at least fourteen adult male emigrants were still living in their birthplaces when they decided to move to New England.

[29] For the connections between cities and Puritanism, see, for instance, Paul S. Seaver, *The Puritan Lectureships: The Politics of Religious Dissent, 1560–1662* (Stanford, Calif., 1970), esp. chs. 4–5; John T. Evans, *Seventeenth-Century Norwich: Politics, Religion, and Government, 1620–1690* (Oxford, 1979); Clark, *English Provincial Society*.

ing their inhabitants more opportunities to work and allocate resources independently than any other part of rural England.[30]

In sum, the New England colonists not only began their migration at a time of life when most of their countrymen were settling down, but they also abandoned the sorts of communities where the range of economic choices and relative freedom of individual behavior were more likely to attract inhabitants rather than to encourage their departure. Moreover, within these communities, the emigrants had apparently attained a degree of economic security that would seem further to have discouraged their transplantation to America. Far from belonging to the poorer segments of English society, most emigrants came from the relatively prosperous middling section – precisely the sort of people for whom the costs of wilderness settlement were quite likely to be high indeed.

Most adult male emigrants worked as artisans prior to their departure for New England, an experience that also distinguished them from most of their fellow countrymen. One late-seventeenth-century observer estimated that, in England as a whole, farmers outnumbered craftsmen by more than seven to one; among the prospective colonists, however, artisans were nearly twice as numerous as farmers.[31] As significant as their numerical preponderance was the fact that the emigrant artisans

[30] Joan Thirsk, "The Farming Regions of England," in Thirsk, ed., *AHEW*, IV, 46–9, 57–9, 67–8, 79–80, quotation from p. 48; David Underdown, *Revel, Riot, and Rebellion: Popular Politics and Culture in England, 1603–1660* (Oxford, 1985), esp. chs. 1–4. Some – though relatively few – emigrants came from England's other predominantly agricultural region, that of sheep rearing and grain growing under cooperative farming regimes.

[31] The observation about England's population was made by Gregory King in 1696; see Charles Wilson, *England's Apprenticeship, 1603–1763* (London, 1965), 239. For a breakdown of the emigrants' occupations, see Table 6 in the Appendix. An even more striking artisanal predominance was noted by N. C. P. Tyack for 147 East Anglian emigrants. He found 16.3 percent of his sample in agriculture, 23.1 percent in cloth trades, 26.5 percent in other artisanal trades, 3.4 percent each in trade and maritime occupations, and 27.2 percent in the professions. This last figure includes a large number of ministers leaving East Anglia in the early 1630s; see Tyack, "Migration from East Anglia," Appendix III.

generally worked only within a narrow range of trades – principally those involved with woodworking, leather working, and the manufacture of cloth. Within these general areas, moreover, the emigrants usually practiced skilled trades that placed them on the middle rungs of the economic ladder. For instance, although nearly half of the emigrant craftsmen worked in the textile trades, together they followed only six out of dozens of possible occupations connected with that highly specialized manufacture. Thirty of the thirty-five clothworkers were either tailors or weavers; the others included two mercers, a clothier, a calenderer, and a fuller. The pattern also held for artisans working outside cloth manufacture; of the forty-six men in this group, over half were either shoemakers or carpenters. Most of the emigrant craftsmen, in other words, worked at trades that demanded a substantial investment of time and money for training and capital equipment and that promised at least an adequate living from the production of finished goods.[32]

Emigrants who made their livings from agriculture likewise came neither from the highest nor the lowest social and economic ranks. At the top of seventeenth-century agrarian society stood the county gentry; below them, in descending order, came yeomen, husbandmen, and landless laborers. This rural hierarchy encompassed both wealth and status, with an individual's position often defined by local opinion as well as income. Landholding, of course, was the key to the system, and the amount of land one held was apparently more important than the kind of tenure under which one held it. Those accorded yeoman status generally farmed substantial estates of fifty acres or more, whereas husbandmen worked smaller plots. It was from this latter group of less affluent –although by no means poor – husbandmen that the rural emigrants principally came: Thirty husbandmen emigrated, compared to just five yeomen and a dozen laborers.[33]

[32] See Table 6 in the Appendix.

[33] See Table 6 in the Appendix. Tyack found a similar result, counting twenty-two husbandmen, one yeoman, and one "farmer"; "Migration from East Anglia," 54–6; Appendix III, vi–via. For a general discussion of these categories, see Wrightson, *English Society,* 31; Mildred Campbell, *The*

Decision

Occupation alone cannot provide a conclusive guide to economic welfare, but when supplemented with other information, it can offer an important clue to the emigrants' relative prosperity. Here it is worth recalling the emigrants' ages. The average age of husbands was thirty-seven years, around midcareer in terms of seventeenth-century life spans. A decade or more past completion of their apprenticeships or terms of service, such men were well established in trades or on farms, yet not so old as to have begun dividing their estates among their children. Several of the urban artisans had been named freemen of their towns, a status that conferred political privileges and indicated some measure of economic stability.[34] Perhaps the most telling evidence of the emigrants' relative prosperity is the fact that all of them managed to procure the funds to pay for their passages and supplies, which could amount to as much as £25 for a family of four.[35] This considerable sum approximated the annual rent for a

English Yeoman in the Tudor and Early Stuart Age (New Haven, Conn., 1942), 11–13, 23–33; Gordon Batho, "Noblemen, Gentlemen, and Yeomen," in Thirsk, ed., AHEW, IV, 301–6; Margaret Spufford, Contrasting Communities: English Villagers in the Sixteenth and Seventeenth Centuries (Cambridge, 1974), 37–9. Husbandmen could, in fact, be quite well off. Benjamin Cooper, a husbandman who sailed on the Mary Anne, died during the voyage in 1637. An inventory of his estate, recorded in Massachusetts that September, amounted to £1,278-12-00; see probate docket no. 4, Suffolk County Registry of Probate, Boston, Mass.

34 For instance, emigrants from Norwich who were freemen included the weavers Nicholas Busby, William Nickerson, Michael Metcalf, Samuel Greenfield, John Gedney, and Francis Lawes; the calenderer Thomas Oliver; the grocer John Baker; the locksmith William Ludkin; and the joiner Samuel Dix; see Jewson, ed., Transcript of Three Registers, 21–2, 30. For their extensive political privileges, see Evans, Seventeenth-Century Norwich, 26–30. Lack of suitable records makes it nearly impossible to assess precisely the economic positions of emigrants prior to their voyages; even the few extant tax lists are inaccurate measures of total wealth; see Breen and Foster, "Moving to the New World," WMQ, 3rd Ser., XXX (1973), 198–9, n. 27.

35 The Massachusetts Bay Company estimated that supplies would cost the emigrants more than £17 per family and that transportation fees would add £8 to £10. See Edmund S. Morgan, "Provisions for the Great Migration," NEQ, XII (1939), 98–9; Nathaniel B. Shurtleff, ed., Records of the Governor and Company of the Massachusetts Bay in New England, 5 vols. (Boston, 1853–4), I, 65.

family farm and equaled a quarter or more of the value of personal property owned by many urban artisans.[36]

Drawn overwhelmingly from England's middle ranks, the emigrant population displayed more social homogeneity than existed in English society as a whole. A fact of considerable significance for the development of New England, this truncated social hierarchy, lacking both rich and poor, caught the attention of several colonial observers. In a letter to an English correspondent, Richard Saltonstall expressed puzzlement concerning New England's peculiar social composition. "It is strange," he wrote, that "the meaner sort of people should be so backward [in migrating], having assurance that they may live plentifully by their neighbors." Richer folk proved to be equally reluctant voyagers, for Saltonstall also hoped that more "gentlemen of ability would transplant themselves," since they too might prosper in the new land. Saltonstall's opinion reflected his assessment of the economic advantages that, he thought, *should* entice members of these two groups to sail. The "meaner sort" might expect good wages in a labor-hungry land, whereas wealthier emigrants – in a somewhat more altruistic vein – would "supply the want we labor under of men fitted by their estates to bear common burdens." Although Saltonstall wrote in 1632, early in the migration decade, succeeding years brought no change in the social composition of the migrating population.[37]

The Great Migration, in other words, defied the usual economic explanations that made sense both of England's internal movement and of emigration to the Chesapeake and West Indian colonies. Even the agricultural depression and industrial

---

[36] Several rural emigrants rented their English property, rather than selling it, and received an annual payment of about £20; see Chapter 2 of this volume. One historian has estimated that most urban weavers in Norfolk owned goods worth no more than £100 during this period; see Allison, "Norfolk Worsted Industry [Part I]," *Yorkshire Bulletin of Economic and Social Research*, XII (1960), 76–7.

[37] Richard Saltonstall to Emmanuel Downing, February 4, 1631–2, in Emerson, ed., *Letters from New England*, 92. Two years later, William Wood noted that "none of such great estate went over yet"; see his *New England's Prospect*, ed. Vaughan, 68.

Decision

difficulties of the early seventeenth century failed to dislodge the sorts of people that Saltonstall and others expected would be natural emigrants. Instead of attracting wealthy men with funds to invest in the colonial enterprise or poor young men seeking to sell their labor in a New World economy, New England lured middle-aged, economically middling families with seemingly little to gain and much to lose by emigration. Indeed, even if economic motives could be discovered among these emigrants, New England would hardly have been a wise choice of destination, for it offered little in the way of improved opportunities. Artisans would be moving to a place with a much smaller population engaged by necessity in subsistence agriculture, with limited buying power, rudimentary market facilities, and shortages of raw materials for their work (especially for those in the textile trades). Men who had endured years of hard work and dependence in order to learn a trade would not lightly abandon it – as they must have suspected would happen – in favor of a primitive agricultural subsistence.[38] Similarly, farmers who might have been attracted by the abundance of New England's land would scarcely have ignored less appealing factors such as its wildness, its lower value, the unfamiliarity of its soils and the region's climate, and the scarcity of labor.

In choosing to emigrate, then, many of these men and women exchanged an economically viable present for a most uncertain future. Moreover, these emigrants, all of whom left England five years or more after the Great Migration began and at least a decade and a half after Plymouth Colony's foundation, had received ample notice from their predecessors that New England was no land of milk and honey. In 1624 Edward Winslow had warned that the "vain expectation of present profit" was the "overthrow and bane" of plantations. Settlers might prosper through "good labor and diligence," but in the absence of a cash crop, great wealth was not to be expected. A decade later, Wil-

[38] Although it is true that many artisans probably had rural backgrounds, and may even have done some part-time farming or gardening in addition to their trades, the transition to full-time agriculture in cleared wilderness settlements would still have been quite drastic.

35

liam Wood delivered a similar message. Some colonists were lured westward by the hope of easy profit but soon fell to criticizing the new society, "saying a man cannot live without labor." These disgruntled settlers, Wood scolded, "more discredit and disparage themselves in giving the world occasion to take notice of their dronish disposition that would live off the sweat of another man's brows. Surely they were much deceived, or else ill informed, that ventured thither in hope to live in plenty and idleness, both at a time." Letters as well as published reports informed would-be settlers not only that New England was no land of instant riches but that it was often, at least at first, a place of privation. In 1631, one young colonist complained to his father in England that "the cuntrey is not so as we ded expecte it" and begged him to send provisions, for "we do not know how longe we may subeseiste" without supplies from home.[39] None of these accounts offered the slightest encouragement to prospective colonists intent solely on economic improvement, a curious feature for literature that was, in large part, intended to promote emigration. Its very peculiarity, however, only gives added force to the principal conclusion derived from the demographic evidence – that the Great Migration was no ordinary migration. Comparisons with other seventeenth-century English population movements, both within the home country and to the other colonies, reveal persistent anomalies in the New England experience. Alone among such movements, the Great Migration uprooted relatively prosperous families with no evident economic reason to depart for the wilderness they knew awaited them. Given the singular character of the New England

[39] Edward Winslow, *Good Newes from New England: or a true Relation of things very remarkable at the Plantation of Plimoth in New-England* (London, 1624), reprinted in Alexander Young, ed., *Chronicles of the Pilgrim Fathers of the Colony of Plymouth, from 1602 to 1625*, 2nd ed. (Boston, 1844), 272–3, 370–1; Wood, *New England's Prospect*, ed. Vaughan, 68; ———, Pond to William Pond, *Winthrop Papers*, III, 18. In *Coming Over*, David Cressy argues that much information about New England exaggerated the bounty of the region; see ch. 1. It is important, however, to distinguish between the celebratory reports of the early seventeenth century and the more subdued accounts of the late 1620s and 1630s that circulated when most migrants actually moved to the region.

emigration, it should come as no surprise that its underlying rationale was correspondingly unique.

III

Despite its ostensibly counterproductive message, the promotional literature for New England settlement was scarcely self-defeating, for its authors *deliberately* aimed at winnowing out people who placed material welfare above all other concerns. For prospective emigrants who passed this motivational test, however, the promotional literature promised that life in Massachusetts might bring improvement of another variety. They learned that the benefits attending migration to New England would mainly accrue not in this world but in the next. A common religious purpose thus animated this special group of settlers, shaping both their experience of migration and the development of their New World society.

Thomas Dudley's account of his first nine months in New England exemplified a thematic pattern common to reports of the region that appeared just when most emigrants were deciding whether or not to move. Dudley, who was deputy governor of the Bay Colony, announced that "if any come hether to plant for worldly ends that canne live well at home hee comits an errour of which he will soon repent him." Emigration to New England, in other words, was more likely to ruin a fortune than to increase it. "But," he went on, if a man emigrated "for spirituall [ends] . . . , he may finde here what may well content him." Dudley wanted to make clear what sort of person would benefit most from emigration. "If any godly men out of religious ends will come over to help us in the good worke wee are about," he wrote, "I think they cannot dispose of themselves nor of their estates more to God's glory and the furtherance of their owne reckoninge."[40]

New England, then, promised its settlers *spiritual* advan-

---

[40] "Gov. Thomas Dudley's Letter to the Countess of Lincoln, March, 1631," in Peter Force, ed., *Tracts and Other Papers Relating Principally to the Origin, Settlement, and Progress of the Colonies in North America, From the Discovery of the Country to the Year 1776*, 4 vols. (Washington, D.C., 1838), II, 12.

tages; men merely seeking wealth would be better advised to seek their fortunes elsewhere, perhaps in the Chesapeake or the West Indies. In a letter to the English secretary of state, Sir John Coke, Emmanuel Downing contrasted Massachusetts's religious mission with Virginia's more mundane purposes. "This plantation and that of Virginia," he explained, "went not forth upon the same reasons nor for the same end. Those of Virginia went forth for profit. . . . These went upon two other designs, some to satisfy their own curiosity in point of conscience, others . . . to transport the Gospel to those heathen that never heard thereof."[41]

Although it seems unlikely that many of the emigrants contemplated new careers as missionaries to the Indians, our skepticism need not extend to Downing's other assertion concerning the emigrants' motivation. Thomas Dudley and Emmanuel Downing were not the only writers to stress the role of religion in Massachusetts's origins. The Reverend John White, an active participant in joint stock ventures that preceded the founding of the Massachusetts Bay Company, proclaimed in *The Planter's Plea* that "the most eminent and desirable end of planting Colonies, is the propagation of Religion." Writing about his first year in Salem, the Reverend Francis Higginson informed prospective settlers that "that which is our greatest comfort . . . is, that we have here the true Religion and holy Ordinances of Almightie God taught amongst us: Thankes be to God, we have here plentie of Preaching, and diligent Catechizing, with strickt and carefull exercise, and good and commendable orders to bring our People into a Christian conversation with whom we have to doe withall."[42]

---

[41] This letter is quoted in Emerson, ed., *Letters from New England*, 93. For a similar statement, see John Winthrop's "General Observations: Autograph Draft," in *Winthrop Papers*, II, 117.

[42] John White, *The Planter's Plea* (London, 1630), reprinted in Force, ed., *Tracts and Other Papers*, II, 12; Reverend Francis Higginson, *New-Englands Plantation with The Sea Journal and Other Writings* (originally published 1630; facsimile, Salem, Mass., 1908), 108. See also the letter from Edward Trelawney to his brother Robert in Emerson, ed., *Letters from New England*, 175–8.

Indeed, New England's Puritan predilections were so well known that colonial leaders feared retribution from the Anglican establishment in England. In *The Planter's Plea* Reverend White specifically sought to dispel rumors that Massachusetts was overrun with Separatists, and during the early 1630s, Edward Howes maintained a steady correspondence with John Winthrop, Jr., concerning similar allegations of New England radicalism. In 1631, Howes reported that "heare is a mutteringe of a too palpable seperation of your people from our church government"; the following year, he informed Winthrop of claims that "you never use the Lords prayer, that your ministers marrie none, that fellowes which keepe hogges all the weeke preach on the Saboth, that every towne in your plantation is of a severall religion; that you count all men in England, yea all out of your church, and in the state of damnacion." Howes worried that the spread of such rumors might endanger not only the colony's reputation but perhaps even its survival.[43]

The concerns of the leaders of the Great Migration – especially the religious leaders – did not, of course, necessarily correspond precisely with the concerns of the bulk of the settlers. But the fact remains that prospective emigrants could hardly have been unaware of the peculiar religious character of New England society. Accounts of the region's commitment to Puritanism were simply too numerous to be overlooked and made it clear that all settlers would have to abide by the "good and commendable orders" designed to bring them "into a Christian conversation." People willing to move to Massachusetts, then, tacitly agreed to become members of the Puritan commonwealth, even if they did not quite agree on what that meant.[44] Puritanism, always an opposi-

[43] White, *Planter's Plea*, in Force, ed., *Tracts and Other Papers*, II, 33–6; Edward Howes to John Winthrop, Jr., November 9, 1631, and November 28, 1632, *Winthrop Papers*, III, 54, 100–1.

[44] In a series of articles, Stephen Foster has been exploring the fluidity of English Puritanism, especially during the crucial decade of the 1630s, investigating the ways in which the timing of the settlers' departure from England influenced their religious outlook. See "The Godly in Transit: English Popu-

tion movement, would evolve in unexpected ways as it became the established religion in the Bay Colony and later in Connecticut. But during the first decade of settlement, it was enough for prospective colonists to know that they wanted to leave England's growing corruption. This shared commitment to Puritan principles, however vaguely defined, became the common thread that stitched individual emigrants together into a larger social and cultural fabric. The Reverend John White recognized that religious motives would not necessarily impel all those who crossed the ocean, but "that the most and most sincere and godly part have the advancement of the *Gospel* for their maine scope I am co[n]fident."[45]

White's confidence was by no means misplaced. The rosters of passengers to New England contained the names of dozens of English men and women whose lives were distinguished by their steadfast commitment to nonconformity, even in the face of official harassment. The *Hercules* left Sandwich in 1635 with William Wetherell and Comfort Starr aboard; both men had been in trouble with local ecclesiastical authorities. Anthony Thacher, a nonconformist who had been living in Holland for two decades, returned to Southampton to embark for New England on the *James*. In 1637, the *Rose* carried Michael Metcalf away from the clutches of Norwich diocesan officials. Metcalf had appeared before ecclesiastical courts in 1633 and again in 1636 for refusing to bow at the name of Jesus or to adhere to the "stinking tenets of Arminius" adopted by the established church. Before his departure, Metcalf had composed a letter "to all the true professors of Christs gospel within the city of Norwich" that chronicled his troubled encounters with church officials and explained his ex-

lar Protestantism and the Creation of a Puritan Establishment in America," in David D. Hall and David Grayson Allen, eds., *Seventeenth-Century New England*, Colonial Society of Massachusetts, *Publications*, 63 (Boston, 1984), 185–238; "New England and the Challenge of Heresy, 1630–1660: The Puritan Crisis in Transatlantic Perspective," *WMQ*, XXXVIII (1981), 624–60. On the variations in Puritan belief, see also Philip F. Gura, *A Glimpse of Sion's Glory: Puritan Radicalism in New England, 1620–1660* (Middletown, Conn., 1984).
45 White, *Planter's Plea*, in Force, ed., *Tracts and Other Papers*, II, 36.

clusively religious reasons for emigration. Thomas and Mary Oliver, Metcalf's fellow parishioners at St. Edmund's in Norwich, had also been cited before the archepiscopal court in 1633, and set sail for Massachusetts the same year as Metcalf. Other emigrants leaving in 1637 were John Pers and John Baker, two more Norwich residents in trouble with church officials; Joan Ames, the widow of the revered Puritan divine William Ames; and Margaret Neave and Adam Goodens, whose names appeared on Separatist lists in Great Yarmouth. Peter Noyes, who emigrated in 1638, came from a family long involved in nonconformist activities in southwestern England.[46]

The Puritan beliefs of other emigrants should not be underestimated merely because they avoided direct conflict with bishops and deacons. John Winthrop's religious motivation has never been in doubt even though he was never convicted of a Puritan offense. Winthrop's "General Observations for the Plantation of New England," like Metcalf's letter to the citizens of Norwich, emphasized the corrupt state of England's ecclesiastical affairs and concluded that emigration "wilbe a service to the church of great consequens" redounding to the spiritual benefit of emigrants and Indians alike. Other explicit statements of motivation likewise stressed the role of religion. Roger Clap, who emigrated in 1630, recalled in his memoirs that "I never so much as heard of *New-England* until I heard of many godly Persons that were going there" and firmly believed that "God put it into my Heart to incline to Live abroad" in Massachusetts. John Dane, who seems to have devoted most of his youthful energies to restraining his evil inclinations, "bent myself to cum to nu ingland, thinking that I should be more fre here then

---

[46] Clark, *English Provincial Society*, 372; Savage, *Genealogical Dictionary*, IV, 270–1; Breen and Foster, "Moving to the New World," *WMQ*, 3rd ser., XXX (1973), 202–3, 207 n. 37; Jewson, ed., *Transcript of Three Registers*, 8; Champlin Burrage, *The Early English Dissenters in the Light of Recent Research 1550–1641*, 2 vols. (Cambridge, 1912), II, 309; Powell, *Puritan Village*, 4; "Michael Metcalfe," *NEHGR*, XVI (1862), 279–84. The incomplete survival of ecclesiastical records in England makes it impossible to discover the full extent of colonists' troubles with the authorities.

thare from temptations." Arriving in Roxbury in the mid-1630s, however, Dane was disappointed to find that relocation did not end his struggle with sinfulness; the devil sought him out as readily in the New World as in the Old.[47]

To assert that most emigrants were prompted by religious sentiment to sail to New England, however, is not to suggest that Nathaniel Tilden, John Emery, or Anne Nickerson – or the thousands of men and women like them – resembled Hawthorne's "stern and black-browed Puritans" in single-minded pursuit of salvation. The decision to cross the ocean was certainly not an easy one to make. Even the most pious – Governor John Winthrop included – wrestled with the implications of removal from family, friends, community responsibilities, and familiar surroundings.[48] Although they strove to subordinate their own interests to the will of God, the New England Puritans never became Christian utopians caught up in a movement whose purpose totally transcended the concerns of daily life.

Perhaps solitary ascetics can happily reject the things of this world in order to contemplate the glories of the next; family men and women certainly cannot. Even as prospective settlers discussed the spiritual benefits that might accompany a move to New England, they worried about what they would eat, where

---

[47] *Winthrop Papers*, II, 111; "Memoirs of Roger Clap," Dorchester Antiquarian and Historical Society, *Collections* (1844), 18–19; "John Dane's Narrative, 1682," *NEHGR*, VIII (1854), 154. Further evidence of the influence of religion may be found in early New England conversion narratives, in which many colonists declared that concern for their spiritual state was a crucial factor in their decision to emigrate; see George Selement and Bruce C. Woolley, eds., *Thomas Shepard's Confessions*, Colonial Society of Massachusetts, *Publications*, LVIII (Boston, 1981).

[48] For instance, Samuel Rogers, scion of a noted Puritan family, ultimately decided against emigration because his father objected to his departure; see Kenneth W. Shipps, "The Puritan Emigration to New England: A New Source on Motivation," *NEHGR*, CXXXV (1981), 83–97. Both Roger Clap and John Dane noted that their fathers, at least initially, protested their sons' emigration; see "Memoirs of Roger Clap," Dorch. Antiq. and Hist. Soc., *Colls.* (1844), 18; "John Dane's Narrative," *NEHGR*, VIII (1854), 154. For Winthrop's difficult decision, see Edmund S. Morgan, *The Puritan Dilemma: The Story of John Winthrop* (Boston, 1958), ch. 3.

they would sleep, and how they would make a living in their new homes. In the spring of 1631, Emmanuel Downing wrote with considerable relief to John Winthrop that the governor's encouraging letters "have much refreshed my hart and the myndes of manie others," for "it was the Judgement of most men here, that your Colonye would be dissolved partly by death through want of Food, howsing and rayment, and the rest to retorne or to flee for refuge to other plantacions."[49] Leaders of the Great Migration sympathized with families struggling with the decision of whether or not to move, and sought to reassure prospective settlers that a decision in favor of emigration would not doom them to cold and starvation in the wilderness. At the same time, the way in which these leaders composed their comforting messages to would-be emigrants underscored the settlers' understanding of the larger meaning of their enterprise.

Several of the tracts and letters publicizing the migration contained favorable descriptions of the new land that were clearly intended to convince godly English men and women that emigration to New England would not foster poverty along with piety. But, on balance, these descriptions of New England's climate, topography, flora, and fauna were modest in scope. Writers consistently focused on those aspects of the region that most closely resembled English conditions, such as the presence of familiar plants or the comparability of Old and New World soils. Their accounts attempted to reassure prospective emigrants that English agriculture could be successfully transplanted to America. When the differences between Old and New England were discussed, they generally proved to be differences of degree, and not of kind, and almost always favored the new land: The New England climate was healthier, the crops were bigger and better.[50]

These descriptions of New England, in fact, were so modest that some readers worried that the region lacked "meanes of

[49] Edward Downing to John Winthrop, 30 April [1631], *Winthrop Papers*, III, 30.
[50] See, for instance, Wood, *New England's Prospect*, ed. Vaughan, 27–57; Higginson, *New-Englands Plantation*, 90–104.

wealth" and therefore was not a good place to settle. In *The Planter's Plea*, Reverend John White provided a most succinct response to this objection. It was "an unanswerable argument," he replied, "to such as make the advancement of their estates, the scope of their undertaking." But New England's modest resources were in "no way a discouragement to such as aime at the propagation of the Gospell, which can never bee advanced but by the preservation of Piety in those that carry it to strangers." For, White concluded, "nothing sorts better with Piety than Compete[n]cy." And the materials to achieve a competency are precisely what these accounts described. Thomas Dudley in effect explicated the meaning of "competency" in a New England context when he listed such goods as "may well content" the colonists. In Massachusetts, Dudley noted, settlers would find "materialls to build, fewell to burn, ground to plant, seas and rivers to fish in, a pure ayer to breath in, good water to drinke till wine or beare canne be made, which togeather with the cowes, hoggs, and goates brought hether allready may suffice for food." Such were the amenities that emigrants not only could but should aspire to enjoy.[51]

Here, then, is the key to the emigrants' willingness to undertake a risky, economically disadvantageous move to a wilderness. With piety as their goal, they could accept a simplification of their economic condition, for that would only help them to achieve their principal end. Promoters of the migration tapped a wellspring of faith and trust in the Lord as they sought to assure the emigrants that a competency would indeed be theirs. For, as John White noted, "all Gods directions" – including the divine imperative to settle New England – "have a double scope, mans good and Gods honour." "That this commandement of God is directed unto mans good *temporall and spirituall*," he went on, "is

---

[51] White, *Planter's Plea*, in Force, ed., *Tracts and Other Papers*, II, 18; "Dudley's Letter to the Countess of Lincoln," ibid., II, 12. See also Wood, *New England's Prospect*, ed. Vaughan, 68; Daniel Vickers, "Competency and Competition: Economic Culture in Early America," *WMQ*, 3rd ser., XLVII, No. 1 (1990), 3–29.

as cleere as the light."[52] The Lord, in other words, would take care of His own. To providentialists steeped in the conviction that God intervened directly in human lives, that divine pleasure or disapproval could be perceived in the progress of daily events, White's statement made eminent sense. Economic concerns were subsumed within an all-encompassing religious vision. The Lord was not likely to reward the emigrants' faithfulness with ruin. Instead, as long as they remained steadfast in their spiritual purpose, they might expect as a sign of divine favor to achieve their competencies.

John Winthrop echoed White's message when he asserted that "such thinges as we stand in neede of are usually supplied by Gods blessing upon the wisdome and industry of man." The governor's firm belief in the connection between divine favor and human well-being explains why, in his "Particular Considerations" concerning his own emigration, he admitted that "my meanes heere [in England] are so shortned (now my 3 eldest sonnes are come to age) as I shall not be able to continue in this place and imployment where I now am." If he went to Massachusetts, Winthrop anticipated an improvement in his fortunes, noting that "I [can] live with 7. or 8: servants in that place and condition where for many years I have spent 3: or 400 li. per an[num]." But this was an "improvement" based on lowered economic expectations to be enjoyed in an atmosphere of heightened religious purpose. Winthrop emigrated in order to undertake the "publike service" that "God [had] bestowed" on him; in return, he hoped that God might reward him if his efforts were successful.[53] Like Winthrop, the other emigrants evidently agreed that the potential achievement of a competency in godly New England far outweighed the present enjoyment of a larger estate in a corrupt England. Only within this context does their willingness to risk the lives and fortunes of their families on a most uncertain venture begin to make sense.

[52] White, *Planter's Plea*, in Force, ed., *Tracts and Other Papers*, II, 2; italics added.
[53] *Winthrop Papers*, II, 143–4, 126.

Puritanism thus played an essential part in convincing otherwise ordinary English men and women to take the extraordinary step of separating themselves from their society and embarking for New England. Very soon, however, the emigrants' religious convictions would come to have another, more creative and demanding role in the drama of the Great Migration. Once the actual movement of people began, shared Puritan beliefs would serve to join disparate individuals from various parts of the country into a unified body, a "great Company of Religious people," to use Winthrop's phrase.[54] But before that union could be accomplished, the emigrants' faith and endurance would be tested in a perilous passage across the ocean.

[54] "A Modell of Christian Charitie," *Winthrop Papers*, II, 282.

2
Passage

After his safe arrival at Salem early in the summer of 1629, the Reverend Francis Higginson concluded his journal of the voyage with a summary of five "remarkeable things" concerning his recent trip. "First," he noted, "through God's blessing our passage was short and speedy," accomplished in just forty-five days. Second, the voyage was "comfortable and easie for the most part"; Higginson and his fellow passengers on the *Talbot* encountered few "stormie and rough seas, saving one night only." Third, most of the emigrants remained healthy during their weeks at sea, avoiding "the great contagion of the scurvy and other maledictions, which in other passages to other places had taken away the lives of many." One seaman and two children – including the minister's own daughter – had died, but the former had been a "wicked fellow that scorned at fasting and prayers," and the two children had both been "very sickly . . . and not likely to have lived long, if they had not gone to sea." Fourth, Higginson found the voyage to be "both pleasurable and profitable," for he and the other passengers were able to appreciate God's glory more fully as they beheld strange fish and other "wonders of the Lord in the deepe waters" that they had never before seen. Finally, Higginson marveled at the fact that "we had a pious and christianlike passage; for I suppose passengers shall seldom find a company of more religious, honest, and kynd seamen than we had."[1]

Not all emigrants would enjoy a voyage so short and so healthy, so comfortable and so "christianlike," as that of Higginson and his companions aboard the *Talbot*. Most passengers spent a longer time at sea, often under harsher conditions. Yet no matter how the details of each ocean crossing varied, the

[1] Reverend Francis Higginson, *New-Englands Plantation with The Sea Journal and Other Writings* (orig. publ. 1630; facsimile, Salem, Mass., 1908), 81–3.

participants all agreed on the singular importance of the event. Every emigrant understood the voyage to be a unique experience, a rite of passage that clearly marked a fundamental shift in the course of his or her life. For months beforehand, the colonists had confronted a welter of unfamiliar tasks in their preparations for departure, having to liquidate their English estates, purchase large quantities of provisions, and arrange for passage on a New England–bound vessel. As they finally made their way to their ports of departure and boarded their respective ships, however, the emigrants, whose preparations had compelled them to dwell on highly individualistic concerns, increasingly recognized the bonds that tied their fates to those of strangers embarking with them. The events of the voyage strengthened those bonds and helped the passengers to understand the meaning of their common enterprise. In a very real sense, then, the voyage marked the beginning of the emigrants' gradual transformation into New Englanders.

I

Although leaders of the Great Migration offered advice on how best to prepare for the move to the New World, the emigrants relied principally on their own common sense, adapting general prescriptions to individual circumstances. Landowners, for instance, faced the particularly delicate task of disposing of their most significant asset – real property – to best advantage. Consider the predicament of Nathaniel Tilden of Tenterden. The Kentish yeoman's decision to emigrate came rather late in life, after he had spent decades accumulating land to pass on to his heirs. This land constituted the family's greatest capital resource, but now Tilden had to figure out how to dispose of it so that the family could leave and yet not ruin their economic position.

Tilden ultimately decided not to sell but to rent his Tenterden estate. Presumably, the rental payments would either find their way across the Atlantic or, more likely, constitute a fund of credit on the books of some English merchant to whom Tilden could turn for imported goods. Either way, the Kentish estate would continue to support the family despite its removal across the ocean. The canny yeoman had contrived a way to furnish his family with much needed capital in the New World at the same time that he kept the title to his Old World property in case they needed to return. Although it is difficult to tell if this scheme worked exactly according to plan, Tilden did include the income from his English estate among his assets when he wrote his will several years later. Far from forcing him to neglect his responsibilities as a husband and father, the decision to emigrate had instead compelled Tilden to be especially creative in fulfilling those same duties.[2]

Ingenious as this solution was, it is not surprising that other landowning emigrants followed suit. Samuel Hall, another Kentish yeoman, left behind "Land in England to the valewe of 20 li p[er] a[nnum]" when he sailed to Charlestown in 1637. Hall did not long enjoy the fruits of his well-laid plans, for he died within a couple of years of his arrival in Massachusetts. His widow, Joan, and infant son, Samuel, however, would benefit from his foresight and find the additional income particularly necessary as they adjusted to life without him. Another emigrant, Peter Noyes, rented out part of his English property to his sister, probably to obtain money to pay for his family's passage. After he sailed in 1638, he retained possession of a house and land near Andover in Hampshire. This property provided Noyes with an annual rent of about £20 during his lifetime and, after his death in 1657, supplemented his three sons' portions. Like Noyes, the surgeon Comfort Starr retained English lands for two decades after his move to Massachusetts, and presumably received some sort of rental payment in cash or credit. Colonists clearly recognized the value of a transatlantic infusion of capital as an addition to the subsistence provided by their New England estates. Both Thomas Besbeech and Edward Johnson

---

[2] Tilden's will is printed in *Mayflower Descendant*, III (1901), 220–2. His inventory (ibid., 222–3) omits real estate and does not mention a rental payment (although the amount of "Debts hopefull & Desprate" was £27), so it is impossible to assess the value of the Tenterden property.

acquired a considerable amount of property in Massachusetts, yet both continued to own English land to their deaths – which occurred some forty years after their emigration.[3]

Renting out property in England and using the income to supplement a New England estate was obviously a prudent solution to one problem of emigration, but it was also a scheme beyond the reach of most emigrants. Virtually all of those who adopted this strategy were older men who had accumulated substantial amounts of land prior to their emigration. Tilden, Noyes, Starr, and Besbeech were all aged forty-five or more, and Edward Johnson was thirty-nine when he rented out his Kentish estate in 1637. Moreover, Tilden, Hall, and Noyes all were yeomen, acutely aware of the value of their freeholds and doubtless reluctant to give them up. Some land might have to be sold or rented to acquire the cash to pay for provisions and passage, but since their estates were clearly substantial, they could afford to retain some portion of them. Other men were less fortunate. Younger emigrants, who had not yet received their inheritances or who had not had the time or means to accumulate property

---

[3] Citations to probate materials will be given by county, followed by docket number, if the original will or inventory survives. Otherwise, if a clerk's copy is available, citation will be made as follows: county, followed by [cc], volume, part, and page number of the copy. Samuel Hall, Suffolk no. 7; Comfort Starr, Suffolk no. 233; Edward Johnson, Suffolk no. 12644; Thomas Besbeech, Middlesex no. 1476; Peter Noyes, Middlesex no. 16074. For Noyes, see also Sumner Chilton Powell, *Puritan Village: The Formation of a New England Town* (Middletown, Conn., 1963), 5. The wills of two other emigrants also mention English estates. Walter Haynes (Middlesex no. 10939) apparently deeded his lands in Dorset to his son-in-law Roger Gourd; in his will he bequeathed "the say[d] deed" to his daughter Elizabeth Gourd – who had remained in England – and her heirs. The will of Joseph Parker, a twenty-four-year-old tanner who sailed on the *Confidence* in 1638, mentions an estate in Romsey, Hampshire. Since Parker listed Newbury as his residence at the time of his removal from England and was quite young when he sailed, this estate was probably bequeathed to him after he had already settled in Massachusetts; his will is printed in *The Probate Records of Essex County, Massachusetts*, 3 vols. (Salem, Mass., 1916–20), III, 278–81. On the emigrants' retention of English property, see also David Cressy, *Coming Over: Migration and Communication between England and New England in the Seventeenth Century* (Cambridge, 1987), 180–90.

through marriage, or saving and purchase, would have to depend almost exclusively on what New England could provide for their livings. Men who had been tenants in England had no choice but to return that land to its owners when they were ready to leave. Husbandmen like John Moulton, Henry Dow, and Richard Carver farmed sizable tracts in Norfolk but could not convert them to capital, and instead had to rely either on their savings or on the sale of personal property for the seed money to fund their transplantation to New England.[4]

For urban artisans, the disposition of real estate proved less of a problem. Since their holdings were usually modest, craftsmen generally divested themselves completely of whatever real estate they held before leaving England. Nicholas Busby, for example, sold his tenement in Norwich to another of the city's weavers rather than leasing it.[5] For Busby and other emigrant artisans, the sale of their property was the simplest and most sensible procedure. Not only could few of them have expected to earn a return comparable to the £20 per annum rents that farmers like Samuel Hall and Peter Noyes could charge for their more extensive holdings, but all would have realized that their earning power derived from their craft work. Artisans could afford to dispose of their English property because their greatest resource – their skill – was eminently transportable.[6]

---

[4] N. C. P. Tyack mentions that these men rented land in Norfolk; see his "Migration from East Anglia to New England Before 1660" (Ph.D. diss., University of London, 1951), 431, n. 44.

[5] Anna C. Kingsbury, *A Historical Sketch of Nicholas Busby the Emigrant* (n.p., 1924), 5–6.

[6] Among the emigrants studied here, eight men listed English property in their wills. Half of these – Thomas Besbeech, Samuel Hall, Peter Noyes, and Nathaniel Tilden – were clearly farmers. Walter Haynes, a linen weaver, and Comfort Starr, a surgeon, lived in small towns (Sutton Mandeville, Wiltshire, and Ashford, Kent) and probably derived part of their living from the land. As mentioned in footnote 3, the tanner Joseph Parker probably inherited his English estate after he moved to the New World. The only urban artisan who, as far as I can tell, retained English land was Edward Johnson, a joiner from Canterbury, and his Old World estate was *not* urban property but land in the "parish of Herron Hill." Farmland, it seems, was the only English land worth retaining.

New England's generation

What artisans did retain were the tools of their trades. Nicholas Busby freely sold his Norwich houselot but evidently never contemplated disposing of his looms. He and other emigrant weavers, such as Nicholas Batt, Walter Haynes, and Thomas Payne, all brought looms and "tackling" to their New England homes.[7] Not to have done so would have seemed an act of utter foolishness, for any artisan arriving in Massachusetts without his tools would have operated under inordinate disadvantages, since adequate replacements could not be bought, and probably could not be made, in New England. Most emigrant craftsmen seem to have assumed that they would earn at least part of their livings in New England through the practice of their trades. With experienced colonial observers like William Wood announcing that the men best suited for the work of settlement included "an ingenious carpenter, a cunning joiner, a handy cooper, such a one as can make strong ware for the use of the country, and a good brick-maker, a tiler and a smith, a leather dresser, a gardener, and a tailor," sensible emigrants could only have concluded that it was worthwhile to pay the freight charges even on bulky equipment. Thus, as they prepared for departure, the ingenious carpenter John Emery and the cunning joiner John Thurston remembered to pack their woodworking implements. Anthony Morse, Joseph Coleman, and William Gault each tucked his wooden lasts and other "toules for the shumaking trad" into the crates and bundles that held his other possessions. In Norwich, the locksmith William Ludkin likewise assembled his wide variety of files, chisels, and hammers to be packed up with the rest of his family's belongings. Such men would no sooner have dreamed of sailing without their tools than without their wives.[8]

---

[7] This information was obtained from probate materials. For Batt, see *Probate Records of Essex County*, III, 187–91; for Lawes, see ibid., II, 49–51; for Busby, see Kingsbury, *Historical Sketch of Nicholas Busby*, 8–14; for Payne, see Nathaniel Emmons Paine, *Thomas Payne of Salem and His Descendants: The Salem Branch of the Paine Family* (Haverhill, Mass., 1928), 16; for Haynes, see Middlesex no. 10939.

[8] William Wood, *New England's Prospect*, ed. Alden T. Vaughan, The Commonweath Series (Amherst, Mass., 1977), 72–3. The information on artisans' tools is from probate materials: John Emery, Essex no. 8976 and [cc]

When faced with the task of gathering other supplies for their voyage, emigrants could rely on more specific advice offered by leaders of the migration. These men constantly reminded prospective settlers of the overwhelming need for careful planning and a realistic assessment of family requirements. The Reverend Francis Higginson explicitly warned of the dangers of inadequate preparation, noting that New England would not supply the wants created by a lack of foresight.

> Before you come be carefull to be strongly instructed what things are fittest to bring with you for your more comfortable passage at sea, as also for your husbandrey occasions when you come to the land. For when you are once parted with England you shall meete neither with taverns nor alehouse, nor butchers, nor grosers, nor apothecaries shops to helpp what things you need, in the midst of the great ocean, nor when you are come to land here are yet neither markets nor fayres to buy what you want. Therefore be sure to furnish yourselves with things fitting to be had before you come.

Higginson's cautionary words nonetheless fell on more than a few deaf ears, for five years later, William Wood felt compelled to repeat the admonition. "Many hundreds," he wrote, "hearing of the plenty of the country were so much their own foes and country's hindrance as to come without provision, which made things both dear and scant. Wherefore let none blame the country so much as condemn the indiscreetness of such as will needs run themselves upon hardship."[9]

Hunger was the hardship that leaders most consistently

Vol. 302, pp. 100–2; John Thurston, Suffolk no. 1504; Anthony Morse, Essex no. 18903; Joseph Coleman, Plymouth [cc] Vol. 3, part I, pp. 140–2; William Gault, in *Probate Records of Essex County*, I, 316–17; William Ludkin, Suffolk no. 122.

[9] Higginson, *New-Englands Plantation*, 121; Wood, *New England's Prospect*, ed. Vaughan, 67–8. For a general discussion of provisioning, see Cressy, *Coming over*, ch. 4.

feared; it was, after all, a problem for which there was ample precedent in other English colonizing ventures. If writers dwelled upon this potential catastrophe, it was because they knew that it could be avoided. Time and again, Bay Colony leaders urged emigrants to bring adequate provisions, emphasizing that food for the voyage alone would by no means suffice. Although New England abounded in arable land, leaders warned, it had not yet begun to produce great surpluses. New arrivals needed to bring along at least a year's supply of food if they hoped to avoid want, and indeed if they wished not to threaten the chances for the survival of the colony as a whole. The specter of starvation clearly haunted John Winthrop during his first New England summer. In a letter to his son John, the governor acknowledged his desire for a continued influx of colonists, "onely people must come well-provided, and not too many at once." Winthrop similarly advised his wife Margaret, who was to emigrate the following year, that she "must be sure to bringe no more companye, then so many as shall have full Provision for a yeare and halfe for though the earth heere be very fertile yet there must be tyme and meanes to rayse it."[10]

The fragile state of colonial food supplies concerned other emigrant leaders no less than the governor. Reverend Francis Higginson, for instance, also warned:

> All that come must have victualls with them for a twelve month, I meane they must have meale, oatmeale, and such like sustenaunce of food, till they can gett increase of corne by their owne labour. For, otherwise, so many may come without provision at the first, as that our small beginnings may not be sufficient to maintayne them.

The minister's sensitivity to this issue was no doubt heightened by the timing of his own arrival in Massachusetts; when he first

[10] John Winthrop to John Winthrop, Jr., July 23, 1630, *Winthrop Papers*, 5 vols. (Boston, 1920–47), II, 306; John Winthrop to His Wife, July 23, 1630, ibid., 304.

set foot in Salem, the struggling settlement was barely three years old. The fleet of five ships, with which Higginson sailed, carried several hundred passengers who, although welcome, had strained the infant town's resources. Seeing land that as yet showed little evidence of English-style farming, Higginson had feared famine and immediately understood what strenuous efforts would be required to avert it.[11]

To help prospective colonists, Higginson appended a "Catalogue of such needefull things as every Planter doth or ought to provide to go to *New-England*" to his account of the voyage. The first seven items on his list constituted what he judged to be "Victuals for a whole yeere for a man" and included eight bushels of meal, two bushels each of peas and oatmeal, two gallons of vinegar, one gallon each of oil and aquavitae, and a firkin of butter. The minister went on to suggest that emigrants bring along a variety of "spices" such as sugar, pepper, cloves, mace, cinnamon, nutmeg, and fruit, and he thought that cheese and bacon would also come in handy. Higginson evidently intended his recommended victuals to be a minimum amount for any passenger able to afford only a minimum of freightage. The daily ration for anyone following his advice would have been decidedly meager: about a cup and a half of meal, two-thirds of a cup each of oatmeal and peas, an ounce of vinegar, a tablespoon or two of oil and of aquavitae, and a bit of butter. No matter how well prepared and seasoned, such a diet would have been both monotonous and nutritionally unbalanced – one that even a nightly swig of spirits would scarcely improve. Fortunately, most emigrants fared better. Higginson himself enjoyed a much more varied diet at sea, and probably on land as well. Along with the minister's recommended supplies, the stores aboard the *Talbot* included ample stocks of bread, beef, cheese, preserved codfish, beer, wine, and mustard seed.[12]

[11] Higginson, *New-Englands Plantation*, 120–1. For the early history of Salem, see Sidney Perley, *The History of Salem, Massachusetts*, 3 vols. (Salem, Mass., 1924), I, 60–142.

[12] Higginson, *New-Englands Plantation*, 111–12; Nathaniel B. Shurtleff, ed., *Records of the Governor and Company of the Massachusetts Bay in New England,*

Provisions for the voyage itself, at least during the early years of the Great Migration, were supplied to passengers by the Massachusetts Bay Company. In December 1629, the company's General Court agreed to charge each emigrant £5 for his or her transportation (including food), with reduced rates for infants and young children. Emigrants and their families could thus expect to receive adequate sustenance from the ship's stock, but writers often urged that they bring along additional items. William Wood, for instance, agreed that passengers would not go hungry if they relied solely on company supplies, but argued that certain other commodities would be required to tempt dulled palates and prevent shipboard illness.[13]

> Although every man have ship provisions allowed him for his five pound a man – which is salt beef, pork, salt fish, butter, cheese, peas, pottage, water gruel, and such kinds of victuals, with good biscuits, and six-shilling beer – yet will it be necessary to carry some comfortable refreshing of fresh victual. As first, for such as have ability, some conserves, and good claret wine to burn at sea. Or you may have it by some of your vintners or wine coopers burned here and put up into vessels which will keep much better than other burnt wine. It is a very comfortable thing for the stomach or such as are seasick. Salad oil likewise. Prunes are good to be stewed; sugar for many things. White biscuits and eggs, and bacon, rice, poultry, and some weather sheep to kill aboard the ship; and fine flour-baked meats will keep about a week or nine days at sea. Juice of lemons well put up is good either to prevent or cure the scurvy.

5 vols. (Boston, 1853–4), I, 26–7; see also John Josselyn, *An Account of Two Voyages to New-England*, 2nd ed. (London, 1675), in Massachusetts Historical Society, *Collections*, 3rd ser., III (Boston, 1833), 222–3.

[13] Shurtleff, ed., *Mass. Bay Recs.*, I, 65–6; Wood, *New England's Prospect*, ed. Vaughan, 69–70. For a similar list of provisions, see also Josselyn, *Account of Two Voyages*, 221.

Prospective emigrants evidently followed the advice of experienced predecessors. As Edward Johnson noted in "Good News from New-England," many passengers brought extra provisions, in large part to satisfy their individual preferences.

> Close Cabbins being now prepar'd with bread, biefe,
>   beere and fish,
> The passengers prepare themselves that they may
>   have their wish.

Colonists seem to have been just as concerned with their palates as with their health, craving a diet that was tasty as well as nutritious. Richard Mather, who sailed to New England in 1635, no doubt expressed the sentiments of many when he proclaimed the merits of this supplementary provisioning.[14]

> And a speciall meanes of the healthfulnesse of the passengers by the blessing of God wee all conceyved to bee . . . the comfortable variety of our food; for seeing wee were not tyed to the ships diet, but did victuall ourselves, wee had no want of good and wholesome beere & bread; and as our land-stomaches grew weary of ship diet, of salt fish & salt beefe and the like, wee had liberty to change for other food which might sort better with our healthes and stomaches; and therefore sometimes wee used bacon & buttered pease, sometimes buttered bag-pudding made with curraynes and raisins, and sometimes drinke pottage of beere & oatemeale, and sometimes water pottage well buttered.

Emigrants like Mather attributed good health to divine providence rather than to the salubrious effects of lemons, raisins, and water pottage, but the care they took in varying their diet could only have reduced shipboard illness and death. Mortality at sea during the Great Migration may in fact have been as low

---

14 Edward Johnson, "Good News from New-England," in Harrison T. Meserole, ed., *Seventeenth-Century American Poetry*, The Stuart Editions (New York, 1968), 159; "Journal of Richard Mather," Dorchester Antiquarian and Historical Society, *Collections*, No. 3 (Boston, 1850), 32.

as 5 percent, prompting contemporary comment. Francis Higginson deemed the healthfulness of his voyage worthy of special mention, and William Wood observed in 1634 that "of six hundred souls not above three or four have died at sea." Granting that Wood's calculation may have reflected his enthusiasm as much as the actual death rate, it seems that few passengers perished during the ocean crossing. Only one of the emigrants in this study – Benjamin Cooper, a husbandman from Brampton, Suffolk – definitely died before reaching New England. Of the hundred-odd ship arrivals that Governor Winthrop mentioned in his journal, fewer than a dozen vessels had experienced mortality, and in only a few cases was the number of deaths very high.[15]

The emigrants' well-being depended as much on the preparation and storage of provisions as on their variety. The fact that many passengers apparently procured much of their own food probably reduced the chances that such items would be poorly packed or in bad condition. Individuals purchasing a few bushels of meal and peas could assess their quality more easily than could a Massachusetts Bay Company representative charged with obtaining supplies for an entire ship. Unscrupulous victualers, however, occasionally evaded the emigrants' watchful eyes and ensured that some passages would be miserable indeed. In 1637, the *Little Neptune* was so afflicted; whether the provisions were bad to start with or deteriorated during the

[15] Relying largely on eighteenth-century data, one scholar has suggested that shipboard mortality for white colonists on the whole averaged about 10 percent; see Henry A. Gemery, "Emigration from the British Isles to the New World, 1630–1700: Inferences from Colonial Populations," *Research in Economic History*, V (1980), 186–90; Higginson, *New-Englands Plantation*, 80–1; Wood, *New England's Prospect*, ed. Vaughan, 70; John Winthrop, *The History of New England from 1630 to 1649*, ed. James Savage, 2 vols. (Boston, 1825), I, 29, 105, 135–6, 205, 267. For 115 passengers on the seven ships used in this study, there was no information concerning their subsequent lives in New England. Even if one were to assume – generously – that half of these passengers died at sea, the death rate would still have amounted to barely 8 percent. Many of them were servants, especially female servants; it is more likely that gender and other biases in the genealogical and historical records are responsible for their disappearance.

voyage scarcely mattered, for the results were the same. Passengers discovered that the "pease were so hard and ill condiconed that they would not be softe though they had never so much seethinge." The cheese had rotted, the butter was blue, and the oatmeal was musty and would not thicken. The owner of the ship returned to sue his supplier, but that did nothing to ease the suffering of dozens of men, women, and children on the passage to New England.[16]

No wonder, then, that emigrants carefully attended to such details as the size and shape of the containers in which their food was packed. Three months before the *Arbella* sailed, Henry Winthrop informed his father that such details could affect the durability of the containers' contents. The governor's wayward second son, who had recently failed to make his fortune as a West Indian tobacco planter, evidently recalled his own seagoing misadventures when he urged his father to pack butter in large hogsheads, not small firkins.

> For to cary it in firkines is fare the worst way for I have sceine the exsperyence of it that one pound of hogsed butter is worth 2 of firkine butter when it comes a shore for the heat of the hould does desoullfe it to oyle in furkines and so it will not keepe when as the other will cut farme.[17]

Besides purchasing and packing ample amounts of food, emigrants concerned themselves with obtaining nonedible supplies. Many other items were needed, and prospective settlers spent a great deal of time and energy rummaging through chests, storerooms, and outbuildings in order to select possessions that would prove to be as indispensable as bread in New England. Advice like Francis Higginson's no doubt echoed in

[16] Dorothy O. Shilton and Richard Holworthy, eds., *High Court of Admiralty Examinations (Ms. Volume 53) 1637–1638* (London, 1932), 54–5, 59.

[17] Henry Winthrop to His Father, Jan. 18, 1629–30, *Winthrop Papers*, II, 194–5; for Henry Winthrop's career, see Darrett Rutman, *John Winthrop's Decision for America: 1629*, The America's Alternatives Series (Philadelphia, 1975), 25.

their minds as they set about their task, reminding them yet again that foresight was essential.

> Therefore be sure to furnish yourselves with things fitting to be had before you come; as meale for bread, malt for drinke, woolen and linnen cloath, and leather for shoes, and all manner of carpenters tools, and a good deale of iron and steele to make nails, and locks, for houses, and furniture for ploughs and carts, and glasse for windowes, and many other things which were better for you to think of them than to want them here.[18]

For additional help to emigrants, the Massachusetts Bay Company published a broadside enumerating necessary supplies. This list, like Higginson's recommendations, bore the marks of experience; it was apparently based on advice sent back to England by John Endicott's advance party, which had gone to Salem in 1628. In addition to victuals, the company suggested that settlers bring four other categories of goods. Apparel was a prime consideration: Each man should carry six pairs of shoes and one of boots, along with leather to mend them, four pairs of stockings, six shirts, twelve handkerchiefs, and one "Sea Cape, or gowne, of course cloth," presumably for foul-weather wear aboard ship. The next category was tools; in addition to the instruments of his trade, each man was advised to bring a spade, a shovel, two hatchets, three axes, a "wood hooke," three hoes, a "wimble, with six piercer bits" (for boring holes), and a hammer. Such items were essential for clearing land and for farming; as for constructing their houses, the emigrants should pack up nails, locks, and hooks for doors. With an eye to the colony's defense, the company recommended that settlers transport a variety of arms and ammunition. Finally, emigrants should bring hooks, lines, and leads for fishing; until agriculture began to prosper, Massachusetts's settlers would depend heavily on what the ocean could provide to supple-

---

[18] Higginson, *New-Englands Plantation*, 121.

ment dwindling stocks of provisions brought from England. In a marginal note on this broadside, the company also acknowledged the need for "bedding, and necessary vessels for kitchen uses." Families presumably would bring what they already had, and not purchase new items. In fact, the company hinted, emigrants might consider disposing of some household goods before leaving for New England, "lesse serving the turne there than would give contentment here."[19]

Emigrants adjusted these suggestions to suit individual requirements. They recognized, however, that there was a common logic inherent in the recommendations offered by experienced travelers. Prospective colonists should give first preference to items not obtainable in New England – principally cloth and other manufactured goods and tools that would see daily use. At the same time, they needed to consider the weight and volume of each item, for bundles, barrels, and unwieldy crates would severely hamper their mobility both en route to their ships and once landed in Massachusetts. On top of that, emigrants had to pay substantial transportation costs. The Massachusetts Bay Company estimated the cost of its recommended supplies – not including freight charges – at £17-07-04. Realizing that this amounted to a sum beyond the reach of many English folk, the company also noted which items "the poore may spare, having sufficient in that which the country affords for needfull sustenance of nature." Yet even if they did without malt, meat, boots, building materials, and pistols, as the company suggested, the "poorer sort" still needed to spend over £10 in preparation for their departure. Then the company levied a £4 charge for every ton of freight, and supplies for a large family quickly added up. John Josselyn estimated that one man's goods amounted to about half a ton, and

19 A facsimile of this broadside, with an introduction by Edmund S. Morgan, appeared in "Provisions for the Great Migration," *New England Quarterly*, IXX (1939), 98–9; see also Higginson, *New-Englands Plantation*, 111–12; Josselyn, *Account of Two Voyages*, 221–5; Wood, *New England's Prospect*, ed. Vaughan, 70–1; John Winthrop to His Wife, July 23, 1630, *Winthrop Papers*, II, 303; John Winthrop to John Winthrop, Jr., Mar. 28, 1631, in ibid., III, 21.

therefore cost him £2 to transport. Since the average emigrant household contained four persons, most groups could expect to pay upward of £25 for freight and passage – a sum that would have exceeded the annual rent for a family farm. Even with fewer goods, less affluent individuals needed close to £15 to cover their expenses. It is clear that, given the many costs of emigration, New England would not be peopled by England's poor.[20]

For an example of one family's preparations for moving to the New World, we can turn to the Coopers of Brampton, Suffolk. Fifty-year-old Benjamin Cooper and his wife, Elizabeth, doubtless spent hours deciding which possessions to take and which ones to sell. The Coopers would be traveling with their four children, a son-in-law named Francis Felmingham, Benjamin's younger sister, and two servants – a large party that would be expensive to transport. Cooper was a prosperous husbandman, but he surely saw no reason to spend more than was strictly necessary for his family's passage; hence, he and his family took care to retain only those goods that were useful and portable. But Cooper did not survive his voyage on the *Mary Anne*, and his family's first, sad task upon disembarkation was to file an inventory of Benjamin's possessions so that his estate could be distributed among his heirs. As a result, the contents of the Cooper family's baggage can be reconstructed – an exercise that indicates that many families must have departed from the spartan suggestions of the company's broadside. In addition to a large quantity of provisions, the Coopers had packed up clothing, bundles of broadcloth, calf skins, and "2 old Carpets." Twenty-eight pairs of sheets lay folded, along with a good supply of table linens, napkins, blankets, and what was perhaps a favorite set of green say curtains. Seven feather beds and three flock beds provided sleeping space for each member of the household, though only six would have pillows. To help him fight in his colony's

---

[20] Morgan, "Provisions for the Great Migration," 98–9; Shurtleff, ed., *Mass. Bay Recs.*, I, 65; Josselyn, *Account of Two Voyages*, 225. A ton was a measurement both of weight and of volume, occupying a space of 40 cubic feet and weighing 20 cwt (2,240 pounds in Great Britain).

defense, Benjamin packed his corslets – tight-fitting garments that protected the torso – along with muskets, swords, and bandoliers. Agricultural tools and harness for horses, eight bullocks, a pair of cart wheels, and an iron chain were brought to help equip the New World farm that Cooper would never see, and miscellaneous pieces of iron and wooden ware, stone and leather bottles, and pewter and brass vessels would stock his widow's kitchen. The Coopers had allowed themselves only a few luxuries – three silver spoons, two bibles and some other books, and a stool covered with velvet – objects that occupied little space and whose sentimental value perhaps more than redeemed the cost of their transportation.[21]

It is equally important to note what the Cooper family did not bring to Massachusetts. Benjamin transported bullocks, but not the heifers that would allow his herd to reproduce. He brought horse harnesses, but no horses; cart wheels, but no cart; flock and feather mattresses, but no bedsteads; and goods enough to fill a house, but none of the materials – neither window glass nor nails nor hinges – necessary to build one. Strive as they might for self-sufficiency, emigrants like the Coopers would have to depend on the local economy for many necessities. Fortunately, New England's forests supplied most of the settlers' needs for fuel, fences, houses, and furniture fairly cheaply. Colonial craftsmen exploited dense stands of red oak, pine, maple, and cedar to create the tables, chests, benches, and bedsteads that filled their neighbors' frame houses. Benjamin obviously intended to rely upon local artisans and the local market to provide the replacements for the housing, furniture, and stock left behind in England. In order to pay for cattle, building materials, and labor, he closely guarded his supply of "ready money" – nearly £400 in cash, probably obtained from the sale of his Suffolk estate – that ultimately helped his widow and children.[22]

[21] Benjamin Cooper's inventory is Suffolk no. 4.
[22] For an examination of early New England woodworkers, see Robert Blair St. George, *The Wrought Covenant: Source Material for the Study of Craftsmen and Community in Southeastern New England 1620–1700* (Brockton, Mass., 1979); for the importance of wood in the domestic economy of early New

New England's generation

Elizabeth Cooper's introduction to Massachusetts was unusually difficult, for she had lost her helpmeet, but all emigrants experienced some degree of disorientation. At least temporarily, the decision to move to New England had turned their worlds upside down. Families that had unquestioningly accepted the logic of accumulation – of land and money, of sheets and quilts and silver spoons – in order to provide for their sons and daughters discovered that migration demanded that they reverse the process, rapidly disposing of goods and land that might well have taken generations to acquire. Ordinarily, couples voluntarily gave up household possessions only when their children entered adulthood – and even then, such acts amounted to a redistribution, not a disposal, of carefully husbanded family resources. The decision to move to Massachusetts, however, forced families to reduce their worldly goods to a minimum, turning household items into a nest egg of cash. For these activities, normal experience provided no guide. Just when their physical, mental, and spiritual resources would be sorely tested, the emigrants deliberately reduced their material possessions to the point of vulnerability. They would have food for a year – if they heeded the experts' advice – and sufficient clothing (until the children grew or fabrics wore thin) and tools for the kitchen and farm. But they no longer had a roof over their heads or even bedsteads on which to lay their mattresses. Once they had pared away the superfluous and the untransportable, they were left in a position that at once fostered individual mobility and encouraged group interdependence.

The emigrants could hardly ignore the precariousness of their position. At the very beginning of the Great Migration, the Reverend Nathaniel Ward sympathized with the plight of colonists awaiting the start of their voyage. In January 1630, Ward interceded on behalf of a group of concerned emigrants when he begged John Winthrop "to reserve roome and passage in your shipps for 2 families, A carpenter and Bricklayer the

England, see William Cronon, *Changes in the Land: Indians, Colonists, and the Ecology of New England* (New York, 1983), ch. 6.

most faithfull and dilligent workmen in all our partes, one of them hath putt of[f] a good farme this weeke and solde all, and should be much dammaged and discouraged if he finds no place amongst yow." Winthrop doubtless did his best to oblige, but even with their berths secure, Ward's carpenter and brick-layer still faced a period of uncertainty, of some financial "dammage," for the passengers on the Winthrop Fleet did not begin to board their ships until the end of March. During the intervening weeks, between the time they disposed of their property and the day of their embarkation, these two families – like hundreds of others in the succeeding decade – would have been compelled to live off their accumulated capital. Every shilling spent for lodging at an inn, or for food and drink at a tavern, was a shilling less to spend in New England. Some may have attempted to minimize the financial strain by postponing the final disposition of their property until the last possible moment, thereby reducing the time during which they would have to live off their savings; others, such as Richard Mather, sought free room and board with charitable Christians in their port town. Yet, few emigrants could have avoided some deple-tion of their funds. Forced to plan according to their vessel's scheduled departure date, they could do little when unforeseen delays or – as in the case of the Winthrop Fleet itself – contrary winds confined ships to their harbor long after they should have been at sea.[23]

Emigrants could, at best, reckon on finding a New England-bound vessel anchored in a port not too far from their homes and assume that the likeliest season for departure would be springtime. Virtually all of the colonists examined here lived within forty miles of their ports of departure; their journeys to dockside would have consumed no more than three or four days. Emigrant ships departed from numerous points along the

[23] Nathaniel Ward to John Winthrop, Jan. 16, 1630, in *Winthrop Papers*, II, 192; "Journal of Richard Mather," 5–6. Winthrop's first letter composed aboard the *Arbella* was dated Mar. 22, 1630; see John Winthrop to His Wife, *Win-throp Papers*, II, 222. The ship did not actually set sail until April 8 (ibid., II, 242).

English coast, including London; Bristol, Barnstaple, Weymouth, and Plymouth in the western counties; Southampton in the south; and such eastern ports as Ipswich, Great Yarmouth, and Gravesend. Sea captains preferred to undertake Atlantic crossings in the early spring: Most emigrant ships set sail in the months of March and April. Ocean voyages were never predictable, but experienced sailors hoped that by embarking in early spring, they would have reasonably good weather both for the westward passage and for the midsummer return trip.[24]

How the colonists actually went about securing passage to New England remains somewhat obscure. In the early years of the migration, the Massachusetts Bay Company apparently played a leading role in obtaining and outfitting emigrant vessels. Arrangements made for the Winthrop Fleet in the winter of 1629–30 were comprehensive: The company agreed to "provyde a sufficient nomber of shipps, of good force" that would be "ready to sett saile from London, by the first day of March." If any passengers wished to board at the Isle of Wight, the ships would stop there for just twenty-four hours. All passengers had to give their names, along with forty shillings toward their freight costs, to the company's undertakers in London by the end of the Michaelmas term. Their baggage had to arrive ten days prior to the scheduled departure date, at which time the remainder of their charges would be paid "ether for mony to bee paid heere, or for com[m]oditie to be deliv[er]ed in the plantacion."[25]

Although the company had similarly superintended the prep-

---

[24] Winthrop recorded ports of departure for twenty-nine ships arriving in Massachusetts between 1630 and 1642. Nine left from London, five each from Bristol and Ipswich, four from Barnstaple, two from Southampton, and one each from Great Yarmouth, Weymouth, Gravesend, and Plymouth. Only one of the ships used in this study, the *James* of Southampton, was mentioned by Winthrop; see Winthrop, *History of New England*, ed. Savage, passim. In his *History*, Winthrop also recorded the dates of departure for thirty-one ships; Charles Banks recorded similar information for eighty-seven emigrant vessels in *The Planters of the Commonwealth* (Boston, 1930). See Table 7 in the Appendix for a presentation of their data.

[25] Shurtleff, ed., *Mass. Bay Recs.*, I, 65–6.

arations for the *Talbot's* crossing a year earlier, one of its passengers offered future colonists advice on an alternative means of arranging their own voyages. "It were a wise course," wrote Francis Higginson, "for those of abilityes to joyne together and buy a shipp for the voyage and other merchandize." The minister readily acknowledged that the "payment of the transportation of things is wondrous deare" and concluded that "a little more than will pay for the passage will purchase the possession of a ship for all together." Never one to skimp on details, Higginson recommended several men to contact about such matters, not forgetting that "my cousin Nowell's counsell would be good."[26]

Whether or not Increase Nowell found himself deluged with eager inquiries about ship purchases, several emigrants did follow Higginson's suggestion. In fact, the practice of cooperative ownership by emigrants of the vessels on which they sailed may have been fairly widespread. At least two of the seven ships studied here were owned by some of their passengers. The *Hercules* of Sandwich was one such vessel. In late November 1634, the emigrants Nathaniel Tilden, Comfort Starr, and William Hatch joined with one "Mr. Osborne" and John Witherley, a local mariner, to purchase a ship. Witherley crossed the Channel to Dunkirk, where he found the 200-ton Flemish-built *St. Peter* available for £340. He and his partners bought it, renamed it the *Hercules,* and brought it to Sandwich to be outfitted for a transatlantic voyage the following spring. By the end of December, 101 emigrants had signed up for the trip to Massachusetts, to be made under the direction of master John Witherley himself. Likewise, some of the passengers on the East Anglian ship, the *Mary Anne,* invested in their vessel. When Thomas Payne wrote his will some seven months after his arrival in Salem, he still owned a share in it. One of Payne's financial partners was the unfortunate Benjamin Cooper, a sub-

26 Ibid., I, 26–7, 36; Frances Rose-Troup, *The Massachusetts Bay Company and Its Predecessors* (New York, 1930), 23–4; Higginson, *New-Englands Plantation,* 119.

stantial portion of whose estate – perhaps as much as £600 – lay in his investment in the ship on which he died.[27]

Higginson's calculation of the financial advantages of emigrant ownership was largely accurate. If the 101 passengers on the *Hercules* paid the going rate for their transportation, the ship's owners would have recouped the vessel's cost in passage fees alone; additional freight charges would have earned them a profit. Moreover, once they settled in New England, the owners could have either sold their shares in the vessel or sought future earnings from subsequent voyages. Most, in fact, probably disposed of their shares fairly quickly: Neither Tilden, Hatch, nor Starr mentioned such investments in their wills. Indeed, this is not too surprising, for of the five known investors, only one – the Sandwich merchant William Hatch – had extensive business experience. Comfort Starr was so unfamiliar with maritime concerns that, when asked by a judge of the High Court of Admiralty to describe his newly purchased vessel, the Kentish physician confessed that, "being noe seaman," he could only guess at its dimensions. In one important way, however, these men were well suited to the task. All of them were older, prosperous men with enough capital to invest in this venture; few of their fellow passengers could have mar-

---

[27] J. R. Hutchinson, "Some Notable Depositions from the High Court of Admiralty," *NEHGR*, XLVII (1916), 332. The passenger list for the *Hercules* is dated December 1634; see Eben Putnam, "Two Early Passenger Lists, 1635–1637," *NEHGR*, LXXV (1921), 218. For Payne, see Paine, *Thomas Payne of Salem*, 16; for Cooper's inventory, Suffolk no. 4. Because of a tear in one corner of Cooper's inventory, it is impossible to know the precise amount of his investment. The total amount of his estate was £1,278-12-00, and the total value of the items still legible equaled £561-14-10. The remaining sum – £716-17-02 – was the total value of the following entries: sacks, a pound of black thread, an apron, eight bullocks, "his part in the ship," "stock in the ship," and "provision in the ship." The first three items together could hardly have been worth more than a few shillings, and the cattle would have been valued at about £80 (Samuel Hall's 1637 inventory lists two two-year-old steers worth £10 each). A good portion of the remaining amount – approximately £600 – was therefore Cooper's ship investment. No inventory of Payne's estate remains; hence the value of his share is unknown.

shaled the same resources. The owners may also have subsidized some of their cotravelers, for the costs of transportation, as we have seen, could be substantial.[28]

The consequences of ownership transcended the realm of finance. Joint purchase of a vessel – and, in a different way, paying the fees of the less fortunate – created strong economic bonds among men who were often recent acquaintances and testified to their common faith in their mission. Their shared liability perhaps helped to dispel the sense of individual vulnerability fostered by the disposal of goods and lands, as Starr, Tilden, Hatch, and others realized that they were not alone in this venture. If their fellow passengers did not have as large a financial stake in the voyage, they had nonetheless pledged their lives as fully as did the ship owners. For weeks prior to their departure from England, the emigrants immersed themselves in a highly individualized process of preparation, but as they made their way to the ships, they increasingly realized that this was a collective adventure. In the busy port towns the emigrants conversed with large groups of similarly committed people, people who had all come to the same decision about the need to move to the New World.

Shortly before each ship's departure, the passengers gathered to meet the king's searchers. These officials, in compliance with a royal proclamation, administered the oath of allegiance to the adults and examined the certificates attesting to their religious conformity that passengers had been required to ob-

---

[28] If the *Hercules's* owners charged the same rate as did the Massachusetts Bay Company (£5 for adults, with reduced rates for children), they would have received between £300 and £350 in passage fees alone. For Comfort Starr's examination, see Hutchinson, "Some Notable Depostions," *NEHGR*, XLVII (1916), 332. The extent to which wealthier emigrants helped poorer ones pay for their passage is unknown. It appears that the Massachusetts Bay Company did pay for the transportation of laborers, at least early in the migration; members who agreed to transport servants received extra allotments of land; see Shurtleff, ed., *Mass. Bay Recs.*, I, 36, 43. Also, in a letter to John Winthrop, Jr., in June 1633, Thomas Gostlin of Groton, Suffolk, mentioned his fruitless attempts to find craftsmen and maidservants to be sent over at Emmanuel Downing's charge; *Winthrop Papers*, III, 124–5.

tain from their parish ministers. Once everything had been judged in order, the searchers dispensed tickets, or "Licenses under their handes and seales, to passe the seas," and cleared the vessel for departure. Thus, unwittingly, Charles I had provided for a ritual that emphasized the emigrants' emerging solidarity. No matter where each passenger came from, no matter what individual circumstances had brought him or her to the ship, every one of them stood on the deck and presented the required documents to the officials. In the process, as passengers received the searchers' stamp of approval, the finality of their decision and their new, shared status as emigrants to New England must have become strikingly apparent. Each emigrant, however, was but a single thread in a fabric of community that was yet to be woven: The voyage itself would begin to weave these disparate strands into a coherent whole.[29]

II

Even if the ocean crossing had done nothing else, it would have given the emigrants something to talk about for the rest of their lives.[30] Even those who had as placid a passage as Francis Higginson had nonetheless embarked on an adventure fraught with potential peril, the outcome of which was never certain. For most passengers, the voyage was an unforgettable introduction to seafaring; their backgrounds as farmers, artisans, and homemakers could hardly have provided much opportunity for maritime excursions. Each trip, of course, differed in its particulars, but all of them reinforced the emigrants' sense of separation from the home country. Both the vast distance covered and

[29] The quotation, and a description of the searchers' visit, are in "Journal of Richard Mather," 6. For the king's proclamation, see Charles Boardman Jewson, ed., *Transcript of Three Registers of Passengers from Great Yarmouth to Holland and New England*, Norfolk Record Society, *Publications*, XXV (1954), 6–7; Carl Bridenbaugh, *Vexed and Troubled Englishmen 1590–1642* (New York, 1967), 468–9.

[30] A different interpretation of several of the themes in this section is discussed by David Cressy in "The Vast and Furious Ocean: The Passage to Puritan New England," *NEQ*, LVII (1984), 511–32; and *Coming over*, ch. 6.

the unfamiliar mode of traveling reminded the colonists that they were no ordinary English migrants.

The duration of the voyage no doubt did much to inculcate a powerful appreciation of the magnitude of their trip. Higginson's six-and-a-half-week passage was, as he himself recognized, a fortunate exception; a crossing of eight to ten weeks was far more common. News of an unusually speedy trip – like that of the *Talbot* or of the *James* of Southampton, which in 1635 sailed to Boston in just thirty-eight days – was offset by accounts of nearly interminable voyages, such as that of a London ship that in 1636 spent a full twenty-six weeks at sea. The problem with this particular crossing, Winthrop explained, was "continual tempests." When the captain finally brought the ship near the New England shore, "the weather was so thick all that time, as they could not make land"; not surprisingly, "the seamen were in great perplexity." The fog cleared briefly, allowing them to see that the ship lay near Cape Ann, but before they could make a move, it "presently grew thick again," forcing them to navigate solely with a compass and their recollection of their position.[31]

Vessels sailing to New England struggled constantly against strong currents and prevailing westerly winds. Instead of the twenty-four hours they had planned to spend at the Isle of Wight, the ships of the Winthrop Fleet lay at anchor for ten days in Yarmouth harbor, until favorable breezes finally sprang up at six o'clock on the morning of April 8. Within hours, however, the winds had died, leaving the *Arbella* and its accompanying ships becalmed in the Channel until ten o'clock that

[31] Higginson, *New-Englands Plantation*, 81. In his journal, Winthrop noted the approximate duration of voyages for twenty-one vessels; Charles Banks provided similar information for twice that number. The length of time for a crossing ranged from five and one-half weeks to half a year; the average voyage – for both Winthrop and Banks – was about nine to ten weeks. The modal durations for Winthrop were six, eight, and twelve weeks (five ships each); for Banks, the mode was eight weeks. See Winthrop, *History of New England*, ed. Savage, passim; the information on the *James* and the London ship is from ibid., I, 161, 205; see also Banks, *Planters of the Commonwealth*, passim.

night. Capricious weather prevented navigators from charting a direct course to their destination, and ships continually tacked against contrary winds, adding miles and days to the trip. Winthrop's detailed account of his crossing testifies to the fortitude of mariners and passengers alike. For every "merry gale" that propelled the ships closer to Massachusetts, there were several days of calm or "stormy and boisterous" seas that impeded progress. During the last week of April, the governor's daily jottings noted "the wind northerly," "the wind still W. and by S.," and after a period of "scarce any wind," the weather obliged with "a pretty gale, so as our ship made some way again, though it were out of our right course." No wonder that six weeks later, on June 5, a northeasterly gale occasioned "in the great cabin, thanksgiving."[32]

Throughout the course of their voyages, the emigrants attempted to maintain a semblance of normal daily routines. Daylight and darkness regulated their lives at sea as much as on land, and there were always meals to prepare and tidying up to do below decks. Although the men obviously abandoned their agricultural or artisanal tasks for the duration of the trip, many ships carried cattle, sheep, and horses that required care. Children demanded their parents' attention as well, and family duties provided one important constant in the emigrants' lives. In fact, the ocean crossing seems not even to have interfered with the reproductive schedules of some families. Three women on the *Rose* were probably pregnant at the time the ship set sail, indicating that at least some couples did not consider the upcoming voyage a sufficient reason to postpone their families' growth. Births and, to a lesser extent, deaths thus continued to punctuate the lives of these families even while they were at sea.[33]

---

[32] Winthrop, *History of New England*, ed. Savage, I, 5, 10, 13, 22. For an account of the circuitous routes taken by ships bound for the Chesapeake in this period, see Melvin H. Jackson, "Ships and the Sea: Voyaging to the Chesapeake," in David B. Quinn, ed., *Early Maryland in a Wider World* (Detroit, 1982), 33–57.

[33] Joan Leeds bore twin sons within two months of the *Rose's* arrival in Massachusetts in mid-June 1637; John and Anne Moulton's son John, as

Passage

Because these familiar activities were performed in such un-usual surroundings, however, they unavoidably assumed a new character. Their cramped quarters below decks ensured that emigrants would experience a lack of privacy unprece-dented even for former dwellers in England's most populous cities. Simple tasks, such as cooking, took on new importance, as those who prepared food needed to plan carefully for a voyage of uncertain duration. Each ship carried a limited quan-tity of provisions (except for the addition of occasional catches of fish) to be consumed during the voyage; food intended for consumption during the first year of settlement was stowed in the vessel's hold and was therefore inaccessible, except for extreme emergencies. Limited supplies of utensils and the ob-vious need to regulate the number of cooking fires probably compelled groups of families to cook and eat together. Even sleeping aboard ship could be an adventure – especially for children – since sheets and mattresses had also been packed

well as Henry and Elizabeth Skerry's daughter Elizabeth, were baptized in March 1638. If the latter two infants were about six months old at their baptism – which seems to have been common practice – both Anne Moul-ton and Elizabeth Skerry were in the advanced stages of pregnancy while aboard ship. For the Leeds family, see Mary Walton Ferris, compiler, *Dawes-Gates Ancestral Lines; A Memorial Volume Containing the American An-cestry of Rufus R. Dawes* 2 vols. (privately printed, 1943), I, 407; for the Moultons, see Henry W. Moulton, *Moulton Annals,* ed. Claribel Moulton (Chicago, 1906), 208; for the Skerrys, see James Savage, *A Genealogical Dictionary of the First Settlers of New England, Showing Three Generations of Those Who Came before May, 1692. . . . ,* 4 vols. (Boston, 1860–2), IV, 104, and Richard D. Pierce, ed., *The Records of the First Church in Salem, Massachusetts 1629–1736* (Salem, Mass., 1974), 16. For the age of infants at baptism, see John Demos, *A Little Commonwealth: Family Life in Plymouth Colony* (New York, 1970), 132. Higginson, Winthrop, and Josselyn all recorded births and deaths in the accounts of their voyages; Higginson, *New-Englands Plantation,* 66, 75–6; Winthrop, *History of New England,* ed. Savage, I, 21, 23; Josselyn, *Account of Two Voyages,* 219. In a letter to his former parishioners in Tarling, Essex, the Reverend Thomas Welde noted that, among his fellow passengers, there were "women big with child," and that "one delivered of a lusty child within forty hours after she landed, she and the child well"; see *Letters from New England: The Massachusetts Bay Colony, 1629–1638,* ed. Everett Emerson, The Commonwealth Series (Amherst, Mass., 1976), 95.

in the hold. In a letter written shortly before his departure, John Winthrop attempted to set his wife's mind at ease about his accommodations, noting that "havinge tryed our shipps entertainment now more than a weeke, we finde it agree very well with us, our boyes are well and cheerfull, and have no minde of home, they lye both with me, and sleepe as soundly in a rugge (for we use no sheets heer) as ever they did at Groton, and so I do my selfe." No doubt the Winthrops found their surroundings somewhat less comfortable once the *Arbella* actually left port.[34]

Much of what the emigrants encountered during their voyages was quite new to them, and by no means pleasant. Seasickness was ubiquitous, plaguing nearly every passenger for at least part of his or her crossing. The first days of the voyage were the worst, for the emigrants had not yet become accustomed to the roll and pitch of the vessel. When the *Talbot* was just one week out of Gravesend, Francis Higginson reported that "the wind blew hard from south west & caused our ship to daunce, & divers of our passengers & my wiffe especially were sea sicke." Richard Mather noted that many of his companions were similarly afflicted on the first day of their trip.

> The 24th [of May 1635] beeing the Lorde's day, the wind was strong in the morning, and the ship daunced, and many of our women and some children were not well; but sea-sicke, and mazy or light in their heades, and could scarce stand or go without falling, unlesse they tooke hold of something to uphold them.

Little could be done to ease the passengers' discomfort; time and gradual adaptation to the ship's movement were the principal remedies for their ills. The only other measure was exercise in the open air, and although afflicted emigrants were understandably reluctant to rise from their sickbeds, their healthy neighbors apparently coaxed them into movement. After two

---

[34] John Winthrop to His Wife, Mar. 28, 1630, *Winthrop Papers*, II, 224.

days of buffeting by "a stiff gale," for instance, many of those aboard the *Arbella* had been laid low. Rather than leaving them to their miseries, Winthrop described how he and other un-affected passengers responded to their companions' distress with rather vigorous ministrations.

> Our children and others, that were sick, and lay groaning in their cabins, we fetched out, and having stretched a rope from the steerage to the mainmast, we made them stand, some of one side and some of the other, and sway it up and down till they were warm, and by this means they soon grew well and merry.

Friendly seamen occasionally joined the passengers in therapeutic recreation. Two days after the previous attack of seasickness, Winthrop noticed that although "the ship heaved and set more than before," fewer people became ill, and of those afflicted, "such as came up upon the deck, and stirred themselves, were presently well again." The ship's captain, who surely wanted his passengers to gain their sea legs as much as they themselves did, "set our children and young men to some harmless exercises, which the seamen were very active in, and did our people much good," although, the governor sniffed, the crew "would sometimes play the wags with them."[35]

Seasickness, however unpleasant, was seldom fatal. Other maladies, particularly smallpox, could wreak much more extensive havoc in the confined quarters of a sailing vessel. Even the relatively "healthfull" voyage of the *Talbot* was marred by this virulent disease; two of its victims were the son and daughter of Francis Higginson.

> This day my 2 children Samuel & Mary began to be sicke of the small-pockes & purples together, which was brought into the ship by one Mr. Browne which

[35] Higginson, *New-Englands Plantation*, 61–2, 64, quotation from 61–2; "Journal of Richard Mather," 6, 8, 9, 11, 12, 14, 17, quotation from 6; Winthrop, *History of New England*, ed. Savage, I, 267.

was sicke of the same at Graves End, whom it pleased
God to make the first occasion of bringing that conta-
gious sicknes among us, wherewith many were after
afflicted.

Despite another outbreak a few weeks later, only young Mary
Higginson succumbed to the infection. John Josselyn witnessed
a similar outbreak of smallpox during his initial voyage to New
England in 1638; although many passengers became ill, Josselyn noted only two deaths. Disease could, of course, inflict
greater damage on shipboard populations. In August 1638, Winthrop recorded the arrival of two vessels "which came over . . .
much pestered, lost many passengers, and some principal
men, and many fell sick after they were landed, and many of
them died."[36] Yet although some degree of shipboard mortality
was probably inevitable, death rates were rarely high. The mi-
crobes transported on these ships had a far worse effect on the
native population of New England than they did on the emigrants, who had developed some degree of immunity to them.
Adequate provisions forestalled serious nutritional deficiencies;
cases of scurvy – the disorder that probably drove young Martin Ivy, a captain's servant, to the extreme of "filching 9 great
Lemmons out of the *Chirurgeons* Cabbin, which he eat rinds and
all in less than an hours time" – were apparently rare. Indeed,
accidents were as much to be feared as disease, as one poor
fellow who "was drowned . . . as he was casting forth a line to
take mackerel" discovered in 1633. Many emigrants doubtless
worried about their survival at sea, but their worst apprehen-
sions of doom went by and large unfulfilled.[37]

[36] Higginson, *New-Englands Plantation*, 65–6, 70–1, quotation from 65; Josselyn, *Account of Two Voyages*, 214, 217, 218, 220; Winthrop, *History of New
England*, ed. Savage, I, 267.
[37] For the effects of European diseases on Indian populations, see, for instance, Francis Jennings, *The Invasion of America: Indians, Colonialism, and
the Cant of Conquest* (Chapel Hill, N.C., 1975), 24–5, 207–8, and Cronon,
Changes in the Land, 85, 87–91. Quotation about scurvy from Josselyn,
Account of Two Voyages, 216. Quotation about accident from Winthrop,
History of New England, ed. Savage, I, 108. For general reports of the healthi-

Passage

If disease threatened the passengers less than they may have feared, inclement weather was justifiably a source of concern. Mid-Atlantic tempests often displayed a ferocity unknown to emigrants whose previous experience was limited to the mild English climate. Francis Higginson, for instance, acknowledged his "land man's" unfamiliarity with ocean storms; the minister's admitted inexperience only heightened his alarm during a storm on May 27, 1629, when

> there arose a South wind, which encreased more and more, so that it seemed to us that are land men a sore & terrible storme; for the wind blew mightily, the rayne fell vehemently, the sea roared & the waves tossed us horribly; besides it was fearfull darke & the mariners maid was afraid; & noyse on the other side with their running here & there, lowd crying one to another to pull at this & that rope. The waves powred themselves over the shippe that the 2 boates were filled with water, that they were fayne to strike holes in the midst of them to let the water out. Yea by the violence of the waves the long boate coard which held it was broken, & it had like to have bene washed overboard, had not the mariners with much payne & daunger recovered the same.

The crew's frantic activity suggests that Higginson's fear was well founded. Emigrants often traveled in convoys of five or six ships, and, at the very least, storms threatened to scatter the vessels all over the North Atlantic. Fierce winds might drive ships miles out of their way, lengthening an already long voyage. What passengers and crews most dreaded, of course, were violent tempests that could reduce the strongest craft to splinters. Perhaps the most vivid passages in the accounts of these seventeenth-century transatlantic voyages are those that de-

ness of voyages, see Higginson, *New-Englands Plantation*, 80–1; "Journal of Richard Mather," 31–2; Thomas Welde to His Former Parishioners at Tarling, June–July 1632, in Emerson, ed., *Letters from New England*, 95–6.

scribe storms and the terror that they struck in the hearts of the emigrants. Richard Mather's depiction of "a sore storme & tempest of wind and raine" is a case in point.

> [M]any of us passengers with wind & raine were raised out of our beds, and our seamen were forced to let down all the sayles: and the ship was so tossed with fearefull mountaynes and valleyes of water, as if wee should have beene overwhelmed & swallowed up.

Less than two weeks later, Mather's ship encountered yet another spell of bad weather near the Isles of Shoals, leading the minister to believe that

> wee were in as much danger as I thinke ever people were: for wee lost in that morning three great ancres & cables; of which cables, one having cost 50£ never had beene in any water before, two were broken by the violence of the waves, and the third cut by the seamen in extremity and distresse, to save the ship and their & our lives. And when our cables and ancres were all lost, we [had] no outward meanes of deliverance but by loosing sayle. . . .[38]

But although sickness and storms often punctuated the voyages of these first-time transatlantic travelers, they seldom dominated the entire experience. Boredom, in fact, more accurately characterized most passages, as days at sea stretched into weeks and weeks into months. Yet the emigrants also shared moments of happiness and thanksgiving, in extraordinary form when children were born or in more commonplace ways when the weather favored their progress; on one such fair day, Richard Mather noted, his fellow passengers were quite "hearty & cheerefull." The voyage, emigrants discovered once they recov-

---

[38] Higginson, *New-Englands Plantation*, 69; see also 71, 78; "Journal of Richard Mather," 24–5, 28–9; see also Winthrop, *History of New England*, ed. Savage, I, 10, 15, 16–19.

ered from initial bouts of nausea, was not an unremitting trial after all.[39]

What seems most thoroughly to have amused – and amazed – passengers was the sighting of unusual sea creatures. Men who kept journals of their crossings regularly reported such events. On one "faire hot summer day," for example, Richard Mather wrote that "wee saw with wonder and delight [an] abundance of porpuyses, and likewise some crampushes as big as an oxe, puffing and spewing up water as they went by the ship." A few weeks later, Mather and his companions were entertained by "a great many of Bonnyetoes leaping and playing about the ship," which, the minister explained, were fish "somewhat bigger than a cod but lesse than a porpuise." In this case, the travelers, weary of pottage, perceived an opportunity for nourishment as well as entertainment. "[O]ur seamen took a Bonyetoe, and opened him upon the decke"; it was, Mather observed, "as good fish in eating, as could be desired." Porpoises likewise permitted culinary experimentation: "[T]he flesh of them was good meate with salt, peper and vinegar; the fat like fat bacon, the leane like bull-beefe."[40]

Mather's ship was by no means the only one to attract porpoises; they seem, in fact, to have escorted most emigrant vessels. Other unfamiliar marine animals, if less ubiquitous, also merited comment and often inspired awe. Whales were occasionally sighted, and, as Francis Higginson remarked, "their greatnes did astonish us that saw them not before: their backs appeared like a little Island." The minister reported seeing grampuses, "a large round fish sayling by the ships side about a yard in length & roundnes," which mariners called "a sunne fish." He also mentioned a glimpse of "a fish very straunge to mee . . . which came by the ships side wafting along the top of

---

[39] "Journal of Richard Mather," 18. For births at sea, see Winthrop, *History of New England*, ed. Savage, I, 21.

[40] "Journal of Richard Mather," 17, 20, 22. Not everyone agreed with Mather's judgment; John Josselyn thought that porpoise flesh tasted like "rusty Bacon, or hung Beef, if not worse"; see his *Account of Two Voyages*, 215. Bonito, on the other hand, made "excellent food" (217).

the water. [I]t appeared at the first like a bubble above the water as bigg as a mans fist[,] but the fish it selfe is about the bignes of a mans thum, so that the fish it selfe & the bubble resembleth a shipp with sailes, which therefore is called a carvell." John Josselyn, on his first voyage to New England, mentioned that the crew of his ship captured "a Sharke, a great one . . . with his two Companions . . . that is the Pilot-fish or Pilgrim, which lay upon his back close to a long finn; the other fish (somewhat bigger than the Pilot) about two foot long, called a *Remora*, it hath no scales and sticks close to the Sharkes belly." Indeed, the frequency and details of these descriptions suggest that emigrants spent a considerable amount of time gazing at the sea and marveling together at its wonders.[41]

The passengers also recognized that the ocean's attractions were by no means limited to the curious creatures that dwelled in its depths. Encouraged by the novelty of their experience to observe with keen eyes scenes and events that might have escaped the notice of more seasoned travelers, they often expressed admiration for the beauty of the sea itself. Richard Mather declared that he and his fellow passengers took pleasure in gazing at the ocean as wind and weather shaped its surface. "It was very delightfull," the minister recalled at the end of his voyage, to have seen such variations, "the sea sometimes beeing rough with mighty mounteynes and deepe valleyes, sometimes againe plaine and smooth like a level meadow, and sometimes painted with a variety of yellow weedes." That Mather resorted to familiar, land-based similes for his descriptions – "mounteynes," "valleyes," and "meadows" – testifies all the more eloquently to the limitations of his previous experience; by employing these homely comparisons, he sought to make an unfamiliar scene more recognizable both to himself and to his readers, using language to conjure up well-

[41] Higginson, *New-Englands Plantation*, quotations from 76, 71, 72; see also 70, 73; Josselyn, *Account of Two Voyages*, quotation from 216; see also 214–15. For other descriptions of unusual sea creatures, see "Journal of Richard Mather," 15, 16, 19, 21; Winthrop, *History of New England*, ed. Savage, I, 16.

known pastoral images in minds unacquainted with the change-
able panorama of the ocean.[42]

As time passed, the passengers gained a greater understanding of the sea, learning to detect changes in the wind and the
onset of storms and to identify different species of Atlantic fish.
Even with this increased knowledge and experience, however,
they never failed to be amazed at natural phenomena. Francis
Higginson eventually considered the appearance of porpoises
worth only a cursory mention in his journal, but his heart quick-
ened when he caught his first glimpse of an iceberg.

> [W]e saw a mountayne of Ice shyning as white as
> snow like to a great rocke or clift on the shoare. [I]t
> stood still & therefore we thought it to be on ground
> & to reach the bottome of the sea. For though there
> came a mighty streame from the north yet it mooved
> not, which made us sound, & we found a banke of 40
> fathom deepe whereupon we judged it to rest: & the
> height above was as much.

There were always new creatures to be seen, new tempests to
endure, or new vistas to contemplate. On rare occasions, passengers may even have marveled, like John Josselyn, at the
sight of "a flame settled upon the main mast, . . . about the
bigness of a great Candle, [which] is called by our Seamen St.
Elmes fire"; this unusual sight, Josselyn added, "comes before a
storm, and is commonly thought to be a Spirit."[43]

If the emigrants refused to take such experiences for granted,
it was because they understood that all the events of their voyage, no matter how seemingly disparate, shared a common
meaning, and they readily saw the pattern that underlay each
day's occurrences. Theirs was a world view that acknowledged
the constant intervention of God in daily affairs. They knew
that the Lord watched over them at sea as well as on land, and

---

[42] "Journal of Richard Mather," 33; for similar descriptive language, see Higginson, *New-Englands Plantation*, 82.
[43] Higginson, *New-Englands Plantation*, 72–3; Josselyn, *Account of Two Voyages*,
215; Josselyn also mentioned seeing an iceberg (218).

that their professed mission in settling New England for His greater glory compelled them to be particularly mindful of His presence in their lives. The accounts of the voyages to Massachusetts, therefore, were not mere catalogues of random occurrences; instead, they provided a continuous record of the Lord's assessment of their progress. Because they believed that all events, all natural phenomena, carried supernatural significance, the emigrants' appreciation of the beauty of the sea could not be merely aesthetic, their fear of violent tempests wholly innocent of even greater dread.

Everything fit into the emigrants' providentialist framework of thought. Strange sea creatures did not just provide diversion and, occasionally, nourishment; they also offered an opportunity to behold "the workes and wonders of the Almighty in the deepe." When favorable winds finally allowed his ship to make progress, Richard Mather perceived a sign of divine favor:

> about one of the clocke the Lord remembered us in mercy, and sent us a fresh gale at south; which though weake and soft, yet did not only much mitigate the heate, but also holpe us something forward in our way.

Similarly, John Hull attributed the freeing of his vessel from a sand bar that it had struck near the Isles of Shoals to the work of the Lord.

> God so ordered it, that (after long beating and much fear) he turned the ship off again into the sea, and the next day gave us a great calm, and, by it, liberty to mend our broken helm, and other things that were amiss.[44]

---

[44] "Journal of Richard Mather," 23; see also 33; "The Diaries of John Hull, Mint-master and Treasurer of the Colony of Massachusetts Bay," *Transactions and Collections of the American Antiquarian Society* (Boston, 1857), III, 142; see also J. Franklin Jameson, ed., [Edward] *Johnson's Wonder-Working Providence, 1628–1651*, Original Narratives of Early American History (New York, 1910), 61–2.

Passage

Both men freely acknowledged the Lord's role in aiding their ships, but neither would have dared to suggest that the passengers *deserved* divine favor. God's ways were more mysterious and hardly depended on human actions. After a severe storm buffeted the *Talbot* near Cape Ann and then quickly abated, Francis Higginson reflected that "hereby the Lord shewed us what he could have done with us, if it had pleased him." Yet although Higginson and his fellow passengers understood divine favor to be a free act of mercy, completely undeserved by humans, they also believed calamities to be a divine rebuke of individual or communal sinfulness. When Winthrop recorded the death of a seaman aboard the *Jewel,* adding that he was "a most profane fellow, and one who was very injurious to the passengers," he never doubted the connection between the sailor's comportment and his fate.[45]

Passengers who could do little to control the behavior of the captain and crewmen were ceaselessly mindful of their own. They knew that in God's eyes they were no less sinful than the vilest mariner, and that the Lord could punish them as swiftly as He did Winthrop's "most profane fellow." Thus when storms or other threats to the passengers' well-being occurred, the emigrants concluded that they had done something wrong and that the Lord was showing His displeasure. Having enjoyed a spell of good weather toward the end of their voyage, for instance, Richard Mather and his companions became complacent, and it was not long before their unwarranted self-satisfaction incurred divine disfavor. "[L]est we should grow secure, and neglect the Lord through abundance and prosperity," admitted Mather, "our wise and loving God was pleased . . . to excercise us with a sore storme & tempest of wind and raine." Several days later, the Lord evidently saw cause once again to remind the passengers of His omnipotence.

> But yet the Lord had not done with us, nor had let us
> see all his power and goodnesse which he would

[45] Higginson, *New-Englands Plantation,* 78; Winthrop, *History of New England,* ed. Savage, I, 20.

have us to take knowledge of; and therefore on Saturday morning about breake of day, the Lord sent forth a most terrible storme of raine and easterly wind, whereby wee were in as much danger as I thinke ever people were.

The tempest had the desired effect: The emigrants acknowledged their weakness and "cryed unto the Lord," who pitied them and ended the storm. "It was," Mather wrote, "a day much to bee remembered," for "the Lord graunted us as wonderfull a deliverance as I thinke ever people had." He concluded with the wish that

> the Lord so imprint the memory of it on our hearts, that wee may bee the better for it, & bee more carefull to please him and to walke uprightly before him as long as wee live; and I hope wee shall not forget the passages of that morning untill our dying day.[46]

Mather's call for remembrance points directly to the heart of the matter. Having observed a most vivid manifestation of the Lord's mercy, the emigrants should strive to "bee the better for it." By constantly recalling this example of divine intervention in their lives, they should remember that God had not – and would not – abandon them. More important, this incident, Mather realized, ought to provoke a *communal* renewal of faith: "I hope *wee* shall not forget," he wrote. Since Mather used his journal to catalogue God's providences for later "improvement" in sermons, one can be sure that his fellow passengers had the opportunity to contemplate the larger significance of the events they experienced. The Lord had bestowed the benefits of His mercy on all of the passengers alike, whether they were adults or children, sinners or saints. Deliverance from the storm, the minister urged, should provide a common spiritual reference point for all of the emigrants on that ship, one that would help inspire them to submit to the Lord to their dying days.

---

[46] "Journal of Richard Mather," 24, 28–30.

Passage

Puritanism was essentially a devotional movement that stressed the importance of a community of believers, drawing upon a complex system of spiritual exercises to give structure and meaning to the daily lives of individuals and their communities. Far from disrupting patterns of devotion, the voyage to New England lent them a new force and immediacy. Since Elizabethan times, for instance, English Puritans had proclaimed days of fasting and prayer as a way of reinforcing their separate identity and of responding to adversity. How much more intense was the same ritual when enacted on a crowded, tossing ship beset by "sicknes & death & contrary winds" in the midst of a vast ocean? Since they were convinced that illness or storms were clear evidence of God's displeasure, the emigrants resorted to days of fasting and humiliation aboard ship to acknowledge their depravity. Such experiences not only strengthened individual piety but also knit together the community of believers. And when these exercises proved efficacious – as after a day of fasting on the *Talbot*, when the Reverend Francis Higginson reported that "we had a fayre gale that night as a manifest evidence of the Lords hearing our prayers" – the emigrants could not help but be encouraged by God's approval of their venture.[47]

Special shipboard devotions in response to extraordinary events augmented a regular schedule of religious exercises. Each vessel became, in effect, a floating congregation. Every day, the emigrants gathered in prayer services; every Sabbath, they listened to sermons. Sabbath keeping at sea was occasionally difficult, especially during bad weather, and could require some sacrifice. Once his ship reached Newfoundland's Grand

---

[47] This discussion relies heavily upon the excellent treatment of Puritan lay devotionalism in Charles E. Hambrick-Stowe, *The Practice of Piety: Puritan Devotional Disciplines in Seventeenth-Century New England* (Chapel Hill, N.C., 1982). For Elizabethan practices, see Patrick Collinson, *The Elizabethan Puritan Movement* (Los Angeles, 1967), 214–19. For evidence of days of fasting, humiliation, and prayer conducted at sea, see Higginson, *New-Englands Plantation*, 67–8, 71, quotation from 67–8, where Higginson also claimed that the *Talbot*'s crew thought "this was the first sea-fast that ever was kept"; Winthrop, *History of New England*, ed. Savage, I, 3, 22.

Banks, the non-Puritan John Josselyn noted how the sailors took advantage of the rich fishing grounds; it being a Sunday morning, however, "the Sectaries aboard threw those their servants took into the Sea again, although they wanted fresh victuals." Since over two hundred clergymen eventually went to New England, passengers could often rely on ministers to lead them in devotions. Francis Higginson and Richard Mather both kept a careful account of the services they conducted aboard ship. Given the strong lay pietistic strain in Puritanism, however, it does not follow that passengers on vessels without clergymen neglected their religious duties; instead, they generally selected one or two of their number to act as lay elders.[48]

Religious leaders constantly sought to interpret the events of the voyage in terms that would be meaningful and spiritually profitable to their listeners. Emigrants were thus constantly reminded that their departure from England had an importance that transcended its effect on their individual lives. The most powerful metaphor pervading Puritan devotion was that of the pilgrimage, and the emigrants could scarcely have failed to see the parallel between the individual's long journey toward salvation and their own communal passage to a New World. When John Cotton selected a text on which to base his farewell sermon for the Winthrop Fleet in 1630, he chose one that emphasized this theme. Drawing on God's promise to Nathan in II Samuel that He would "appoint a place for my people Israel, and will plant them," Cotton intertwined the dual themes of

---

[48] Quotation from Josselyn can be found in his *Account of Two Voyages*, 218; see also 216. For evidence of daily prayer and Sabbath keeping, see Higginson, *New-Englands Plantation*, 61, 62, 63, 65, 72, 74, 79; "Journal of Richard Mather," 6, 9, 11, 13, 14, 18, 19, 20, 22, 24, 31, 34; Winthrop, *History of New England*, ed. Savage, 1, 9, 15. Plymouth Colony lacked an ordained minister for nearly a decade after its founding; see George D. Langdon, Jr., *Pilgrim Colony: A History of New Plymouth, 1620–1691* (New Haven, Conn., 1966), 116–23. Of the seven ships studied here, three carried ministers: Reverend William Wetherell on the *Hercules* (who listed himself as a schoolmaster), Reverend Joseph Hull on the Weymouth ship, and Reverend John Youngs on the *Mary Anne*.

the community's transplantation and the individual's path of devotion.[49]

Given the importance of typology – of seeking biblical analogues for current events – in Puritan theology, it is scarcely surprising that Cotton and other ministers explored their bibles to discover precedents for the experiences of their own lives and then explained the connections to their fellow emigrants. Such discoveries established a link between the New England settlers and biblical forebears and infused the migration with unmistakable spiritual significance. One scriptural passage in particular seems to have appealed to emigrant ministers. Francis Higginson, for example, suddenly "saw the truth" of Psalm 107, verses 23 to 32; he and others almost certainly communicated to their fellow passengers the fervor of their discovery. For the verses do indeed sum up the ordeal and sublimity of passing beyond the seas.

> They that go down to the sea in ships, and occupy
>   their business in great waters;
> These men see the works of the Lord, and his
>   wonders in the deep.
> For at his word the stormy wind ariseth, which
>   lifteth up the waves thereof.
> They are carried up to the heaven, and down again
>   to the deep; their soul melteth away because
>   of the trouble.
> They reel to and fro, and stagger like a drunken
>   man, and are at their wit's end.
> So when they cry unto the Lord in their trouble,
>   he delivereth them out of their distress.
> For he maketh the storm to cease, so that the
>   waves thereof are still.

[49] Hambrick-Stowe, *Practice of Piety*, 23–4, 42–3, 54–90. Cotton's text was II Samuel 7:10: "Moreover I will appoint a place for my people Israel, and will plant them, that they may dwell in a place of their own, and move no more; neither shall the children of wickedness afflict them any more, as beforetime."

Then are they glad, because they are at rest; and
    so he bringeth them unto the haven where they
    would be.
O that men would therefore praise the Lord for his
    goodness; and declare the wonders that he
    doeth for the children of men!
That they would exalt him also in the congregation
    of the people, and praise him in the seat of
    the elders!

The emigrants had all gone down to the sea in ships and had seen the Lord's wonders in the deep. All had staggered on their vessels' decks in tempests that the Lord had raised and had mercifully ended. Gathering in their congregations, they had not failed to exalt the Lord in all His power and mercy. No less for ordinary emigrants than for Francis Higginson, the truth of these verses was as plain as if they had been written about their own voyages. For indeed, in a way, they had.[50]

The voyage to New England marked a dramatic turning point in the lives of the emigrants. Shared experiences of wonder and dread, given point by the biblical glosses of their leaders, provided the settlers with a profound sense of physical and spiritual separation from England. The ocean passage, above all else, identified New England's founding generation, distinguishing its members from ancestors and descendants alike. But if the events of each voyage served to knit together strangers into shipboard communities while at sea, those communities did not remain intact on land as passengers dispersed upon their arrival. The emigrants would hold powerful memories in common with their shipmates but generally would not settle together with them. Having abandoned their English towns and villages to form temporary communities at sea, they would regroup to form new communities in the New World.

[50] Hambrick-Stowe, *Practice of Piety*, 54–8; Sacvan Bercovitch, *The Puritan Origins of the American Self* (New Haven, Conn., 1975), ch. 2. For references to Psalm 107, see Higginson, *New-Englands Plantation*, 69–70; "Journal of Richard Mather," 17.

3

Transplantation

No single trait defined the New England settlers – and distinguished them from other English emigrants to the New World – more clearly than their self-conscious commitment to communalism. Aboard ship, strangers wove the strands of a common religious spirit and a common decision to emigrate (although a decision arrived at separately by individuals and families) into a web of community that sustained them in the face of a dangerous transatlantic voyage. The experience of the voyage would always be remembered as a shared one, and in a very real sense, the beginnings of New England society date less from the moment of the settlers' arrival in Boston or Salem than from the time of their departure from Southampton or Great Yarmouth. But shipboard communities were, in the end, temporary expedients created in response to a powerful but temporary event, and they disbanded upon arrival in New England. Once the settlers had landed, they soon embarked on the formation of new, permanent communities based on the principle of voluntary association.

Constructing new communities was an endeavor without precedent in the lives of the settlers; none of them had ever founded a town or village in England. Yet it is clear from their activities that there was a general, if unarticulated, consensus about how that process should be carried out. Settlement would be a corporate enterprise as groups of colonists voluntarily gathered together to establish towns, each with its church, where the spiritual and secular communities would be coterminous. Agriculture would provide the principal economic basis of these communities, and within the larger communal framework of each town, individual economic needs would be addressed through the equitable (though not equal) distribution of land. It was precisely this determination to maintain a careful balance between the needs of individuals and those of the community as a whole that distinguished New Englanders so thoroughly from other English settlers in North America.

New Englanders, for instance, were no less eager than their Chesapeake counterparts to obtain land in the New World, but their eagerness was tempered by a concern for community integrity. Chesapeake settlers, unconstrained by an ideological commitment to dwelling in towns, settled first and developed community ties later. Establishing their plantations where the land seemed richest and access to water transportation easiest, they created a society with widely dispersed settlement where neighbors often lived a considerable distance from each other. Community ties in the Chesapeake ultimately proved strong and durable, but they appeared only gradually as settlers formed connections with their neighbors through marriage, mutual interdependence, and economic exchange.[1]

The distinctive New England approach to settlement, however, was not one that the Puritans imported from England in its final form. Rather, they groped toward it once they had arrived, and once it had become apparent that the form of land distribution they had initially contemplated would work at cross-purposes to their communal ideal. For initially – before any settlement had actually taken place – the Massachusetts Bay Company proposed to allocate land according to a headright system, evidently modeled on the one the Virginia Company had used. Emigrating householders would receive plots for themselves, plus additional acres for each family member or servant ("head") they brought with them. Such a system would certainly have attracted land-hungry recruits to the region, much as it did in Virginia, but it was hardly consistent with the Bay Colony leaders' commitment to community settlement. Under a headright system, colonists might well have scattered

[1] Kevin P. Kelly, " 'In dispers'd Country Plantations': Settlement Patterns in Seventeenth-Century Surry County, Virginia," in Thad W. Tate and David L. Ammerman, eds., *The Chesapeake in the Seventeenth Century: Essays on Anglo-American Society and Politics* (Chapel Hill, N.C., 1979), 183–205; Darrett B. Rutman and Anita H. Rutman, *A Place in Time: Middlesex County, Virginia, 1650–1750* (New York, 1984), esp. chs. 3, 4.

throughout the countryside, planting themselves and their families as the Virginians did, wherever they thought the land looked most promising. Once they had reached New England, however, the colony leaders recognized the difficulties a headright system posed for community integrity and so adopted instead a settlement policy more congenial to their communal ideals. By the mid-1630s, the General Court was regularly granting land not to individuals by headrights, but to towns as corporate entities as a way of ensuring that New Englanders would settle together and stay together in geographically coherent communities.[2]

This false start by Bay Colony leaders demonstrates that, instead of carrying with them some utopian blueprint for their society's organization, colonists arrived with a general set of

---

[2] For the original Massachusetts headright scheme, see Nathaniel B. Shurtleff, ed., *Records of the Governor and Company of the Massachusetts Bay in New England*, 5 vols. (Boston, 1853–4), I, 42–3. The precise timing of the transition to a town-grant system is unclear, although by 1634 the court made such a grant to the inhabitants of Newtown (Cambridge) who sought a more "convenient" habitation; ibid., I, 119. For evidence that individual grants could promote disorder in the first year of settlement, see Darrett B. Rutman, *Winthrop's Boston: A Portrait of a Puritan Town, 1630–1649* (Chapel Hill, N.C., 1965), 45–6. For a description of the Virginia headright system, see Edmund S. Morgan, *American Slavery, American Freedom: The Ordeal of Colonial Virginia* (New York, 1975), 93–4, 171–3.

For the town-grant system, see Roy Hidemichi Akagi, *The Town Proprietors of the New England Colonies: A Study of Their Development, Organization, Activities, and Controversies, 1620–1770* (Philadelphia, 1924), 30–8. New England assemblies did occasionally grant land to individuals, often to prominent men either as a reward for public service or as an incentive to promote the formation of towns; see John Frederick Martin, "Entrepreneurship and the Founding of New England Towns: The Seventeenth Century" (Ph.D. diss., Harvard University, 1985), chs. 1–7. Although this general discussion focuses on land policy in Massachusetts (where the bulk of New Englanders lived), similar practices of granting land to communities prevailed elsewhere. For Plymouth, where a town-grant policy eventually replaced communal ownership, see George D. Langdon, Jr., *Pilgrim Colony: A History of New Plymouth, 1620–1691* (New Haven, Conn., 1966), 30, 42, 48–53; for New Hampshire, see David E. Van Deventer, *The Emergence of Provincial New Hampshire, 1623–1741* (Baltimore, 1976), 21–33; for Connecticut, see Bruce C. Daniels, *The Connecticut Town: Growth and Development, 1635–1790* (Middletown, Conn., 1979), 119.

shared principles, which through experimentation and adaptation formed the basis of an emergent structure of community. The abandoned headright scheme was but one episode in what proved to be the greatest ongoing challenge facing the colonists – that is, the task of accommodating the very real subsistence needs of anxious settlers while preserving a communal ideal that emphasized the subordination of the individual to the community. The experience of Plymouth had demonstrated the futility of seeking to found a society on pure communalism, and that of Virginia had warned of the dangers of unrestrained individualism.[3] Maintaining the critical balance between the two became, in the end, the colonists' greatest achievement.

Paradoxically, the triumph of Puritan communalism ultimately depended upon a highly individualistic process of geographic mobility within New England – a Great Reshuffling of population that succeeded the Great Migration, a process by which colonists sorted themselves out into the communities in which they would remain for the rest of their lives. Yet this inland migration, although inspired by the settlers' search for economic opportunity, never threatened the communal goals of New England society but instead supported them in a complex and subtle way. In fact, the colonists' patterns of movement within New England demonstrated more forcefully than anything else how fully ordinary settlers – as well as ministers and magistrates – were committed to preserving the communal ideals of Puritanism.

I

The reshuffling of the emigrant population occurred as a direct but unanticipated consequence of the system of communal land distribution. Although this town-based system was established by the colonial legislatures, ordinary colonists imple-

---

[3] After a seven-year experiment with communal ownership of property, in 1627 Plymouth settlers divided up the colony's land and other assets into private holdings; see Langdon, *Pilgrim Colony*, 29–31, 38–40.

mented it, controlling, to a remarkable degree, access to land within their communities. Colonial governments exercised little supervision over the townspeople's activities; once the Massachusetts Bay General Court granted land to a group of petitioners, for instance, it subsequently left the critical business of organizing the town up to the inhabitants, requiring only that no town order be "repugnant" to colony law.[4] But as they set up their towns and divided town lands, the inhabitants also created a set of conditions that ensured that their fellow colonists would – at least for a brief period after their arrival in New England – be compelled to move around the region before finding a permanent residence.

It was clear from the start that these New World communities would not simply replicate former patterns of English life.[5] New England towns, unlike English villages and boroughs that dated from time out of mind, existed above all to be the secular counterparts of religious congregations: There could be no town without its church and no church without its town. Settlers agreed that both church and town should be modeled on the scriptural precedent of the covenanted community of believers.[6] When they turned to the division of land within their communities, the colonists made no attempt to reproduce the complex English tenurial system and instead adopted a nearly universal system of freehold ownership.[7] Unlike copyholders or leaseholders, whose property rights were limited to a fixed time, freeholders owned their land outright, enjoyed its fruits

[4] Shurtleff, ed., *Mass. Bay Recs.*, I, 167, 172.

[5] There were, of course, some similarities between New England towns and the English villages from which emigrants came; for the most complete exposition of this theme of transatlantic persistence, see David Grayson Allen, *In English Ways: The Movement of Societies and the Transferal of English Local Law and Custom to Massachusetts Bay in the Seventeenth Century* (Chapel Hill, N.C., 1981).

[6] The pioneering study of this process is Kenneth A. Lockridge, *A New England Town: The First Hundred Years* (New York, 1970).

[7] There were renters as well as freeholders in early New England, but their experience proved to be the exception rather than the rule; see Stephen Innes, "Land Tenancy and Social Order in Springfield, Massachusetts, 1652 to 1702," *William and Mary Quarterly*, 3rd ser., XXXV (1978), 33–56.

exclusively, and passed it along to their heirs as they wished. It was precisely because of this widespread consensus about the form and meaning of New England towns and land tenure that colony governments could afford to leave the process of settlement up to the settlers themselves.

Indeed, despite its decentralized nature, New England settlement followed a singularly consistent pattern, proceeding in several well-defined stages. First, before inhabitants could move to a new plantation, a number of preliminary tasks, such as surveying the land and laying out roads, had to be completed. These tasks of town development demanded an investment of time and money far beyond the capabilities of most ordinary settlers. Colony officials therefore turned to a relatively small group of prosperous colonists eager to carry out these functions in return for grants of land as proprietors in the new towns. Such men as John Winthrop, Jr., and John Pynchon, with capital resources greatly surpassing those of most of their fellow colonists, operated throughout New England and played an essential role in the foundation of towns. At first glance, the entrepreneurial behavior of these proprietors, who held speculative rights to land in towns they never intended to inhabit, seems to stand in sharp contrast to the communal ideals of New England society. Yet their actions as entrepreneurs were in fact sharply constrained by the communitarian imperatives of their society. Their efforts and resources encouraged town formation; towns – and churches – were the communitarian ends that justified their speculative means. Furthermore, they operated under legal restraints by which colony governments forbade actions (such as hoarding land to drive up the price) that would discourage settlement.[8] Finally, these proprietary entrepreneurs had an important stake in promoting community growth, even if they did not intend to live in such places themselves. Any land grant they received as nonresident proprietors remained worthless until

---

[8] See, for instance, Shurtleff, ed., *Mass. Bay Recs.*, I, 114; Martin, "Entrepreneurship and the Founding of New England Towns," 224, 235–8.

permanent settlers arrived. In land-rich New England, only the influx of colonists into a town, increasing the demand for (and thus the price of) real property, could make the entrepreneurs' financial ventures profitable. This first stage in the settlement process, rather than challenging the society's ideological commitment, successfully harnessed individual economic initiative to benefit Puritan communalism.[9]

In the second phase of settlement, inhabitants arrived in the towns and composed the town and church covenants that expressed their shared ideal of community. At the same time, they engaged in more mundane matters, dividing up town land in ways intended to ensure each family a comfortable subsistence. In each town, the inhabitants themselves – or, more specifically, those prominent settlers who were, as Edward Johnson put it, "men of good and honest report" – undertook the delicate task of allocating land among their neighbors and themselves.[10]

In so doing, these settlers – like the developers before them – carefully weighed individual and community needs. They took care of individual families by assigning plots according to "quality" or social standing, so that no one would suffer a comparative diminution in status because of migration. These were, after all, seventeenth-century Englishmen thoroughly accustomed to the idea of hierarchy and hoping to use it to stabilize their New World society. New England's social pyramid, however, would be sharply truncated, partly as a result of the homo-

[9] The best account of this first stage of New England settlement is in Martin, "Entrepreneurship and the Founding of New England Towns," especially chs. 1–6. Martin's research provides a new perspective on the communitarian origins of New England towns; it should be noted that he places greater emphasis on the role of individual initiative than appears here. For more on the careers of John Winthrop, Jr., and John Pynchon, see Richard S. Dunn, *Puritans and Yankees: The Winthrop Dynasty of New England, 1630–1717* (Princeton, N.J., 1962; paperback, New York, 1971), chs. 3, 5; Stephen Innes, *Labor in a New Land: Economy and Society in Seventeenth-Century Springfield* (Princeton, N.J., 1983), esp. ch. 2.

[10] Edward Johnson, *Johnson's Wonder-Working Providence, 1628–1651*, ed. J. Franklin Jameson, Original Narratives of Early American History (New York, 1910), 213. See also Akagi, *Town Proprietors*, chs. 3, 4.

geneous character of the emigrant population and partly due to the deliberate manipulation of land policy. For if a man's quality was important in determining his land allotment, so too was the size of his household. In upholding hierarchical standards, in other words, the proprietors could not ignore the very real subsistence needs of the settlers. Edward Johnson, one of the "good and honest" men who divided Woburn's land in 1640, noted that even "the poorest had six or seven acres of Medow, and twenty five of Upland, or thereabouts," enough for a decent subsistence. Such grants represented, moreover, freehold land in quantities utterly beyond the reach of most English farmers. From the town's perspective, individual settlers' desire for land commensurate with their social standing had to be balanced against the community's need to provide "the poorest" with sufficient means to prevent them from becoming an economic burden on their neighbors.[11]

The real economic advantage to becoming a proprietor in a New England town, however, lay not only in the size and quality of one's original land grants but also in the rights that accompanied proprietary status. Of primary importance was the right to share in future divisions of the land that the town initially held as common property. The townsmen charged with making allotments usually carved up only a small proportion of each community's total land reserves when the town was being settled. This seeming parsimony in fact bespoke a keen understanding of long-run economic benefits. Very few colonists

---

[11] For land distribution in individual towns, see, for instance, Lockridge, *A New England Town*, 10–12; Philip J. Greven, Jr., *Four Generations: Population, Land, and Family in Colonial Andover, Massachusetts* (Ithaca, N.Y., 1970), 45–9. For contemporary English notions of hierarchy, see Keith Wrightson, *English Society 1580–1680* (London, 1982), ch. 1, and Peter Laslett, *The World We Have Lost*, 2nd ed. (London, 1971), ch. 2. The classic New England statement concerning hierarchy appears in John Winthrop's "A Model of Christian Charity," *The Winthrop Papers*, 5 vols. (Boston, 1929–47), I, 294; see also Stephen Foster, *Their Solitary Way: The Puritan Social Ethic in the First Century of Settlement in New England* (New Haven, Conn., 1971), ch. 1. The quotation from Edward Johnson is in Johnson, *Wonder-Working Providence*, ed. Jameson, 213.

could have marshaled sufficient labor resources to bring more than a fraction of their property under cultivation anyway. For instance, when Joseph Bachelor died in 1647, a decade after his arrival in Salem, only six of his seventy acres of land had been "broken up." By limiting the size of initial land grants, immense (by English standards) reserves of town land were set aside for later distribution, when actual cultivation would be practicable and – more important – when the land would be needed for the support of future generations.[12]

The key to the system lay in restricting access to the undivided common lands to "original proprietors," those settlers who received allotments during a town's early years. Shares in future divisions would be allocated according to the size of each proprietor's original grant. Few proprietors failed to realize that their interests would be best served by limiting entry into their group. Uncontrolled admissions to the town, given the widespread commitment to providing virtually all inhabitants with land, meant not only the multiplication of original grants but a corresponding reduction in the size of future shares of undivided land. Thus all over New England, proprietors began to limit the number of townsmen who could partake of the same advantages they enjoyed. The "closings" of proprietorships could occur quite soon after initial land divisions. As early as January 1636 – barely six years after its founding – Dorchester's proprietors denied new arrivals access to the town's undivided land. Dedham's leaders prohibited a further influx of proprietors only a few *months* after the town's founding. But Dedham's founders, like settlers in other communities, came to realize that an effective proprietary pol-

12 The best description of the proprietary system, and the one that informs much of the following discussion, is in Martin, "Entrepreneurship and the Founding of New England Towns," esp. chs. 8, 9. Older treatments of the subject include Akagi, *Town Proprietors*, and Melville Egleston, "The Land System of the New England Colonies," *Johns Hopkins University Studies in Historical and Political Science*, 4th ser., XI (1886), 549–600. Joseph Bachelor's land is described in his inventory, in the Essex County Probate Records, Salem, Mass., docket no. 2089. On the initial limitation of land grants, see also Greven, *Four Generations*, 48–9; Lockridge, *New England Town*, 12.

icy required a sense of balance. Admitting too many landholders had obvious repercussions, but it was equally disadvantageous to close the proprietorship too early, for that might leave a town with too few settlers to be viable. Dedham's founders thus soon reopened the proprietorship, admitting new members until 1656. Responding to similar calculations in their communities, the settlers in twenty-two towns scattered from Maine to Rhode Island either closed or drastically restricted entry into the proprietorship within the first ten years of settlement; the inhabitants of thirty-four towns did so within thirty years of their founding.[13]

For those who arrived early, then, proprietorship could confer considerable economic security – not only on themselves, but also on their children and even their grandchildren. Their town's undivided property constituted a sort of territorial trust fund that would help to support their descendants. Thus proprietary policies gave the founding generation of settlers in any town an economic stake commensurate with their ideological investment in their community's welfare even as they provided the settlers' descendants with an incentive to remain that ensured the community's survival and growth.

But the process of settlement did not cease at this point, with dozens of new communities inhabited by satisfied proprietors and their expectant children. A third phase began with the arrival of new settlers seeking accommodation in established towns. In most cases, if the newcomers were well-behaved, God-fearing Christians, they would be accepted into the community and granted (or sold) land for their present use, although often they would not be entitled to share in future divisions of town land. In towns where proprietorships were closed, a fundamental split therefore appeared within the body of landholders, dividing the early arrivals who would enjoy the

---

[13] City of Boston, *Fourth Report of the Record Commissioners* [Dorchester Town Records], 2nd ed. (Boston, 1883), 14; Akagi, *Town Proprietors*, 71–2; Lockridge, *New England Town*, 8–9; Martin, "Entrepreneurship and the Founding of New England Towns," tables 3, 3a.

special privileges of proprietorship from the latecomers who would not.[14]

This two-tiered system of landholding in New England towns spawned local disputes, but the position of the original proprietors as a group was never seriously threatened. Tension was defused in part by the fact that there were always some settlers for whom the benefits of proprietorship were not particularly attractive. Older emigrants, those who were either childless or who had adult offspring, had little incentive to augment their present estates with shares of land that might well be allocated after their deaths. Without large families to help provide labor, such settlers also faced difficulties in cultivating even their initial allotments. Single young men, at least temporarily, confronted similar problems; in a land where labor was scarce and expensive, such men might find it initially advantageous to hire themselves out, rather than to burden themselves with estates they could not yet afford to improve.

The generally low level of conflict over landholding and proprietary privileges, however, also owed much to the fact that new communities appeared throughout the lifetimes of the first generation of settlers. In Massachusetts, the founding of twenty-three towns during the 1630s signaled the high point, but scarcely the end, of the expansion of settlement; sixteen new towns were begun in the 1640s, nine in the 1650s, nine in the 1660s, and twelve in the 1670s. Only the outbreak of King Philip's War in 1675 halted the outward movement of colonists, and the return of peace brought the resumption of town foundings.[15] The fourth and final phase of settlement began as latecomers left established communities where they were denied accessible farms or proprietary privileges and moved on to found new towns where they could control the distribution of land themselves. These settlers faced a prolonged period of mobility, but

---

14 Martin, "Entrepreneurship and the Founding of New England Towns," 291–302; Greven, *Four Generations*, 62–4.
15 The timing of town foundings has been compiled from data in Paul Guzzi, ed., *Historical Data Relating to Counties, Cities and Towns in Massachusetts* (Boston, 1975).

for emigrants who had already uprooted themselves from England and had survived a transatlantic voyage, this no doubt seemed a bearable price to pay for economic security.

It is clear from their behavior in New England that settlers quickly learned how this unique system of land distribution and town founding worked and what its implications were. Yet even as they embraced the communal ideals that the system was meant to uphold, average colonists were free – and indeed compelled – to address familial concerns, the most important being the acquisition of the farms that would support them. Personal circumstances dictated how often families moved, where they settled, and how well they adapted to their new surroundings. In the end, the colonists examined here dispersed into no fewer than forty-five communities scattered from Maine to New Jersey.[16]

Different patterns of mobility and settlement emerged, but through them all ran a common thread of concern for community: No matter how the settlers took advantage of the opportunities New England offered, the search for secure livelihoods never overrode the search for spiritual fulfillment. Indeed, in the most fundamental sense, their attempts to satisfy both their economic and spiritual needs were inseparable aspects of the settlers' desire to live their lives, as completely as possible, within the communion of saints.

II

We cannot know if John and Anne Moulton thought that their journey would be over once the *Rose* docked in Boston harbor.

---

[16] The distribution of the household heads' destinations was as follows: ninety-two to Massachusetts Bay (76.7 percent); sixteen to Plymouth Colony (13.3 percent); four to New Hampshire (3.3 percent); two each to Connecticut, Long Island, and Rhode Island (1.7 percent each); and one each to New Haven and New Jersey (0.8 percent each). Two families moved back to England. Emigrants who arrived during the first wave of settlement early in the 1630s would, of course, have moved less frequently than did the colonists in this study, who arrived between 1635 and 1638.

If they did, they soon discovered their mistake, for their migration was, in fact, beginning a new and equally challenging phase. Once John and his servant, Adam Goodens, retrieved the family's baggage and rejoined Anne, her maidservant, Alice Eden, and the five young Moulton children, the couple had to decide what to do next. Fortunately for them, the port of Boston by 1637 already offered weary passengers a few rudimentary amenities. The family may have sought a warm meal and information about temporary lodging at Samuel Cole's tavern, and they undoubtedly visited the town's weekly market, where goods damaged at sea or left behind could be replaced and where news about the colony's outlying settlements could be heard. Yet even as John Moulton welcomed the warmth of the June sun after weeks of cold Atlantic winds, his experience as a husbandman no doubt warned him against complacency. He knew that he had arrived too late to plant for that year's harvest, and now could fully appreciate the urgency of warnings about provisioning. The best he could hope to do was to settle his family within the next few months, so that he and Adam could take advantage of warm weather to construct shelter for the household and to begin to clear ground for next spring's planting.[17]

By October, the Moultons had settled in Newbury, some twenty-five miles north of Boston.[18] Why John chose to settle his family in this particular village cannot be determined; what *is* clear is that he soon regretted his decision. Less than a year later, he joined sixteen other Newbury inhabitants in signing a

---

17 For the Moulton household, see Charles Boardman Jewson, ed., *Transcript of Three Registers of Passengers from Great Yarmouth to Holland and New England*, Norfolk Record Society, *Publications*, XXV (1954), 22; for early Boston, see Rutman, *Winthrop's Boston*, 37, 180–1. The most recent genealogical research on the Moulton family can be found in William Haslet Jones, "The English Background of Some Early Settlers of Hampton, New Hampshire, from Ormesby St. Margaret, Norfolk [continued]: The Moulton Family," *New England Historical and Genealogical Register*, CXLI (1987), 313–29.

18 Henry W. Moulton, *Moulton Annals*, ed. Claribel Moulton (Chicago, 1906), 208; Joshua Coffin, *A Sketch of the History of Newbury, Newburyport, and West Newbury, from 1635 to 1845* (Boston, 1845), 24.

petition requesting the General Court's permission to begin a new community at Winnacunnet, a site across the Merrimack River that later became the town of Hampton. The petitioners declined to give a reason for their request, but it is likely that they were unhappy with Newbury's provisions for their accommodation. The town's first settlers had arrived in the spring of 1635, more than two years before the Moultons set foot in Massachusetts. Naturally, the founders of Newbury first assigned lots near the town center fronting the river; later arrivals such as the Moultons received more distant and less desirable holdings, subordinating them both economically and politically to their predecessors, who controlled the board of selectmen to whom the power of land distribution had been entrusted.[19]

Moulton's willingness to seek other, and presumably better, accommodation elsewhere probably intensified in the spring of 1638, when Anne gave birth to their sixth child. He evidently realized that if he helped to found a new town, he could shape its land policy in ways that had been, and probably always would be, denied him in Newbury. There were also other undeniable, if less immediately tangible, attractions in being a town founder. Besides participating in land distribution, Moulton could contribute to the organization of the new community's civil and ecclesiastical institutions. As a firstcomer, he would have a say in the selection of the town's minister and could likewise offer his opinions – and perhaps his services – as Hampton chose its first board of selectmen. All of these factors undoubtedly weighed in Moulton's decision to move his family another ten miles or so north to the new village of Hampton.

The move paid off handsomely, for Moulton's economic circumstances improved in Hampton and he soon became prominent in town affairs. In December 1639, he received one of the largest lots initially granted by the town, a parcel of 250 acres. Within a few years he became Hampton's fourth largest land-

---

[19] Shurtleff, ed., *Mass. Bay Recs.*, I, 236; Coffin, *History of Newbury*, 18–19. In his analysis of early Newbury, David Allen discovered that the town's distribution of land was highly stratified, more so than in the four other towns that he examined; see *In English Ways*, 110–11.

holder, for his initial grant entitled him to a considerable share of property in subsequent divisions. Moulton achieved political recognition as well, gaining election as Hampton's first representative to the General Court.[20]

John Moulton's experience was no isolated success story, but rather exemplified – at least up to the point of his election to the General Court – the predominant pattern of early New Englanders' lives. Most colonists arrived, like the Moultons, during the summer and spent several weeks in the port towns where they had disembarked.[21] There they sought information about good places to settle, and – usually before winter set in – most had selected a nearby town and moved there. But for many settlers, the first choice of destination proved as unsatisfactory as John Moulton's choice of Newbury. Whether their complaint concerned discriminatory land policy or some other factor, many chose to move to a new town, generally one less than two years old.[22]

---

[20] Joseph Dow, *History of the Town of Hampton, New Hampshire*, 2 vols. (Salem, Mass., 1893), I, 12, 17–18; Van Deventer, *Emergence of Provincial New Hampshire*, 22. In 1645, when Hampton's freemen resolved to divide the town's cow commons according to individual need and projected actual use, Moulton objected strenuously – to the point of petitioning the General Court for redress – because the scheme ignored both a man's wealth, as measured by tax rates, and the number of children in his family. By that time, Moulton was the father of seven and obviously sensitive to the issue; see Van Deventer, *Emergence of Provincial New Hampshire*, 22.

[21] According to Winthrop's record of incoming ships, the vast majority of vessels (seventy-five of ninety-three, 80.6 percent) arrived between May and August. See John Winthrop, *The History of New England from 1630 to 1649*, ed. James Savage, 2 vols. (Boston, 1825), passim.

[22] More than half of all household heads for whom there is information on New England residence settled in towns that were no more than five years old when they arrived (64 of 122, 52.5 percent). In most of those cases, in fact, the destination was two years old or less when the newcomers arrived (56 of 64, 87.5 percent; or 45.9 percent of the total of 122 household heads). Most of these settlers of infant towns (30 of 56) repeated Moulton's experience of moving first to one town and then to the newly established community. Although these general patterns of movement are clear, precise measurements are hampered by three factors. First, the ports of arrival for these ships are unknown and must be deduced from the distribution of the passengers' first known residences. (It seems likely that the *Hercules*, the

The channels of information alerting settlers to the establishment of a new town remain obscure, but the likeliest purveyors of news were the original developers of a tract, eager to entice colonists in order to make good on their investments.[23] Settlers investigating these frontier opportunities formed groups, the character of which indicates the rapidly increasing complexity of connections binding New England society together. In some cases, a common English regional background united settlers of a particular New England community. Many emigrants from Kent, for instance, crossed the border into Plymouth Colony in order to settle at Scituate, whereas the Bay Colony town of Weymouth became home to several families from Somerset. When Robert Page and Henry Dow moved their families to Hampton, they settled near the Moultons, who had also been their neighbors back in the Norfolk village of Ormesby. Shipboard acquaintanceship may also explain aspects of New World settlement patterns, as when the *James* passengers John and Richard Knight of Romsey in Hampshire and Anthony and William Morse of Marlborough in Wiltshire all brought their families to Newbury in 1635. Perhaps most important, however, were connections forged in the settlers' first New England residences. John Moulton joined several of his Newbury neighbors in petitioning for permission to settle Hampton, and many of the families who would settle Sudbury first met in Watertown. Groups that would find their way to the Connecticut and New Haven colonies originally formed in Charlestown, one of

James, the Weymouth ship, the *Rose*, and the *Confidence* landed in Boston, the *Mary Anne* in Salem, and the Sandwich ship of 1637 in Charlestown.) Second, migration can be detected only by settlers' appearances in the records, usually through official admission to a town or church or a grant of land; since brief moves generally went unrecorded, evidence of movement is necessarily understated. Third, it is not always clear when a settler arrived in a town; hence, it is often impossible to calculate how old that town was when the settler moved in. The figures given here, and elsewhere in the chapter, are based on a conservative reading of the evidence and should thus be considered as minimum figures.

23 See, for instance, Martin, "Entrepreneurship and the Founding of New England Towns," chs. 1, 2.

the principal ports of arrival during the Great Migration.[24] The early phases of the settlement process clearly served to create ties among emigrants who had not known one another in England. As new groups formed prior to setting out for their new town, their members would find themselves increasingly dependent upon the good will of their new-found neighbors.

Establishing a new town was no easy undertaking, even after developers had surveyed the area and laid out roads. Settlement spread from the region of Boston north and south along the coast, as colonists first occupied open land that had been cleared for agriculture by its previous native inhabitants – most of whom had recently (and, their successors believed, providentially) succumbed to European diseases. Once the most attractive sites had been taken, colonists moved into increasingly wilder regions, where they often found their physical stamina sorely tested.[25]

[24] Of the sixteen settlers in the study who are known to have settled permanently in Scituate, fourteen came from Kent. Similarly, seven of the eight permanent settlers in Weymouth, Massachusetts, came from the West Country counties of Dorset and Somerset. (These numbers exclude settlers who lived in these towns for a while but may have moved on, i.e., settlers whose deaths were not recorded either in Scituate or in Weymouth.) For the Page and Dow families in Hampton, see Robert Piercy Dow, ed., *The Book of Dow; Genealogical Memoirs of the Descendants of Henry Dow 1637, Thomas Dow 1639 and Others of the Name, Immigrants to America during Colonial Times* (Rutland, Vt., 1929), 29–30; Charles Henry Pope, *The Pioneers of Massachusetts, a Descriptive List, Drawn from Records of the Colonies, Towns and Churches, and Other Contemporaneous Documents* (Boston, 1900), 339. On the persistence of English local connections in New England, see also Allen, *In English Ways*. For Sudbury's settlers, see Sumner Chilton Powell, *Puritan Village: The Formation of a New England Town* (Middletown, Conn., 1963); for Charlestown emigrants, see Ralph James Crandall, "New England's Haven Port: Charlestown and Her Restless People. A Study of Colonial Migration, 1629–1775" (Ph.D. diss., University of Southern California, 1975), 50.

[25] On the colonists' geographic dispersal, see Howard S. Russell, *A Long, Deep Furrow: Three Centuries of Farming in New England* (Hanover, N.H., 1976), 22; Lois Kimball Mathews, *The Expansion of New England: The Spread of New England Settlement and Institutions to the Mississippi River, 1620–1865* (Boston, 1909), 11–42. On Indian mortality, see Neal Salisbury, *Manitou and Providence: Indians, Europeans, and the Making of New England, 1500–1643* (New

Settlers seldom seem to have been fully aware of the difficulties they would face in "traveling through unknowne woods, . . . sometimes passing through the Thickets, where their hands are forced to make way for their bodies passage," to establish their new homes. Edward Johnson, who vividly described the hardships of settlement, detected (as usual) a divine purpose behind the colonists' ignorance of what lay ahead. The Lord, he wrote, was "pleased to hide from the Eyes of his people the difficulties they are to encounter withall in a new Plantation, that they might not thereby be hindered from taking the worke in hand."[26] Providential or not, the colonists' ignorance would often subject them to financial no less than physical hardships. The costs could be especially high for those who had settled for a couple of years in one town, expecting it to be their permanent home, before moving on to a new place. So Zacheus Curtis discovered when he decided to leave his home of three years in Reading in order to follow up on a promise of employment in Gloucester. In his rather hasty preparations for the move, Curtis had to "put off" most of his possessions, including five or six loads of hay, for which he received "not halfe the worth of it." The costs of changing his residence also included the "42s in english corne it cost me bringing my goods downe to Salem & waiting there a fortnight with my family for the boat" and the "2 Bushells [of] Corne it cost me fore store house roome for my goods," plus three pigs lost in transit.[27]

York, 1982), 175–7, 183–4, 191–3, 209–20; Francis Jennings, *The Invasion of America: Indians, Colonialism, and the Cant of Conquest* (Chapel Hill, N.C., 1975), ch. 2. For a contemporary description of the difficulties of inland settlement, see Johnson, *Wonder-Working Providence*, ed. Jameson, 111–13.

[26] Johnson, *Wonder-Working Providence*, ed. Jameson, quotations on 112, 111.

[27] This information comes from a suit entered by Curtis against his prospective Gloucester employer, William Bartholomew, who backed out of the agreement when Curtis failed to show up for a fortnight's trial at his new job; see George F. Dow, ed., *Records and Files of the Quarterly Courts of Essex County, Massachusetts*, Vol. 2 (1656–62) (Salem, Mass., 1912), 132. For more information about Curtis, who was a passenger aboard the *James*, see Mary Audentia Smith Anderson, compiler, *Ancestry and Posterity of Joseph Smith and Emma Hale, with Little Sketches of Their Immigrant Ancestors* . . . (Indepen-

Even if they had fully understood the difficulties that lay ahead, many of the colonists who set out for new towns on the frontier would probably have deemed their efforts worth the risk. For most of these migrants to new towns were families with young children, and the benefits of early settlement, particularly the proprietary privileges, promised a unique opportunity for fathers to bestow upon their offspring a considerable inheritance of land.[28] These families usually found a permanent residence within five years of their arrival in New England – and often in as little as one year. The parents were in their thirties and forties, with children ranging in age from infancy to adolescence.[29] They were, in other words, families suited both to deal with the special demands of settling in a new town and to reap the advantages of such efforts. Once again, the experience of John Moulton typified that of many of his fellow emigrants. When the forty-year-old Moulton moved his family to Hampton in 1639, he could count on the labor of his oldest son, Henry, who was then sixteen, along with that of his servant, Adam Goodens, to help with the hard work of starting a farm. Two of his four daughters were in their early teens and thus able to help Anne Moulton in setting up the household and

dence, Mo., 1929), 89–90; Sidney Perley, *The History of Salem, Massachusetts* 3 vols. (Salem, Mass., 1924), II, 145–6. Although, in moving from Reading to Gloucester, Curtis did not follow the general pattern of moving to a new plantation, others who did move to the frontier surely encountered similar tribulations.

28 Of the fifty-six household heads who ended up settling in towns no more than two years old when they arrived, at least 39 (69.6 percent) had minor children. (Since this figure includes only children born before emigration, omitting American-born offspring, the actual number of families with children was probably greater.)

29 Half (twenty-nine of fifty-six, 51.8 percent) of those household heads who settled in new towns arrived within a year of disembarkation. Nearly three-quarters (forty of fifty-six, 71.4 percent) settled in a new town within five years of their arrival from England. The bulk of these household heads were in middle age when they reached the new town. Of the forty-seven for whom there is adequate information, nine (19.1 percent) were in their twenties, thirteen (27.6 percent) were in their thirties, seventeen (36.1 percent) were in their forties, six (12.8 percent) were in their fifties, and two (4.3 percent) were in their sixties.

performing domestic work. By the time Henry married and his father was in his fifties, young John, Jr., had matured to take his older brother's place in the family economy. The labors of both Moulton brothers would be amply rewarded because of their father's decision to move to Hampton: Henry and John, Jr., each received a sizable portion of their father's estate in the town, land that they had been working as much for themselves as for their father.[30]

The principal inhabitants of newly founded towns, therefore, were families whose composition enhanced their ability to do well in these infant communities. Middle-aged fathers had sufficient resources, in terms of capital brought over from England and the labor of their sons, to transform wilderness into farmland. Their families provided both the incentive to seek out communities with generous land policies and the means to develop their holdings. Moreover, the fathers' mobility ensured their sons' persistence: By seeking out places where they could become proprietors, fathers also acquired the means to settle their sons locally on estates created either from the original paternal grant or from shares in later divisions.[31]

Sons were not the only source of labor in the new towns, of course: Servants accompanied more than half of the emigrant families on the voyage, and most probably stayed with their masters for at least a year or two as they moved within New England.[32] Servants also discovered that their economic chances

---

[30] Moulton, *Moulton Annals*, 208–9. On the importance of sons' labor in the establishment of family farms, see Daniel Vickers, "Working the Fields in a Developing Economy: Essex County, Massachusetts, 1630–1675," in Stephen Innes, ed., *Work and Labor in Early America* (Chapel Hill, N.C., 1988), 49–69. For a discussion of the contributions of women to the household economy, see Laurel Thatcher Ulrich, *Good Wives: Image and Reality in the Lives of Women in Northern New England 1650–1750* (New York, 1982), chs. 1, 2.

[31] On the persistence of the second generation, see Greven, *Four Generations*, 39–40; Linda Auwers Bissell, "From One Generation to Another: Mobility in Seventeenth-Century Windsor, Connecticut," *WMQ*, 3d ser., XXXI (1974), 86–8.

[32] Fifty-five of ninety-nine emigrant families (not including solitary travelers) traveled with servants. The length of their terms of service is difficult

often improved as a result of relocation. Their status, of course, temporarily limited their opportunities, for servants could not own land until their terms were completed.[33] Most, however, were free within a couple of years, and if they had followed their masters to new towns, they often managed to become proprietors too. In fact, service in husbandry dramatically declined as a source of labor in the New England economy in large part because access to land was so easy.[34] Two of Nathaniel Tilden's servants, Thomas Lapham and George Sutton, for instance, traveled with their master to the new town of Scituate, and when their terms were completed, both became Scituate proprietors.[35]

to calculate, but several were evidently freed within a year or two of their arrival, as they were recorded as having married or acquired land – both of which were forbidden to servants. Although one in six of the emigrants included in this study came to New England as a servant, as a group they are very difficult to track through the available records. Maidservants in particular left barely a trace in the evidence. Difficulties in following their migration patterns – only 39 (all males) of the total of 114 can be followed with any accuracy – result from the fact that within a year or two of their arrival, many servants apparently left the households with which they had emigrated. Since migration is measured here largely through appearances in local records, former servants can slip through the researcher's net because a time lag of months or years frequently separated the conclusion of their service and the acquisition of land, membership in a church, or marriage – time when the former servant could have moved almost anywhere.

[33] Shurtleff, ed., *Mass. Bay Recs.*, I, 127.

[34] On the decline of service in New England, see Vickers, "Working the Fields," in Innes, ed., *Work and Labor in Early America*, 49–69.

[35] Each former servant also married a Tilden daughter. For Lapham, see James Savage, ed., *A Genealogical Dictionary of the First Settlers of New England, Showing Three Generations of Those Who Came before May, 1692 . . .*, 4 vols. (Boston, 1860–2), III, 56; Samuel Deane, *History of Scituate, Massachusetts, from Its First Settlement to 1831* (Boston, 1831), 154, 302. For Sutton, see ibid., 346, and Edward F. H. Sutton, *Genealogical Notes of the Sutton Family of New Jersey* (New York, 1900), with an unpaginated typescript addendum bound into the volume at the library of the New England Historic Genealogical Society in Boston. This last source mentions that the Suttons moved to North Carolina because of their Quaker beliefs. There were Quakers in Scituate in the seventeenth century (see Deane, *History of Scituate*, 47–57), but there is no evidence that the Suttons were of their number. Colony records include prosecutions of Scituate Quakers, but Sutton's name does not appear (see Nathaniel B. Shurtleff, ed., *Records of the Colony of New*

Although the former servants would most likely have become proprietors anyway, the fact that they did not have to move to realize that status was due to their former master's decision to make the new town of Scituate his home.

In all, one in four male servants became a landowner in the town to which he had been brought by his master.[36] But for all male servants, the timing of their freedom – and the related factor of their age – critically affected their migration history and subsequent economic trajectory. Edward Jenkins, another of Nathaniel Tilden's servants, was compelled to postpone his entry into the ranks of Scituate proprietors because of a set of factors beyond his control. He was perhaps ten years younger than Tilden's other servants, and his term of service continued long after theirs had ended.[37] By the time he was ready for a farm of his own, Scituate's inhabitants no longer agreed on the proper basis for allotments and thus obstructed Jenkins's efforts to obtain one. The former servant ultimately acquired his farm by marrying the daughter of a locally prominent land-

Plymouth in New England, 12 vols. [Boston, 1855–61; reprinted New York, 1968], III, 130, 147, 165, 200–1, 204, 213; VIII, 103, for mentions of Quakers). The Suttons may in fact have moved out of Scituate, for there is no record of their burial there and the Plymouth probate records contain no information on their estate. If they did move, they probably did so after their children were grown, since their son John married a local woman and stayed in Scituate.

36 Fourteen of the thirty-nine traceable servants (all males) ended up staying in the same town as their masters; in ten of the fourteen cases (or 25.6 percent of the total thirty-nine) that destination was a new town. There is no information on the migration patterns of female servants.

37 In his will of 1641 (at which time both Lapham and Sutton were married), Nathaniel Tilden bequeathed the rest of Jenkins's contract to his son Joseph. Jenkins does not appear as a free agent until 1645. Although the birth dates of the three servants are unknown, the fact that Lapham and Sutton married within a few years of their arrival in New England suggests that they were in their early twenties when they emigrated in 1635. Jenkins, in turn, did not marry until 1645. For data on Jenkins, see Pope, *Pioneers of Massachusetts,* 257; Lula May (Fenno) Woolson and Charles Amasa Woolson, *The Woolson-Fenno Ancestry and Allied Lines, with Biographical Sketches* (privately printed, 1907), 115–16. Tilden's will appears in *Mayflower Descendant,* III (1901), 220–2.

owner (who, as it happened, had married the widow of Jenkins's former master, Tilden).[38]

But prosperous and well-connected brides were never abundant enough to ensure other former servants entry into the ranks
of proprietors in their masters' towns. For them, the route to
economic security was the same as it had been for many of their
masters – migration. Thus men who came to New England as
servants generally found it necessary to make one more move
during their lifetimes than did men who arrived as the heads of
households.[39] Such mobility often enabled them to replicate –
and occasionally to exceed – the economic achievement of their
former masters. The career of Andrew Hallett illustrates the re-
wards that might accrue to those willing to move. When Hallett's
master, Richard Wade, arrived in Dorchester in 1635, he obtained land for himself barely two weeks before the town decided that newcomers would no longer enjoy rights of proprietorship. Hallett left town as soon as he could. Family ties as well
as the hope for better opportunities drew him some sixty miles to
the southeast, first to Sandwich and then to Yarmouth, where
his father lived. There the former servant prospered, combining
proprietary grants with additional purchases and, in 1647, a generous share of his father's estate. By the time of Hallett's own
death in 1684, his estate was worth nearly £1,200.[40]

---

38 Deane, *History of Scituate*, 4–6, 10–11, 281; for Jenkins's marriage, see Mary
Lovering Holman, *Ancestry of Colonel John Harrington Stevens and His Wife
Frances Helen Miller* (privately printed, 1948), 486. Thomas Doggett, a servant who emigrated on the *Mary Anne*, also prospered through a series of
judicious marriages; see T. H. Breen and Stephen Foster, "Moving to the
New World: The Character of Early Massachusetts Immigration," *WMQ*,
3rd ser., XXX (1973), 210–11.
39 Twenty-three of thirty-nine traceable servants (58.9 percent) lived in three
or more New England towns, whereas only 59 of 122 household heads (48.3
percent) did so. These are conservative figures – especially for servants.
40 City of Boston, *Fourth Report of the Record Commissioners*, 14, 31; for Hallett,
see C. W. Swift, *Genealogical Notes of Barnstable Families, Being a Reprint of the
Amos Otis Papers, Originally Published in the Barnstable Patriot*, 2 vols. (Barnstable, Mass., 1888) I, 473–507. A clerk's copy of Hallett's will and inventory are in Vol. 4 of the Plymouth probate records, 134–5, at the Plymouth
County Registry of Probate, Plymouth, Massachusetts.

New England thus proved to be a place where servants could eventually prosper as fully as did their masters. Individual achievement, of course, depended considerably upon a servant's own abilities. Yet migration – undertaken either as part of the master's household or independently – often constituted an essential element in the strategy for economic security. Their dependent status at the time of emigration did not hinder servants' subsequent standing; it may, in fact, have helped them ultimately to set up independent households. Usually arriving in New England as single young men with neither the funds nor the labor resources to improve a farm, they gained valuable assets in service. By providing experience in working New England land, the modest cash payment often accorded to servants completing their terms, and a local network of acquaintances with whom they might exchange labor and goods in the process of establishing their own farms, servitude offered young New Englanders what it seldom conferred in Old England: opportunity.

Young, single men who emigrated independently, and not as servants, also managed to acquire farms, but like the servants, they often delayed their entry into the ranks of New England's landowners. They too had to obtain the tools, livestock, and other goods necessary to convert a land grant into a working farm. Colony law in fact interfered with their attainment of independence; Bay Colony legislation dictated that unmarried persons could not live on their own, but had to be subject to regular "family government."[41] This supervision did not necessarily mean residence with actual kin, although a few bachelors could draw on family connections for help. John Bachelor, for instance, followed his two older brothers to settle in Salem and probably boarded with either Henry or Joseph, earning his keep by working on their farms until he could manage his own.[42] William Morse likewise joined his married brother, An-

---

[41] Edmund S. Morgan, *The Puritan Family: Religion and Domestic Relations in Seventeenth-Century New England* (New York, 1966), 145–6; John Demos, *A Little Commonwealth: Family Life in Plymouth Colony* (New York, 1970), 77–8.
[42] F. C. Pierce, *Batchelder, Batchellor Genealogy* (Chicago, 1898), 343–9.

thony, in Newbury and may have worked out a similar arrangement until he married and could afford to set himself up as an independent freeholder.[43] But many single men had no close kin in New England to help them get a start. More than half of the young bachelors, however, were artisans, and probably boarded with strangers and practiced their trades while saving for farms of their own.[44] Joseph Parker probably worked for several years as a tanner in Newbury before moving on to become a proprietor in Andover.[45] Similarly, Thomas Bonney, a shoemaker, and Jarvis Boykett, a carpenter, both plied their trades in the busy port of Charlestown before becoming substantial landowners in Duxbury and New Haven, respectively.[46] Indeed, new towns often sought to lure men skilled in particular crafts by offering them monopolies of production or additional land if they would set up shop in the community. Philemon Dickerson was just one of many settlers who availed

---

[43] Pope, *Pioneers of Massachusetts*, 320–1.

[44] Of the twenty-nine unmarried young male emigrants for whom there is information on New England mobility, eighteen (62.1 percent) were named as artisans on the ship lists. The comparable figure for emigrant household heads was 45.4 percent artisans (forty of eighty-eight with information on New England mobility).

[45] Savage, *Genealogical Dictionary*, III, 353; Greven, *Four Generations*, 46–7. Parker apparently lived in Newbury from the time of his arrival in New England in 1638 until he moved to Andover in 1645. He is not listed among the original proprietors of Newbury; see Allen, *In English Ways*, appendix 3, 261–7.

[46] Bonney owned only a houselot in Charlestown, but later became an original proprietor in Bridgewater, adjoining Duxbury. For biographical information, see Savage, *Genealogical Dictionary*, I, 211; Pope, *Pioneers of Massachusetts*, 58; Sherman Grant Bonney, Calvin Fairbanks Bonney, Harriott Cheney Bonney, *A Tribute* (Concord, N.H., 1930), 4–5; Thomas Bellows Wyman, *The Genealogies and Estates of Charlestown, in the County of Middlesex and Commonwealth of Massachusetts, 1629–1818*, 2 vols. (Boston, 1879), I, 99. For Boykett, see Savage, *Genealogical Dictionary*, I, 226; Wyman, *Genealogies and Estates of Charlestown*, I, 105; Edward G. Atwater, *History of the Colony of New Haven to Its Absorption into Connecticut* (New Haven, Conn., 1881), 111. There is no direct evidence that either of these men worked at their trades in Charlestown, but their limited landholdings in that town strongly suggest that they could not have been engaged full-time in agriculture.

themselves of such offers when he accepted a supplemental land grant to set up tan pits in Salem.[47]

Most emigrants, then – whether male or female, married or single, household head or servant – eventually conformed to a common pattern in settling New England. They would spend their first year or two moving about the region, and most would finally choose for their permanent home a newly founded community where they might still obtain farms near the town center and enjoy proprietary privileges. There they would stay and improve the family farms that eventually supported their children and even many of their grandchildren.

This pattern of short-run mobility followed by long-run persistence was so widespread – characterizing more than eight out of ten household heads and virtually all male servant emigrants – that it overwhelmed the small number of exceptional cases.[48] Only a minority of settlers distinguished themselves in one of two ways: either by unusual stability, in that they simply remained in their port of disembarkation, or by unusually frequent mobility. Such atypical behavior, by its very infrequency as well as its lack of pattern, only underscores the significance of the predominant experience of settlement.

Fewer than one in six household heads stayed in the principal port towns of Boston, Charlestown, or Salem, and several of these were widows who presumably moved in with relatives who had emigrated earlier.[49] The principal common characteristic linking the others who remained was occupation: Three out of

---

[47] Nathaniel Emmons Paine, *Thomas Payne of Salem and His Descendants: The Salem Branch of the Paine Family* (Haverhill, Mass., 1928), 22. Dickerson later moved to Southold, Long Island.

[48] Those fitting the predominant pattern include 102 of the 122 traceable household heads (83.6 percent) and 37 of the 39 traceable male servants (94.8 percent). A similar result, also obtained from genealogical materials, was found by John W. Adams and Alice B. Kasakoff, "Migration and the Family in Colonial New England: The View from Genealogies," *Journal of Family History*, Vol. 9, No. 1 (Spring 1984), 28–9; see also Ralph J. Crandall, "New England's Second Great Migration: The First Three Generations of Settlement, 1630–1700," *NEHGR*, CXXIX (1975), 347–60.

[49] Twenty of the 122 household heads stayed in port towns; the three widows (Katherine Rabey, Margaret Neave, and Emme Mason) all stayed in Salem.

four were craftsmen who apparently found the relatively more populous port towns, with their constant incoming streams of emigrants throughout the 1630s, the most congenial setting for the practice of their trades.[50] Their decision to remain in such places must be put in context, however, for most artisans moved out to the countryside, where comparatively few of them could earn their living from the full-time practice of their crafts. Indeed, at least some of the artisans living in port towns may have expected to remain just long enough to accumulate the price of a farm in another community, only to find that bad luck or poor trade forced them to remain indefinitely. The fortunes of the fuller Maudit Ingles, for instance, clearly declined during his years in Boston: When he joined the church after five years in town, he was identified simply as a "laborer." Similarly, William Gault never prospered as a shoemaker in Salem; once his debts were paid after his death, his estate amounted to only £27.[51] Those who succeeded economically in the port towns as often as not abandoned former occupations for new endeavors better suited to a commercial environment. Two Salem residents – Edmund Batter, a maltster turned merchant, and John Gedney, a weaver turned tavernkeeper – prospered from their occupational changes.[52]

As early as 1634, one commentator noted that Boston was better suited to commerce than farming; it was a town "fittest for such as can trade into England for such commodities as the country wants."[53] Moreover, Boston and the other ports at Sa-

---

[50] Thirteen of the seventeen men (76.5 percent) who remained in a port town were identified as artisans on the ship lists.

[51] Six of the artisans remaining in port towns were bachelors when they emigrated. For Maudit Ingles, see Pope, *Pioneers of Massachusetts*, 157; for Gault, see Perley, *History of Salem*, II, 30–1; *The Probate Records of Essex County, Massachusetts (1635–1681)* (Salem, Mass., 1916–20), I, 316–17.

[52] For Batter, see Pope, *Pioneers of Massachusetts*, 39; Perley, *History of Salem*, I, 198; Essex will, docket no. 2137, Vol. 302, p. 147 [cc]. For Gedney, see Pope, *Pioneers of Massachusetts*, 184; Henry Fitzgilbert Waters, *The Gedney and Clarke Families of Salem, Mass.* (Salem, Mass., 1880), 4–8.

[53] William Wood, *New England's Prospect*, ed. Alden T. Vaughan, The Commonwealth Series (Amherst, Mass., 1977), 59.

lem and Charlestown were among New England's longest-settled towns, whose best land had already been granted to the earliest inhabitants.[54] Yet throughout the 1630s, some farmers continued to settle in these ports instead of one of the large farming towns in the interior. The small number of latecomers to port towns usually had to be satisfied with less attractive estates located on the outskirts of the community. For instance, John Parker, who arrived in Boston in 1635, got forty acres at Muddy River, an area that later became the town of Brookline. Thomas Brigden of Charlestown and William King of Salem likewise acquired farms distant from the town center.[55] Still others found satisfactory accommodation only by spending money derived from their liquidated English estates – an option generally open only to older men who had had prosperous English careers. Francis Lawes, a forty-two-year-old Norwich weaver, apparently bought the Salem property of a departing townsman and only later petitioned the town for a "ferder portion of lande" to supplement his purchase.[56] Another Norwich weaver who settled in Salem, fifty-year-old Thomas Payne, used his English savings to buy a houselot and directed that his investment in the emigrant ship *Mary Anne* be sold to provide estates for his children – none of whom, by the way, remained in town.[57]

[54] Rutman, *Winthrop's Boston*, 68–71, 84–7; Crandall, "New England's Haven Port," 27, 59; Christine A. Young, *From "Good Order" to Glorious Revolution: Salem, Massachusetts, 1628–1689* (Ann Arbor, Mich., 1980), 17.

[55] For Parker, see Savage, *Genealogical Dictionary*, III, 351; "Suffolk County Deeds, Vol. III," *Essex Antiquarian*, XI (1907), 83. For Brigden, see City of Boston, *Third Report of the Record Commissioners* [Charlestown Land Records, 1638–1802] (Boston, 1878), 61. For King, see William P. Upham, communicator, "Town Records of Salem, 1634–1659," *Essex Institute Historical Collections*, 2nd ser., Vol. I, Pt. 1 (1868), 80.

[56] Lawes did receive land grants in Salem, but evidently only after he had acquired a house lot by other means; see Upham, comm., "Records of Salem," 59.

[57] Again, Payne seems to have been granted land after he acquired a houselot in Salem; see ibid., 57; H. D. Paine, *Paine Family Records: A Journal of Genealogical and Biographical Information Respecting the American Families of Payne, Paine, Payn &c.*, quarterly issues bound in 2 vols. at the New England Historic Genealogical Society (New York, 1880), I, 12–17; Nathaniel Emmons Paine, *Thomas Payne of Salem*, 15, 18–19, 23, 30, 35, 38.

The settlers who decided to forgo the arduous but advantageous experience of moving out to found new towns probably responded to a variety of temperamental and personal factors. Some may have preferred the local minister, others perhaps found satisfaction within the more complex structure of economic opportunity in the more populous port towns, and still others were no doubt simply reluctant to attempt wilderness settlement. Thomas Payne, already aged fifty, evidently preferred his less strenuous plan for providing for his children through investment rather than further migration. Francis Lawes, who emigrated with his wife and only one child – an adult daughter who was soon married – probably saw little need to amass a substantial landed estate for his small family. Perhaps too some of these port town dwellers, who had previously lived in Norwich or Canterbury, found in Boston or Salem the closest New England equivalents to the busy English provincial centers they had left behind.[58]

Even less numerous – although more easily explained – are the instances of settlers who moved repeatedly throughout their lives. Only about one in twenty household heads – and an even smaller proportion of servants – lived in four or more

Payne's will, in which he directs his ship investment be sold to provide bequests for his children, is reprinted in ibid., 16; no inventory has survived, so it is impossible to know the value of that investment. His oldest son, Thomas, Jr., purchased a farm in Dedham and eventually became a proprietor there, whereas the other children moved to Southold, Long Island after their father's death. Another port town resident, Thomas Brigden of Charlestown, also purchased his houselot, although he later received grants of land; see Wyman, *Genealogies and Estates of Charlestown*, I, 126–7.

[58] For Payne, see footnote 57; for Lawes, see Jewson, *Transcript of Three Registers*, 21–2; Walter Goodwin Davis, *The Ancestry of Sarah Stone, Wife of James Patten of Arundel (Kennebunkport) Maine* (Portland, Me., 1930), 57. Fourteen of the twenty household heads who remained in port towns came from the English towns of Canterbury, Marlborough, Norwich, Salisbury, or Great Yarmouth – each of which had more than 6,000 inhabitants in the early seventeenth century. See John Patten, *English Towns, 1500–1700* (Folkestone, 1978), 106, 251; Marion K. Dale, "The City of New Salisbury," in Elizabeth Crittall, ed., *A History of Wiltshire*, VI, The Victoria History of the Counties of England (London, 1962), 72.

towns in New England.[59] For some of these, frequent migration was nothing less than a quest for economic survival. The feckless Zacheus Curtis, for instance, moved at least five times in search of a prosperity that always eluded him.[60] William Nickerson, with nine children to support, ended up in Plymouth Colony after moving at least six times. At Monomoit (later Chatham) he ran afoul of Old Colony authorities when he illegally purchased land directly from the Indians – an honest mistake, he protested, occasioned by his need to provide a "comfortable subsisting" for his numerous offspring.[61] Thomas Doggett, a servant who emigrated in 1637, lived in at least four towns; his search for economic security entailed not only migration but also marriage – to a succession of three prosperous widows.[62]

But necessity of another sort compelled some colonists to live always on the move. The most frequent movers among these emigrants include a handful of religious dissidents, who found that in crossing the Atlantic they had not journeyed far enough to find liberty of conscience. These colonists discovered that the New England Way was as intolerant of dissent as the Anglican regime from which they had fled, and availed themselves once again of migration as the means to self-preservation. Among this group was John Greene, whose support first of Roger Williams and later of Samuel Gorton did nothing to endear him to the Bay Colony's magistrates and

---

[59] The precise number of frequent movers was seven household heads and one servant.

[60] Curtis first appeared in Salem; he then moved to Reading, then to Gloucester, back to Salem, then to Rowley Village (Boxford), and finally to Topsfield; see Perley, *History of Salem*, II, 145–6; Anderson, *Ancestry and Posterity*, 89–90. At the time of his death in 1682, Curtis's estate amounted to £185 16s. 8d, and the debts against that estate equaled £134 6s. 8d.; Essex Probate Records, docket no. 6940, copy in Vol. 302, p. 33.

[61] William C. Smith, *A History of Chatham, Massachusetts, Formerly the Constablewick or Village of Monomoit* (Hyannis, Mass., 1909), 55–64; Shurtleff, ed., *Records of the Colony of New Plymouth*, II, 129; III, 101, 165; IV, 44, 49, 58–9, 64, 97, 101–2, 134–5, 153–4; quotation from IV, 153.

[62] Samuel Bradlee Doggett, *A History of the Doggett-Daggett Family* (Boston, 1894), 325–42; see also Breen and Foster, "Moving to the New World," 210–11.

ultimately necessitated several moves within Massachusetts and Rhode Island.[63] For Anthony Emery, Quaker predilections combined with accidental misfortune to produce a life on the move. After nine years' residence in Newbury, he apparently had had enough of the Bay Colony and moved north to Dover, where he signed a civil compact repudiating Massachusetts's claim of jurisdiction over the town. In Dover, Emery opened an inn that within a few years burned to the ground. That twist of fate – or providence – probably contributed to his decision to move to Kittery, only to find that, in 1652, the settlements of Maine agreed to submit to the Bay Colony government. Disfranchised by Massachusetts for his Quaker sympathies, Emery finally moved to Portsmouth, Rhode Island, leaving behind a long-suffering wife who sued for the rights to Emery's Kittery property rather than move yet again.[64]

Interestingly, two of the emigrant ministers in this study also moved frequently, by no means conforming to the image of the "faithful shepherd" tending his spiritual flock.[65] William Wetherell's fourth and final move to Scituate aroused considerable controversy, as his former congregation at Duxbury refused to dismiss him when he was invited to head Scituate's newly founded Second Parish.[66] And the peripatetic Reverend

63 Greene also made one trip back to England. See Louise Brownell Clarke, *The Greenes of Rhode Island with Historical Records of English Ancestry 1534–1902* (New York, 1903), part I, 52–8; Almira Torrey Blake, *The Ancestry and Allied Families of Nathan Blake 3rd and Susan (Torrey) Blake; Early Residents of East Corinth, Vermont* (Boston, 1916), 88–90.

64 Elizabeth Bartlett Sumner, *Ancestry and Descendants of James Henshaw Coltman and Betsey Tobey* (Los Angeles, 1957), 66–7; Reverend Rufus Emery, *Genealogical Records of the Descendants of John and Anthony Emery, of Newbury, Mass. 1590–1890* (Salem, Mass., 1890), 309–10; Rhode Island Historical Society, *The Early Records of the Town of Portsmouth* (Providence, R.I., 1901), 96, 134, 140, 150, 158, 168, 187.

65 The other, Reverend John Youngs, followed the predominant pattern of remaining briefly in port (Salem) and then moving to a new town (Southold, Long Island). See Selah Youngs, Jr., *Youngs Family: Vicar Christopher Yonges, His Ancestors in England and His Descendants in America; A History and Genealogy* (New York, 1907), 38–41.

66 A graduate of Corpus Christi College, Cambridge, Wetherell identified himself as a schoolmaster when he emigrated on the *Hercules* in 1635. After

119

Joseph Hull moved with truly astonishing frequency over a vast geographical range. His travels commenced when he brought his congregation of West Country neighbors to Weymouth in 1635. Although many of them stayed, he did not: He left in 1639 and spent the next three years in three nearby towns (Hingham, Barnstable, Yarmouth). The congregation at Barnstable heartily disapproved of their footloose pastor and excommunicated him for going to head Yarmouth's church without a proper dismissal from their group. Hull evidently ignored the reprimand until the Plymouth General Court ordered his arrest if he attempted to practice his ministry. He then returned to Barnstable – but not for long. At this point, Hull's reputation extended far beyond the several towns that he, at one time or another, called home. In 1643, John Winthrop noted Hull's next move when, with undisguised horror, he recorded in his journal that the inhabitants of the Maine hamlet of Agamenticus (York) "had made a taylor their mayor, and had entertained one Hull, an excommunicated person, and very contentious, for their minister." After an uncharacteristically lengthy five-year stay, the preacher was off again, this time back to England, where he served a Cornish parish until he was ejected from his living by the 1662 Act of Uniformity. By this time, Hull headed an enormous family; he already had seven children when he first came to New England in 1635, and some two decades later an Englishman commented that the minister "has a very greate charge of children[,] neare twenty. Some say more." By now as unwelcome in Old England as in the Bay and Plymouth colonies, Hull next settled in as minister in Oyster River (Durham), New Hampshire.

a brief stint teaching at Charlestown, he moved to Cambridge and was in Duxbury by 1638. There is no evidence that he served as minister in that town or even as assistant to Duxbury's Reverend Ralph Partridge. When Scituate's church split over the issue of baptism by immersion in 1645, both Wetherell's former congregation at Duxbury and the elders at Plymouth refused to agree to his move to head Scituate's new Second Parish. For biographical information, see Savage, *Genealogical Dictionary*, IV, 492; Pope, *Pioneers of Massachusetts*, 488; Samuel Deane, *History of Scituate, Massachusetts, From Its First Settlement to 1831* (Boston, 1831), 33, 35, 82–4.

Before long, he made his eighth move to a final resting place at the Isles of Shoals, where he died in 1665.[67]

Hull's odyssey departed dramatically from the common experience of New Englanders, although his travels did fit the general pattern in one significant particular: With the exception of his return to Cornwall, he consistently moved to new communities on the edges of settlement. The source of his "contentiousness" is unclear, but given his repeated moves to new congregations, it was almost certainly religious in origin. If so, Hull's migratory habits, along with those of known religious dissidents, reveal an important and distinctive feature of New England society. As the much more spectacular cases of Roger Williams and Anne Hutchinson attest, the most effective way to deal with religious controversy in a society lacking a central authority with strong coercive power was simply to allow (or compel) the offending party to leave. Conscious of the threat posed by these individuals and their heterodox beliefs, yet often unsure of how best to deal with them, the Bay Colony government almost invariably chose banishment as the easiest and most effective response.[68] It was a response, however, that could succeed only in a land with space enough to separate the offenders from the majority.

Such conditions did not obtain in densely settled England, where conflict between the authorities and dissidents routinely

[67] George Walter Chamberlain, *History of Weymouth, Massachusetts*, 4 vols. (Weymouth, Mass., 1923), III, 300–1; Charles H. Weygant, compiler, *The Hull Family in America* (n.p., 1913), 245–9. The quotation from Winthrop is in his *History of New England*, ed. Savage, II, 100; the statement by the Englishman is in A. G. Matthews, *Calamy Revised, Being a Revision of Edmund Calamy's Account of the Ministers and Others Ejected and Silenced, 1660–62* (Oxford, 1934), 283.

[68] The Bay Colony's reliance on a policy of exiling dissidents is also seen in its treatment of Quakers; only when offenders ignored the sentence of banishment did the authorities resort to capital punishment. See Jonathan M. Chu, *Neighbors, Friends, or Madmen: The Puritan Adjustment to Quakerism in Seventeenth-Century Massachusetts Bay* (Westport, Conn., 1985), 40–9. Chu also describes the weakness of central authority in Massachusetts; when localities chose to accept peaceful Quakers, there was little that colonial officials could do to intervene.

erupted. In the end, New England served as the region where English religious offenders could be isolated, but this resulted more from the choice of the dissidents than from the command of the authorities. Once begun, such processes of self-selection went on uninterrupted for some settlers in the New World. If the experiences of John Greene or Anthony Emery offer any guide to those of other dissenting colonists, self-exile was at least as common – and probably more frequently exercised as an option – as exile under compulsion for those of tender conscience. Most Puritans took the difficult step of leaving home for the sake of their spiritual welfare just once in their lives, but dissenters from the New England Way did so again and again.[69]

III

For every Joseph Hull, however, there were more than a dozen John Moultons. The vast majority of settlers found permanent homes after a brief period of mobility and remained in those communities for the rest of their lives. For all but a tiny minority, migration within New England was not an extension of the Great Migration to flee religious persecution but rather a short-term strategy to ensure their economic security. Yet this is not to

[69] It should be noted that, despite recent scholarship emphasizing the significance of remigration back to England, the evidence in this study suggests that repatriation was in fact quite rare. Only two families are known definitely to have returned. Those families were William and Christian Cockram, who moved from Hingham, Massachusetts, back to Suffolk and John Sanders and his family, who lived in Salisbury and Newbury before returning to Wiltshire. See Pope, *Pioneers of Massachusetts*, 106–7, 399; Hingham, Massachusetts, *History of the Town of Hingham, Massachusetts*, 2 vols. ([Hingham, Mass.], 1893), II, 134; David W. Hoyt, *The Old Families of Salisbury and Amesbury, Massachusetts, with Some Related Families of Newbury, Haverhill, Ipswich, and Hampton*, 3 vols. (Providence, R.I., 1897), I, 309. For discussions of remigration, see William L. Sachse, "The Migration of New Englanders to England, 1640–1660," *American Historical Review*, LII (1948), 251–78; David Cressy, *Coming Over: Migration and Communication Between England and New England in the Seventeenth Century* (Cambridge, 1987), ch. 8; Andrew Delbanco, "Looking Homeward, Going Home: The Lure of England for the Founders of New England," *New England Quarterly*, LIX (September 1986), 358–86.

suggest that upon their arrival in New England the settlers simply jettisoned their religious scruples in order to pursue purely economic ends. What they sought in the New World was a material life that would support – not threaten – their spiritual goals. They knew only too well the dangers of wealth and covetousness, and scarcely wished to ride the proverbial camel trying to squeeze through the eye of the needle.[70] But they also understood that the incessant demands of poverty would likewise undermine their capacity to concentrate on their spiritual duties. Most colonists therefore carefully chose a middle path, aiming for the modest prosperity that they called "competency."

When in 1630 the Reverend John White identified a competency as the earthly reward for which the colonists, as God's faithful servants, might strive, he saw no need to define the term because his contemporaries knew very well what he meant by it. He who possessed a competency had a sufficiency, although not an abundance, of this world's goods. But the term, as seventeenth-century English people understood it, connoted more than simply an economic status. It also signified independence, the possession of property sufficient to free oneself from reliance on others. Early modern English people in general valued such independence as an ideal, but only in New England did so many actually achieve it.[71] Colonists understood that their competencies would not necessarily entail an improvement in their economic condition. Indeed, had they reasoned in those terms, many settlers might have anticipated an absolute decline in their standard of living. At least one broadside warned that they would find "lesse serving the turne there [in New England] than would give contentment" in England. Other writers, describing the material comforts of a New

---

[70] For a discussion of the complicated Puritan attitude toward wealth, see Foster, *Their Solitary Way*, ch. 4.

[71] Daniel Vickers traces the origins of the idea of competency and explores its transformation over a period of centuries in his excellent article "Competency and Competition: Economic Culture in Early America," *WMQ*, 3rd ser., XLVII, No. 1 (1990), 3–29.

England residence, listed clean air, good water, healthy livestock, an abundance of fowl and fish, plenty of wood for fuel
and building, and, of course, land – hardly the ingredients of
more than a modest prosperity.[72] But that, in the end, was
precisely the point. They sought property enough to enable
them to support their families, to follow the bidding of their
consciences, and to contribute to the maintenance of their new
communities. A modest prosperity would reinforce spiritual
integrity; as Reverend White explained, "nothing sorts better
with Piety than Competency."[73]

Migration within New England functioned as the means by
which colonists reached these mutually sustaining goals. Their
general preference for moving to new communities demonstrated that the competencies they sought would be based on
the ownership of freehold farms, preferably obtained through
grants and not purchase, and of sufficient size (augmented by
subsequent shares of common land) both to support themselves and to ensure their descendants competencies comparable to their own. The colonists' relatively generous practice of
land distribution and their commitment to freehold tenure
meant that emigration often brought less a new prosperity than
a new status. But at a time when only a minority – perhaps one
in seven household heads – owned freehold land in England,
when almost all of them owed at least token payments to a
manorial lord, the colonists keenly appreciated the importance
of such a change in their lives.[74] Richard Carver, a husbandman

<hr>

[72] Edmund S. Morgan, "Provisions for the Great Migration," *NEQ*, XII
(1939), 99; Thomas Dudley, "Gov. Thomas Dudley's Letter to the Countess
of Lincoln, March 1631," in Peter Force, ed., *Tracts and Other Papers Relating
Principally to the Origin, Settlement, and Progress of the Colonies in North America, From the Discovery of the Country to the Year 1776*, 4 vols. (Washington,
D.C., 1838), II, 12; Wood, *New England's Prospect*, ed. Vaughan, 68–9.
[73] John White, *The Planter's Plea* (London, 1630), reprinted in Force, ed.,
Tracts and Other Papers, II, 18.
[74] The prevalence of freeholdership varied from region to region in England;
see Joan Thirsk, ed., *The Agrarian History of England and Wales (1500–1640)*
(Cambridge, 1967), IV, 63, 684–5. In 1696, Gregory King estimated that
freeholders headed approximately 180,000 families, or about 13.2 percent

who emigrated in 1637, claimed for himself the title of yeoman less than a year later, after he had acquired a freehold farm in Watertown. William Stephens, an Oxfordshire husbandman, similarly began to call himself a yeoman after settling in Newbury. Nathaniel Tilden, Nicholas Butler, and Peter Noyes – who had all been called yeomen in England – concluded that their freehold ownership of substantial New England estates (and, perhaps, their ability to leave the task of actually working those farms to others) entitled them to assume the rank of gentleman.[75]

The eagerness with which these colonists assumed their new titles suggests that they took satisfaction in their new status as independent freeholders. But their efforts to obtain the farms that conferred that status always occurred within a social, economic, and cultural framework that strictly circumscribed individualistic behavior. Preachers warned their flocks that, as one of them put it, "a man that hath competency may not pray for more enlargement in the world"; he might move his family to obtain an adequate subsistence, but he could not seek merely to gain "more worldly advantage to himselfe."[76] To do otherwise risked valuing one's temporal above one's spiritual estate. Moreover, colonists understood that their efforts to gain eco-

of the total of 1,360,586 families; see Charles Wilson, *England's Apprenticeship 1603–1763* (London, 1965), 239.

[75] The term "yeoman" did not have a precise legal definition in this period, but it generally indicated freehold status; see Mildred Campbell, *The English Yeoman in the Tudor and Early Stuart Age* (New York, 1942), 23–6. Carver called himself a yeoman in his will (see Suffolk County Probate Records, Vol. 1, 22–3), as did Stephens (*Probate Records of Essex County*, I, 153). Tilden was labeled a gentleman in his inventory (see *Mayflower Descendant*, III [1901], 220), as was Noyes in his (Middlesex County, docket no. 16074). Butler was called a gentleman in a 1652 deed (see *Suffolk Deeds* [Boston, 1880–1906], Liber I, 196). Although Tilden, Butler, and Noyes called themselves yeomen at the time of their voyages, their English estates may not have been held exclusively as freeholds. Noyes, for instance, held land in copyhold in Weyhill, Hampshire; see Powell, *Puritan Village*, 8.

[76] [John Wilson], "Certeyne Questions with their Answers tending to declare how farre Church-covenant binds the Members to Cohabite togeather and so to continue [ca. 1648]," in the Mather Family Papers, Box 13, Folder 8, pp. 8, 9; American Antiquarian Society, Worcester, Massachusetts.

nomic security had to be carried out in union with their fellow Christians. They should not strike out on their own, but move either as individuals to established communities or as groups to found new towns.

At least for the first generation or two, the reality of New England society approximated the communal ideal remarkably well. Despite the abundance of available land, only a handful of colonists rejected membership in a community in order to try carving out isolated farmsteads of their own.[77] Equally rare were attempts to subvert the normal process of community formation for selfish ends. The treatment of transgressors in the few cases that did occur was notable for the evidence it offers that early New Englanders voluntarily submitted to communal control. Colonial authorities had few effective sanctions to employ against those who lived outside of the community and mainly resorted to persuasion in their attempts to lure them back.[78]

William Nickerson was one of the few colonists who perceived the limits of colonial authority and tried to exploit them for his own benefit. His long-running battle with the Plymouth General Court began in 1655, when Nickerson was charged with illegally purchasing land at Monomoit (later Chatham) from the Indians. The court unleashed an array of penalties, including disfranchisement and heavy fines (and a stint in the stocks for defaming public officials), but Nickerson fought back and managed to prolong the case for nearly a quarter of a century. In the end, although he failed in his bid to become sole owner of what was apparently a town-sized tract, he did receive permission to keep and improve 100 acres of arable land

[77] This is not to suggest that colonists lived in compact, nucleated communities but simply that they overwhelmingly resided in organized towns; on the dispersed pattern of New England settlement within towns, see Joseph S. Wood, "Village and Community in Early Colonial New England," *Journal of Historical Geography* 8, no. 4 (1982), 333–46.

[78] For an example of Plymouth authorities' efforts to encourage a wayward colonist to move to a settled community, see Shurtleff, ed., *Records of the Colony of New Plymouth*, III, 6–7.

plus additional meadow, a parcel that the court deemed "a competency" sufficient to his needs. Ironically, Nickerson and his children then informed the Plymouth Court that "wee doe not desire to live alone" and petitioned to be allowed to recruit more settlers to form a new township.[79]

Nickerson posed a threat to good order in Plymouth not only because he sought to live temporarily beyond the bounds of an established community but also because he obviously wanted to found a town for the purpose of enriching himself. His original – and ultimately thwarted – scheme clearly involved speculating in those Monomoit lands not reserved for his own use and that of his family. The willingness of the Plymouth Court to pursue its case against him for decades on end demonstrated its determination that such individualistic behavior should not go unchecked. At the same time, however, it is important to recognize that Nickerson's obstreperousness had few parallels in Plymouth or any other New England colony in this period. Most settlers accepted the communal restraints of their culture and sought to achieve their goals within them.

Certain practical considerations, of course, also encouraged communal settlement in New England. Isolated farmsteads were less easily defended, and colonists were notably wary of the wilderness and its unknown dangers.[80] Especially during the early years of settlement, New Englanders depended on the help of neighbors in order to establish their family farms. Four years after his arrival in New England, John Winthrop noted that "we are like to have 20 [plows] at worke next yeare," a tiny number that suggests how widely crucial tools were shared. House and barn raisings, more frequent in the earliest years of New England than ever after, could not have taken place without the cooperation of many hands. Perhaps even more than

---

[79] Ibid., III, 101, 120, 165; IV, 44, 49, 58–9, 64, 87, 96–7, 101–2, 134–5, 140, 153–4, 157–8, 162–3, 183–4; V, 147, 154, 155, 171; VI, 14; VII, 155, 171. The court granted Nickerson his 100 acres despite his inability to produce the deed proving his original purchase.

[80] Peter N. Carroll, *Puritanism and the Wilderness: The Intellectual Significance of the New England Frontier 1629–1700* (New York, 1969), ch. 4.

men, women depended on others for assistance in a wide range of activities from household work to childbirth.[81] None of this is to deny or minimize the extent to which the settlers' preference for communal life also derived from their experience in England, where all had lived in towns or villages. But this factor, like the practical necessity of cooperation, is hardly sufficient by itself to explain the character of New England settlement. English background and the task of overcoming the physical challenges of colonization pertained with equal force to settlers elsewhere in British North America, yet nowhere else was the impulse to communalism so strong and so enduring as in New England.

The distinctiveness of New England's experience lies in the fact that its inhabitants adopted not only the practice of communal life but also a religious and ideological commitment to a communal way of life. Because of their profound belief in the necessity of worship in gathered congregations of the saints, they sought to organize their temporal lives in a manner consistent with their religious convictions. Drawing upon their understanding of the relationship between the believer and God as a contractual bond, they organized both their churches and their communities by means of covenants. Covenants embodied their unique cultural imperative to live with and through their fellow Christians. And because covenants relied on the voluntary submission of their subscribers, they provided the ideal mechanism for keeping order in a society made up of comparative equals. Notwithstanding a few William Nickersons, order in early New England would be safeguarded not by coercion but by conscience.[82]

The emerging social order of New England was not, of

---

[81] John Winthrop to Sir Nathaniel Rich, May 22, 1634, in *Winthrop Papers*, III, 167; Abbott Lowell Cummings, *The Framed Houses of Massachusetts Bay, 1625–1725*, (Cambridge, Mass., 1979), 69; Ulrich, *Good Wives*, chs. 1–3, 7.

[82] The Puritan idea of the covenant is explored in detail in the works of Perry Miller; see especially his "The Marrow of Puritan Divinity," in *Errand Into the Wilderness* (Cambridge, Mass., 1956), 48–98. See also Lockridge, *New England Town*, chs. 1, 2.

course, without its tensions; it was, after all, a society made up of colonists pledged to live in communal harmony with each other who were simultaneously working to achieve their families' competencies. At what point did improving a farm, bargaining for an adequate share of new dividends, or purchasing additional acreage cross the fine line between seeking a competency and competing with one's neighbors in the undue pursuit of worldly advantage? Where did the commercial activities of Boston or Salem merchants, for whom competition no less than profit was necessary to survive, fit into the static scheme of competency? Such issues affected every colonist and were not easily resolved.[83]

Communities as well as individual settlers faced challenges posed by the cultural imperative to keep spiritual and worldly interests in equilibrium. Disputes over land presented a particular danger, since they generally pitted anxious settlers, concerned about their economic well-being, against equally anxious town leaders, upset by attacks on their authority, worried by the prospects of diminished tax revenues, and concerned with the preservation of their community. Yet such disputes revealed both the limits of the system and its capacity for containing conflict at tolerable levels. If arbitration, either by townsmen or disinterested neighbors, failed to bring satisfaction, the aggrieved inhabitants as often as not simply departed to form a new town. However temporarily wrenching, their removal helped to restore harmony to the original community, and in the new town, the inhabitants once again pledged – perhaps with heightened intensity – to live in peace with one another.[84]

[83] For discussions of the difficulties in reconciling commercial activity with Puritan ideals, see Bernard Bailyn, *The New England Merchants in the Seventeenth Century* (Cambridge, Mass., 1955); *The Apologia of Robert Keayne: The Self-Portrait of a Puritan Merchant*, ed. Bernard Bailyn (New York, 1964); Paul Boyer and Stephen Nissenbaum, *Salem Possessed: The Social Origins of Witchcraft* (Cambridge, Mass., 1974). Christine Heyrman has demonstrated that such difficulties were not insurmountable; see *Commerce and Culture: The Maritime Communities of Colonial Massachusetts, 1690–1750* (New York, 1984).

[84] See, for instance, Powell, *Puritan Village*, chs. 8, 9.

As a means of resolving conflict, of course, this process was constrained by New England's ability to expand geographically. Once the accessible land had been taken up, the colonists would either have to find some other way to mend their differences or learn to accept a measure of permanent disunity in their midst. To a considerable extent, in fact, the character of New England's emerging social order depended as much upon the availability of farm land as it did upon the colonists' determination to put their Puritan principles into action. The abundance of land permitted communities to proliferate and also to preserve their internal harmony by providing a way of isolating malcontents – whether they were religious dissenters intent on challenging the New England Way or contentious townsmen unhappy with their accommodation. It likewise allowed the majority to gain, without destructive competition, the competencies so crucial to both their economic and spiritual welfare.

Choosing a town and acquiring land were only the first steps toward providing for one's family. These gave households the means to a competency, but not the competency itself. For that to be realized, colonists had to turn their land grants into functioning farms – never an easy task, and one aggravated by the fact that a majority of the emigrants had not worked as farmers in England. Most colonists would discover that although moving to New England allowed them to worship as they wished, it also required fundamental changes in the ways in which they earned their living.

4
Competency

As long as hundreds of emigrant families disembarked at New England ports each year, the region's economic survival seemed assured. The newcomers' stores of goods, reserves of cash, and lines of credit with English merchants added wealth to a colonial economy that could not depend upon the lucrative staple crops that supported British settlements in other parts of North America. Thus New England's early prosperity was intimately tied to the annual appearance of emigrant ships; inhabitants regularly flocked to port towns in order to exchange their small agricultural surpluses for whatever scarce manufactured goods and even scarcer currency newcomers willingly relinquished. Once emigration ceased with the coming of the English Civil War, however, the precariousness of such economic arrangements was fully revealed and New England suffered its first economic depression. The flow of specie dried up, and prices for all sorts of local commodities – particularly land, cattle, and corn – plummeted. The crisis put many people into "an unsettled frame of spirit" and tested the ability of leaders to discern divine approbation in what must have seemed at least an equivocal judgment on their success in building a Christian commonwealth. If New England were to survive, it would have to sell something other than its reputation for piety.[1]

[1] General works that inform this brief discussion of the early New England economy include John J. McCusker and Russell R. Menard, *The Economy of British America, 1607–1789* (Chapel Hill, N.C., 1985), 91–111; Howard S. Russell, *A Long, Deep Furrow: Three Centuries of Farming in New England* (Hanover, N.H., 1976), parts 1, 2; Darrett B. Rutman, "Governor Winthrop's Garden Crop: The Significance of Agriculture in the Early Commerce of Massachusetts Bay," *William and Mary Quarterly*, 3rd ser., XX (1963), 396–415; Marion H. Gottfried, "The First Depression in Massachusetts," *New England Quarterly*, IX (1936), 655–78; Bernard Bailyn, *The New England Merchants in the Seventeenth Century* (Cambridge, Mass., 1955); Terry

New England's economic problems were exacerbated by the fact that, unlike other British colonies, the region produced little that consumers in the home country wanted to buy. Without staple crops such as sugar or tobacco, and with a fur trade that diminished as the economic depression lengthened, settlers faced formidable challenges in their search for economic stability. Moreover, the region's healthy rate of population growth, which under other circumstances might have fueled economic expansion, seemed instead to threaten it – in large part because this growing population demanded manufactured goods for which it could not pay. In the midst of the depression, colonial leaders accurately concluded that New Englanders needed to increase exports and cut back on imports. Defining the problem, however, proved easier than solving it.

Colonial governments, particularly in the Bay Colony, attempted to spur economic development by various means, but in the end success depended more on private initiative than on public incentives. The Massachusetts General Court offered land grants, bounties, and trade monopolies to encourage local production of items such as cloth, glass, and iron that otherwise had to be imported from England. Such measures met with mixed success, but meanwhile colonists began to exploit the region's most abundant natural resources. If there was little demand for New England fish, timber, livestock, and agricultural produce in the home country, enterprising merchants soon found markets for these commodities in southern Europe, the Wine Islands, and the West Indies, establishing elaborate trade networks that would endure for the rest of the colonial period. Where commerce advanced, the shipbuilding and maritime trades followed, and soon became leading sources of the specie and credit vital to the region's economic health. By

L. Anderson and Robert Paul Thomas, "White Population, Labor Force and Extensive Growth of the New England Economy in the Seventeenth Century," *Journal of Economic History*, XXXIII (1973), 634–67. The quotation is from John Winthrop, *The History of New England from 1630 to 1649*, ed. James Savage, 2 vols. (Boston, 1825), II, 85.

the end of the seventeenth century, New Englanders had created a thriving, diversified economy in which the labors of
farmers, shipbuilders, fishermen, and merchants combined to
make "a greate Martt and Staple" of their corner of the British
Empire.[2]

For individual colonists, too, survival depended on the ability to adapt to a new environment and to a different set of
economic arrangements than those they had known in England. If, at first, "the straits of the whole country were such,
that every Plantation and family had enough to do, to know
how to subsist," settlers soon organized their economic lives
in ways that provided them with somewhat more than a bare
minimum of worldly goods. Most became farmers, producing
crops and raising herds that supplied their families' subsistence needs and generated a modest surplus that could be
exchanged in the marketplace for items that could not be
grown or made at home. Many of them sought additional
economic security by practicing one or more trades as well as
working in agriculture. But this choice of occupation – for
farmers or for artisans – seldom meant the simple resumption
of an English way of life. Most colonists, as one commentator
noted, found it necessary to look to "the providence of God
[to] put them into another way of livelihood than formerly
they had been acquainted with."[3]

The Great Reshuffling of the population, then, was followed
by an equally important restructuring of the colonists' economic lives. New England's limited endowment of natural resources, its abundance of arable (if stony) land, and, perhaps
most important, its chronic shortages of labor and capital
sharply restricted the range of economic opportunities and compelled first-generation settlers to make fundamental adjust-

---

[2] The quotation comes from a complaint made by London merchants in 1676
who were concerned about New England competition; cited in McCusker
and Menard, *Economy of British America*, 84.

[3] Quotations are from Reverend William Hubbard, *A General History of New
England, from the Discovery to MDCLXXX*, 2nd ed. (Boston, 1680); reprinted
in Massachusetts Historical Society, *Collections*, 2nd ser., V (1815), 244.

ments in their working lives. Even so, New England's growing prosperity, resting as it did upon the achievement of economic security by thousands of hardworking and enterprising families, testified to the ability of settlers to seek out and develop whatever economic advantages the region afforded. In the end, most colonists indeed achieved the competency to which they aspired, and in so doing created a setting where the piety with which it sorted best could flourish.

I

In the Bay Colony, official efforts to stimulate domestic manufacturing in order to curtail foreign imports concentrated on the development of a homegrown textile industry. Although such policies might have encouraged the one out of four emigrant men who had worked in cloth manufacture in England to resume their accustomed trades, few were destined to follow their former occupations in the colonial setting. The failure to establish a thriving New England textile industry, however, did not occur for want of effort on the part of the settlers. Beginning in 1640, the Massachusetts General Court passed a series of measures intended to encourage local production. The legislature instructed town selectmen to identify those within their communities who were skilled in textile work, and the colonial government offered bounties for whatever "linnen, woollen, and cotton clothe" they might manufacture.[4] Within a year, hard times compelled the court to cease paying bounties, leaving officials to cast about for other ways of encouraging production. The magistrates' concern evidently was not purely economic; in 1645, the Bay Colony legislature noted that, for want of good woolen clothing, "many pore people have suffered much could and hardship, to the impairing of some of their healths," and some of their children had been "much scorched with fire, yea, divers burnt to death" trying to keep warm.

---

[4] Nathaniel B. Shurtleff, ed., *Records of the Governor and Company of the Massachusetts Bay in New England*, 5 vols. (Boston, 1853–4), I, 294, 303.

Touching though they were, such exhortations did little to stimulate cloth manufacture.[5]

In their efforts to establish domestic textile production, settlers faced several obstacles that proved too difficult to surmount completely. There were, for instance, serious problems with the supply of materials to turn into fabric. Although thousands of sheep were imported into New England, they were slow to thrive. Sheep required a better quality of fodder than the region's wild meadows afforded, and colonists, at least at first, could not take time from their other pressing tasks to prepare good pasturage. Moreover, the docile sheep proved no match for predators – particularly wolves – and therefore required closer supervision than more self-sufficient livestock, such as cattle, goats, and swine.[6] Sheep production increased somewhat in the second half of the seventeenth century as colonists moved into areas with better pasturage, particularly the Connecticut Valley, and onto offshore islands, like Nantucket, that offered natural protection from predators.[7] Nevertheless, few families bothered with sheep rearing, and those who did generally raised less than a dozen animals – enough to support the domestic production of homespun but not much more.[8]

At the same time that officials sought to encourage wool growing and weaving, they also suggested producing other materials, such as hemp and flax, for cloth manufacture. Enough of this

[5] Ibid., I, 320, 322; II, 105, 251–2; III, 355–6; quotation from II, 105. For general discussions of efforts to encourage cloth production, see Arthur Harrison Cole, *The American Wool Manufacture*, 2 vols. (Cambridge, Mass., 1926), I, 34–7; William B. Weeden, *Economic and Social History of New England 1620–1789*, 2 vols. (Boston, 1896), I, 170–1, 197–8; Bailyn, *New England Merchants*, 71–4.

[6] Russell, *Long, Deep Furrow*, 34.

[7] Stephen Innes, *Labor in a New Land: Economy and Society in Seventeenth-Century Springfield* (Princeton, N.J., 1983), 37; Edward Byers, *The Nation of Nantucket: Society and Politics in an Early American Commercial Center 1660–1820* (Boston, 1987), 42.

[8] Of the fifty-seven adult male emigrants whose inventories included livestock, twenty-six (45.6 percent) owned sheep. The median number per flock was ten, with a range from two to forty animals.

was done to allow at least one emigrant hempdresser, Faintnot Wines, to continue working part-time at his trade in Charlestown, but hemp and flax never became mainstays of textile production either. Efforts to import West Indian cotton likewise amounted to little, probably because England preferred to ship cotton to its own spinners and weavers rather than to encourage colonial competition.[9]

Perhaps as great an obstacle as the scarcity of suitable raw materials was the region's chronic labor shortage. Clothmaking proceeded in many labor-intensive stages, from the initial washing and combing of the wool to spinning the yarn and then weaving, fulling (done at a mill), and dyeing the finished product. Many of these productive steps required relatively unskilled labor, but even that was in short supply. Official recognition of this difficulty appeared in a directive of the Massachusetts General Court of 1656, which ordered that "all hands not necessaryly imployd on other occasions, as woemen, girles and boyes, shall, and hereby are, enjoyned to spin according to their skill and abillitie[.]" Town selectmen were to visit all families, count the number of potential spinners, and then set quotas for household production. Spinners were supposed to labor for thirty weeks a year and produce three pounds of yarn per week. Compelled by financial exigency to suspend the positive inducement of bounties, the government found it necessary to threaten to fine those who failed to fulfill their quotas – an impractical measure and one evidently never enforced. The very fact that the court felt compelled to try it, however, reveals the depth of official anxiety over the "necessities of the country in respect of clothing[.]"[10]

The development of a domestic cloth industry in New England was by no means a complete failure, but it never proved to be more than a disappointment to its promoters. Small gains were made, for instance in Rowley, where emigrant weavers from Yorkshire transported the equipment for a fulling mill,

---

[9] Shurtleff, ed., *Mass. Bay Recs.*, I, 294, 322; Bailyn, *New England Merchants*, 72; Faintnot Wines's inventory lists undressed flax and dressed hemp; see Middlesex County Probate Records, docket no. 25234.
[10] Shurtleff, ed., *Mass. Bay Recs.*, III, 396–7.

which was in operation as early as 1643, and where a substantial proportion of the inhabitants engaged in household production of cloth. Other mills operated in other towns, but the domestic supply of cloth never approached the domestic demand. Most colonists concluded that it was simply easier to sell produce from their farms and purchase better-quality fabrics from England. Those who could not find sufficient markets for their crops or skills turned to other expedients, such as careful mending and passing down of clothing from one generation to the next (obviously a temporary solution) or the use of coarse homespun. Those who maintained connections with English relatives called on them for help. Comfort Starr of Boston, for example, agreed to bequeathe his estate in Kent to his son Comfort, Jr. (who had returned to England), on the condition that he would send his New England nieces and nephews "good Kersey & Peniston . . . to the worth of forty shillings a peece."[11]

Without a strong domestic textile industry, all colonists encountered similar problems in obtaining cloth, but for former English clothworkers, those difficulties were compounded by the more immediate question of how they would earn their living. These artisans had spent years learning the mysteries of their crafts, and had invested in looms and other equipment that they had paid to transport across the ocean. Once settled in New England, they had to wrestle with the decision of whether to cling to their trades or to abandon them in response to the limited economic opportunities in their new home.

Most emigrant clothworkers tried to work part-time at their former trades while devoting most of their efforts to managing farms. Many of the weavers who had brought their looms with them apparently continued to use them, mainly producing fab-

---

[11] David Grayson Allen, *In English Ways: The Movement of Societies and the Transferal of English Local Law and Custom to Massachusetts Bay in the Seventeenth Century* (Chapel Hill, N.C., 1981), 29–30; Weeden, *Economic and Social History*, I, 176–7, 193–4, 304–7; Edward Johnson, *Johnson's Wonder-Working Providence, 1628–1651*, ed. J. Franklin Jameson, Original Narratives of Early American History (New York, 1910), 211; for Starr's will, see Suffolk County Probate Records, docket no. 233.

rics for themselves and their neighbors. Thomas Antrim of Salem, for instance, died possessed not only of a loom and tackling but also of various amounts of cotton, woolen, and linen cloth, along with several pairs of "cource" sheets that were probably of his own making. Even so, Antrim's principal support came from his farm and herd of cattle. John Pers of Watertown, who likewise earned his living mainly from agriculture, persisted in calling himself a "weaver" until his death. Nicholas Busby initially tried to combine weaving and farming in Watertown but – evidently finding rural life not to his liking – soon moved to Boston, where he opened a dry-goods shop and continued to weave part-time. At the time of his death, he had six pounds' worth of "Cloth in the Looms."[12]

Other emigrant clothworkers pursued several activities at the same time, obviously hoping that their multifarious efforts would produce economic security. Thomas Payne, formerly a Suffolk weaver, owned a farm in Salem, wove cloth part-time, and also became involved in running a local mill. His bequest of

---

[12] Evidence from probate materials indicates that at least seven of the fourteen emigrant weavers brought looms with them to New England. For Thomas Antrim's inventory, see George Francis Dow, ed., *Records and Files of the Quarterly Courts of Essex County, Massachusetts*, 8 vols. (Salem, Mass., 1911–21), III, 72–3. Pers's inventory is printed in Frederick Clifton Peirce, *Peirce Genealogy, Being the Record of the Posterity of John Pers, An Early Inhabitant of Watertown, in New England, Who Came from Norwich, Norfolk County, England* (Worcester, Mass., 1880), 19. For Busby, see Watertown, Massachusetts, *Watertown Records*, 8 vols. (Watertown, Mass., 1894–1939), I, 50–1, 135; City of Boston, *Second Report of the Record Commissioners [The Book of Possessions, 1652]* (Boston, 1877), 207; Anna C. Kingsbury, *A Historical Sketch of Nicholas Busby the Emigrant* (privately printed, 1924), 12. Busby received a bounty from the General Court for cloth he produced, before the court suspended the payments; see Shurtleff, ed., *Mass. Bay Recs.*, II, 51. Three other weavers – Nicholas Batt, Francis Lawes, and Walter Haynes – also continued their trade in New England. Batt's inventory is in *The Probate Records of Essex County, Massachusetts (1635–1681)*, 3 vols. (Salem, Mass., 1916–20), III, 187–8. Lawes's inventory is in ibid., II, 49–51. Haynes's will is in the Middlesex County Probate Records, docket no. 10939. For a general discussion of occupational change in New England, see also T. H. Breen and Stephen Foster, "Moving to the New World: The Character of Early Massachusetts Immigration," *WMQ*, 3rd ser., XXX (1973), 213–17.

his "Loomes & Slaies" to his son Thomas "concerning his trade of a weaver" indicated a commitment to keep his craft alive within the family. Anthony Thacher, originally trained as a tailor, tried his hand at numerous tasks once he settled in Yarmouth. At the time of his death, this jack-of-all-trades owned – besides a farm and agricultural implements – "Coopers Tooles," "trucking Cloth" (for trade with the Indians), a thousand boards, and "surgery Instruments."[13]

The least attractive solution to the occupational dilemma was to abandon completely the old craft and take up a new one. To start all over again with a lengthy and rigorous period of training was evidently more than most men could stand – or afford. Only William Parsons, an unmarried twenty-year-old tailor from Wiltshire, chose this option. He shrewdly adopted the trade of joiner, an occupation greatly in demand in New England. When John Gedney, a Norwich weaver who settled in Salem, decided to give up his former occupation, he chose a new endeavor that required no new skills but rather a little capital and a friendly, law-abiding nature. Gedney was "called by the towne to keepe an Inne" and soon became the proprietor of the prosperous Ship Tavern by marrying (as his second wife) the former owner's widow. At one point, in 1640, Gedney was approached by his neighbors to "enquire about fustean spinsters" who might help Salem develop its own textile industry, but there is no evidence that Gedney himself made any attempt to return to his former trade.[14]

---

[13] For Payne, see Nathaniel Emmons Paine, *Thomas Payne of Salem and His Descendants: The Salem Branch of the Paine Family* (Haverhill, Mass., 1928), 16. Thacher's inventory is in the Barnstable County Probate Records, volume of pre-1685 records, 291–3.

[14] Parsons called himself a tailor on the *James* passenger list (see Louise Brownell Clarke, *The Greenes of Rhode Island, with Historical Records of English Ancestry, 1534–1902* [New York, 1903], 768–9; in a deed of 1674, he is identified as a joiner (see *Suffolk Deeds*, 14 vols. [Boston, 1880–1906], VIII, 417). For Gedney, see William P. Upham, ed., "Town Records of Salem, 1634–1659," *Essex Institute Historical Collections*, 2nd ser., I (1868), 94; Sidney Perley, *The History of Salem, Massachusetts*, 3 vols. (Salem, Mass., 1924), II, 100, 183–4.

Several emigrant clothworkers chose yet another option – abandoning their trades in order to devote themselves to full-time farming. Thomas Hayward, a Kentish tailor, eventually settled in the new town of Bridgewater, where he became an original proprietor and began to call himself a yeoman. Others followed Hayward's example in becoming New England farmers. Their possessions generally included land, agricultural tools, and household goods, but gave no indication that they ever attempted to practice their former trades. Even Michael Metcalf, one of Norwich's more successful weavers (and one of the town's fieriest Puritans), took up full-time farming when he settled with his large family in Dedham. No loom appeared among his possessions at the time of his death, apparently indicating that Metcalf had relinquished all connections with his former trade when he moved to New England.[15]

II

Artisans working in trades not related to clothmaking likewise had adjustments to make in New England, but the nature of those adjustments depended upon their specific craft. Men with highly specialized skills found the transition most difficult, for the primitive colonial economy had no place for their abilities. Again, their choices essentially amounted to abandoning their old trade or trying to work at it part-time. Edmund

[15] Nine of the nineteen clothworkers whose occupational histories can be traced became full-time farmers. For Thomas Hayward, see Charles Henry Pope, *The Pioneers of Massachusetts, A Descriptive List, Drawn from Records of the Colonies, Towns and Churches, and Other Contemporaneous Documents* (Boston, 1900), 224; Justin Winsor, *A History of the Town of Duxbury, Massachusetts, with Genealogical Registers* (Boston, 1849), 266; see also his will and inventory in the Plymouth County Probate Records, Vol. 4, Pt. 1, pp. 82–4. For Michael Metcalf, see Daniel M. Wheeler, *The Wheeler Family of Rutland, Massachusetts, and Some of Their Ancestors* (n.p., 1924), 19–20; L. M. Harris, communicator, "Metcalf Family," *New England Historical and Genealogical Register,* VI (1852), 171; his will and inventory are in the Suffolk County Probate Records, Vol. 1, 497–500; Vol. 4, 214–15.

Hawes, who had completed eight years of training as a cutler in London only months before his voyage, evidently decided that setting up shop in New England would not be worth the effort. Instead he settled in the newly incorporated town of Yarmouth, where he began to learn the mysteries of agriculture.[16] William Ludkin fared somewhat better when he moved to Hingham, for there he found some demand for his skills as a locksmith. But in order to make ends meet, he found it necessary to broaden the scope of his trade and thus took up blacksmithing, which allowed him to supply his neighbors' constant demand for spades and shovels, in addition to their less frequent requests for locks and keys.[17]

The existence of a colonial demand for their skills, however, did not always ensure that certain artisans would continue at their trades. Henry Bachelor, a brewer from Kent, could no doubt have found many an eager consumer near his Ipswich, Massachusetts, home had he resumed his English occupation, but decided to raise cattle and corn rather than work to quench his neighbors' thirst. Nicholas Holt likewise forsook a useful trade – tanning – to become a farmer at a time when some towns were offering generous inducements to tanners who would settle in their communities. The reasons for these men's decisions will never be known, but the likeliest explanation – since both became original proprietors in their respective New England towns – is that landownership appeared to offer

[16] John W. Hawes, "The English Ancestors of Edmond Hawes of Yarmouth, Mass.," *Library of Cape Cod History and Genealogy,* no. 92 (1912), 1–12; Charles F. Swift, *History of Old Yarmouth, Comprising the Present Towns of Yarmouth and Dennis, from the Settlement to the Division in 1794 with the History of Both Towns to These Times* (Yarmouthport, Mass., 1884), 54–5. Hawes's inventory indicates that he worked as a farmer; see the Barnstable County Probate Records, Vol. 1, 83–5.

[17] Ludkin drowned in 1652, and thus his inventory lists his work in progress. Among other items, his shop contained "two ould spring lockes an 2 ould playt lockes," an account of money due for "worke doune about old locks and keyes," "seven duzen and thre shovell trayes," and "a duzen of spayd trases," clearly indicating the diversity of his business. His inventory is in the Suffolk County Probate Records, docket no. 122.

greater economic security for their families than did labor at their English occupations.[18]

But some craftsmen found that opportunities to continue practicing their trades were too good to pass up. New England conditions particularly favored those artisans who worked in wood and leather; thus carpenters, joiners, and shoemakers were the craftsmen most consistently able to carry over their English trades to New England. The colonial demand for woodworking skills was incessant, particularly in the first decades of settlement, since every family needed shelter and furniture (which was generally too expensive to transport from England). The extent of the building boom in early New England can hardly be exaggerated: During the decade of the Great Migration, thousands of barns and houses had to be constructed, as well as meetinghouses and other public buildings. As for shoes, these proved to be one portable commodity that was cheaper and easier to produce locally than to import from the home country. In addition to the high domestic demand for the products of their labor, both shoemakers and woodworkers enjoyed another advantage in New England in that the raw materials used in their work were readily available. Farmers' early dependence on cattle raising provided constant supplies of leather, and the region's seemingly limitless stands of timber (which farmers were eager to clear) furnished carpenters and joiners with more wood than they could use.[19]

[18] Bachelor's inventory gives no evidence of brewing activities; see the Essex County Probate Records, docket no. 2070; for biographical details, see Mary Lovering Holman, *The Scott Genealogy* (Boston, 1919), 207; Abraham Hammatt, "The Early Inhabitants of Ipswich, Mass., 1633–1700," *The Hammatt Papers*, no. 1 (1880), 26. For Holt, see Daniel S. Durrie, *A Genealogical History of the Holt Family in the United States: More Particularly the Descendants of Nicholas Holt of Newbury and Andover, Mass., 1634–1644, and of William Holt of New Haven, Conn.* (Albany, N.Y., 1864), 11–13; Philip J. Greven, Jr., *Four Generations: Population, Land, and Family in Colonial Andover, Massachusetts* (Ithaca, N.Y., 1970), 46–7, 59–60, 88–92. In 1639, Salem granted Philemon Dickerson (a passenger on the *Mary Anne*) land on which to dig tan pits; see Perley, *History of Salem*, II, 71.

[19] Occupational continuity was principally measured by the appearance of woodworker's or shoemaker's tools in probate inventories. Of the nine

Competency

The high demand for their services conferred economic advantages on these workmen that worried colonial officials. Accustomed to comparatively low English wage rates – a consequence of England's perennial labor glut – and suspicious of the willingness of workers to demand higher payment than they had traditionally received, colonial legislators imposed wage and price controls in an attempt to restrict the earnings of New Englanders within familiar bounds. As early as August 1630, the Massachusetts General Court prohibited men in the construction trades from earning more than two shillings a day; somewhat later, Connecticut officials set prices for shoes instead of trusting the fluctuations of the market. Governor John Winthrop worried that high wages encouraged "those who had commodities to sell" to raise their prices accordingly, "sometime double to that they cost in England," which in turn hurt those colonists who did not work at lucrative trades. What worried Winthrop and the other magistrates about this was not only the economic hardship it caused for some, but its manifest tendency to erode the moral fiber of the emerging society. The governor lamented that because workmen "could get as much in four days as would keep them a week," they spent their ample leisure time in idleness – or worse, in indulging their appetites for "tobacco and strong waters."[20]

Although subject to repeated accusations of greed, craftsmen

shoemakers for whom there is evidence, at least five continued at their trades; of the five carpenters, four pursued their trade in New England. The one sawyer also worked as a sawyer in New England, and the one joiner for whom there is information, evidently continued to work at least part-time at his trade. For general information on the woodworking trades, see Abbott Lowell Cummings, *The Framed Houses of Massachusetts Bay, 1625–1725* (Cambridge, Mass., 1979), ch. 4; Robert Blair St. George, *The Wrought Covenant: Source Material for the Study of Craftsmen and Community in Southeastern New England 1620–1700* (Brockton, Mass., 1979), 22–102. On New England's timber resources, see William Cronon, *Changes in the Land: Indians, Colonists, and the Ecology of New England* (New York, 1983), ch. 6. Edward Johnson commented on the availability of leather for New England shoemakers; see *Wonder-Working Providence*, ed. Jameson, 248.

20 Shurtleff, ed., *Mass. Bay Recs.*, I, 74, 109; Weeden, *Economic and Social History*, I, 308; Winthrop, *History of New England*, ed. Savage, I, 116.

continued to flex their newfound economic muscle. Carpenters, for example, insisted on three shillings a day for their labor – a wage half again higher than the one set by the General Court.[21] The craft proved so profitable that many youths who sought training in carpentry did not even wait to finish their training before embarking on their careers.[22] Such abuses encouraged artisans working in particularly favored crafts to try to exert corporate control over entry into their fields. It was no accident that the first craftsmen to try to organize guildlike societies were those in the wood- and leather-working trades, for they had the most to gain from efforts to restrict entry into their crafts and establish monopolies of production in important towns, such as Boston.[23]

If a shoemaker like Joseph Coleman or a carpenter like Joseph Tilden found an unexpectedly salubrious economic climate in New England, he also had to adapt his working life in ways familiar to all New England craftsmen. Virtually all artisans, whether they lived in Boston or in one of the outlying towns, worked at farming as well as manufacturing. Moreover, the dispersed pattern of settlement in New England often meant that artisans served wide geographical areas inhabited by people of varying levels of wealth; they could not afford to specialize in the practice of their trades if they wanted to earn a good living. Joseph Tilden, for instance, fashioned ornate chests and cases for his wealthier customers but also plainer objects for less prosperous patrons. Edward Johnson, who had been trained as a joiner, was called upon at different times to construct both a bridge and a boat. John Emery's possession of "carpenter turner and joyners tools" suggests that he built everything from houses to chairs to chests. And even if their trades were in considerable demand, some artisans found it expedient to diversify still further. The farmer and shoemaker

---

[21] Winthrop, *History of New England*, ed. Savage, I, 116.

[22] Cummings, *Framed Houses*, 40–1.

[23] Darrett B. Rutman, *Winthrop's Boston: A Portrait of a Puritan Town, 1630–1649* (Chapel Hill, N.C., 1965), 232, 250–1; Robert F. Trent, "New England Joinery and Turning before 1700," *New England Begins: The Seventeenth Century*, 3 vols. (Boston, 1982), III, 508.

Joseph Coleman also owned "Cooper stuffe," suggesting that he worked part-time in at least two trades.[24]

The experience of these artisans reveals much about the structure of opportunity in New England and the economic expectations of colonial workers. No one who had been in the Bay Colony for long could fail to recognize that its economy differed significantly from that of the home country. The settlers had left a land where labor was plentiful and cheap, whereas land was both scarce (relative to population) and dear, only to arrive in a place where that traditional economic relationship was inverted. Colonial land supplies seemed limitless – towns actually gave it away free to their inhabitants – whereas the scarcity of laborers pushed wages to disconcertingly high levels. Easy access to land created an overwhelmingly agricultural economy, more so than that of England itself.[25] Although wage rates were high and certain kinds of skilled labor were in considerable demand, circumstances peculiar to the colonial setting dictated that few craftsmen would be able to take advantage of these conditions to grow wealthy at the practice of their trades. Outside of Boston, perhaps, no community was populous enough to employ its artisans full-time. Moreover, the chronic scarcity of currency in early New England hampered the development of a vigorous market economy, and if for no other reason than to play it safe, artisans usually acquired farms with which to support their families.[26] Even such successful carpen-

---

[24] St. George, *The Wrought Covenant*, 17, 70; Cummings, *Framed Houses*, 202–3; Trent, "New England Joinery," in *New England Begins*, III, 503; for Emery's inventory, see Essex County Probate Records, docket no. 8976 [clerk's copy, Vol. 302, pp. 101–2]; for Coleman's inventory, see Plymouth County Probate Records, Vol. 3, Pt. 1, pp. 140–2.

[25] In 1696, Gregory King estimated that nearly 1 million persons (about 18 percent of the English population) made their livings in nonagricultural pursuits – through trade, "handicrafts," military service, the law, seafaring, or in the "Sciences and Liberal Arts." Although similar estimates are not available for seventeenth-century New England, it seems likely that over 90 percent of the population was primarily engaged in agriculture. For King, see Charles Wilson, *England's Apprenticeship 1603–1763* (London, 1965), 239.

[26] Keith Wrightson suggests that many English artisans, particularly in rural areas, also combined farming and craft work. Even so, New England arti-

ters as John Emery of Newbury devoted most of their efforts to agriculture. Emery's farm, orchard, and numerous livestock could not be tended adequately only when woodworking did not otherwise occupy him.[27] Owning land in amounts unobtainable by most English artisans, New England craftsmen necessarily subordinated work at their trades to work on their farms. Moreover, land provided the only source of security in the uncertain economic climate of early New England. It was no coincidence that the bulk of official complaints about high wages occurred before the depression of the 1640s; during the difficult years, the Massachusetts Court was compelled to set rates of commodities, or "country pay" (including corn, wheat, rye, barley, peas, hemp, and flax seed), for the repayment of debts.[28] In such circumstances, few if any artisans could afford to try to make ends meet through the practice of their crafts alone.

The conditions that discouraged colonial artisans from craft specialization likewise marked a departure from English experience. Some rural artisans in England tried their hands at several trades simultaneously, but for the most part, the home country supported an elaborate occupational structure, and because there was sufficient demand for their skills many artisans worked full-time at their trades. This was so particularly in the cities, where many of the emigrant artisans had lived.[29] But even in Boston, early New England's largest – indeed only – "urban" area, the occupational structure was highly idiosyncratic, with craftsmen concentrated in trades concerned with

sans would have noticed differences in that, no matter what their specific craft, their primary economic activity was probably farming. Moreover, many of the emigrant artisans came not from rural England but from its large provincial towns, where they had presumably managed to make their livings mainly at their trades. See Keith Wrightson, *English Society 1580–1680* (London, 1982), 35.

27 Evidence of Emery's concentration on agriculture appears in his will and inventory; see the Essex County Probate Records, docket no. 8976, Vol. 302, pp. 100–2.

28 Shurtleff, ed., *Mass. Bay Recs.*, I, 304.

29 Wrightson, *English Society*, 35; John Patten, *English Towns 1500–1700* (Folkestone, 1978), 273; Wilson, *England's Apprenticeship*, 67–9.

processing agricultural produce (e.g., as butchers, millers, brewers), with servicing the emerging shipping industry (e.g., as coopers and shipbuilders), and with construction.[30] Not until the later seventeenth century would there be greater occupational diversity, with some craftsmen turning to luxury trades such as silversmithing, and not until then would significant numbers of artisans be able to make their livings solely by their crafts.[31] And even if Boston was becoming more cosmopolitan by 1650, these trends did not transform the essentially agrarian character of most other towns throughout New England.

These general economic conditions, quite different from those that obtained in England, dictated the boundaries within which colonial artisans would organize their working lives. No matter what their trade, most colonial craftsmen concluded that economic security lay primarily in landownership and farming. When newly arrived artisans decided on a town in which to settle, as often as not they made their choice on the basis of favorable land policy rather than a congenial location for their trade. Many of them fanned out into newly founded towns, such as Duxbury, Yarmouth, or Scituate in Plymouth Colony or Haverhill, Dedham, Sudbury, or Andover in Massachusetts Bay Colony, where they could become original proprietors. And even the minority who settled in the older, more populous coastal towns such as Boston, Salem, Charlestown, and Newbury usually obtained farms there, if not proprietary privileges.[32]

The behavior of these men bespoke their common goals in the ordering of economic life. More than wealth, they sought economic security for their families and the possession of farms that, together with proprietary privileges, permitted them to

[30] Rutman, *Winthrop's Boston*, 190–3.
[31] Ibid., 194–5; Albert S. Roe and Robert F. Trent, "Robert Sanderson and the Founding of the Boston Silversmiths' Trade," in *New England Begins*, III, 480.
[32] Of the twenty-two emigrant artisans for whom there is adequate information concerning New England residence and occupation, eleven settled in older towns (Boston, Charlestown, Salem, Newbury) and eleven chose newly formed communities. Probate evidence indicates that only five of these men owned no farmland, but only their houses and shops.

provide for their children (and even their children's children) in ways that craft work alone could not. The experience of John Thurston, a part-time carpenter of Medfield, provides an example of the way in which such judicious decisions conformed to the limited economic opportunities in early New England. At the time of his death in 1686, Thurston was owed just over £100, the bulk in "common" or country pay, evidently as reimbursement for carpentry work. Although a sizable sum, this would have made for a paltry (and perhaps difficult to collect) bequest when divided among his eight children. But as a town proprietor, in addition to being a carpenter, Thurston had sufficient resources in real property to provide all of his offspring with land and marriage portions before his death. At least two of his sons remained in Medfield, and both apparently enjoyed a standard of living comparable to that of their father.[33]

The settlers' decisions about earning their livings, in short, were made in a way consistent with their overall goal of acquiring the competencies that they had been assured could be theirs. Whether or not conditions favored the practice of their English trades, artisans took advantage of New England's plentiful land in order to ensure that their families would have the means to maintain their economic independence into the next generation. In establishing farms on which they might occasionally work at their trades, however, these settlers scarcely aimed to achieve self-sufficiency along with competency. Undeveloped though their region's economy might have been during the first decades of settlement, New Englanders striving for competencies regularly exchanged goods and services with

---

[33] Brown Thurston, *Thurston Genealogies 1635–1880* (Portland, Me., 1880), 356–7; Suffolk County Probate Records, dockets no. 1504, 3291, 3392. The listing of property in John Thurston's inventory indicates that he distributed most of his land prior to his death (at the age of seventy-nine). Two of Thurston's sons carried on their father's practice of combining farming and carpentry; see St. George, *The Wrought Covenant*, 99. James Henretta explored a similar theme of concern for the family's economic security, reaching somewhat different conclusions than those presented here, in "Families and Farms: *Mentalité* in Pre-Industrial America," *WMQ*, 3rd ser., XXXV (1978), 3–32.

their neighbors and resorted to the marketplace to sell their surpluses and to buy whatever necessities or luxuries they could not produce at home. For these farmer-craftsmen, periodic engagement in a market economy – whether to sell their skills or the products of their farms – by no means contradicted their adherence to the ideal of competency. Commercial activity instead simply provided one more means by which that ideal might be realized.[34]

III

Men who had worked as farmers in England faced an easier transition to colonial life than did former artisans, for they could all anticipate a return to a familiar way of life once they settled in a New England town.[35] There was no question that their services would be welcomed in a setting where rapid population growth meant more mouths to feed and where port town merchants eagerly purchased whatever surplus grain and cattle they could sell in order to sustain emerging overseas commercial links and improve the region's balance of trade. Thus farmers, unlike the majority of artisans, suffered no radical disjunction between their old and new ways of life. Their families' patterns of work would continue to be governed by the rhythm of the seasons, the vagaries of the weather, the demands of planting and harvesting crops, and the cycles of raising and slaughtering livestock. Nonetheless, their pursuit of familiar tasks in a new environment required certain adjustments in daily life that, if less difficult than those faced by many emigrants, nevertheless reflected the limitations imposed by the colonial setting.

Some of those adjustments were basic indeed. For instance, in New England farmers encountered a climate far from identical to that of England. Assuming that weather patterns were

---

[34] On this point, see Daniel Vickers, "Competency and Competition: Economic Culture in Early America," *WMQ*, 3rd ser., XLVII (1990), 3–29.

[35] Every one of the twenty-six emigrant farmers whose New England careers can be traced continued to work as a farmer in the New World.

constant along lines of latitude, colonists expected New England to have a climate resembling that of northern Spain, warmer than that of England itself. They found instead that the region experienced wide extremes of weather and were particularly surprised by the bitter winters. Notwithstanding the Reverend Francis Higginson's optimistic observation that "though it bee here somewhat cold in the winter, yet here we have plentie of Fire to warme us," the unexpected severity of the climate posed greater problems than that of simply keeping warm. The growing season differed from that in the home country, a factor that perhaps contributed to initial difficulties in introducing English cereal crops to New England. Habits of livestock rearing had to be altered as well. England's moderate climate permitted cattle to roam outside all year long, whereas New England's frigid winter temperatures discouraged this practice. Near the end of December 1630, John Winthrop lamented that "[m]any of our cows and goats were forced to be still abroad for want of houses," for he guessed that many animals would not survive until spring. But during the first years of settlement, colonists had to construct shelter for themselves before they could begin to provide for their livestock.[36]

Another fundamental adaptation was the wholesale adoption of a crop unknown in England – maize. Long a dietary staple of the region's Indian population, maize quickly assumed equal importance in the agriculture of the English newcomers. Corn yields were reliable at a time when the cultivation of English grains was not, and therefore provided a steady source of food for humans and fodder for animals. Moreover, corn yielded more grain with less labor and grew successfully

[36] Karen Ordahl Kupperman, "The Puzzle of the American Climate in the Early Colonial Period," *American Historical Review*, 87, no. 5 (1982), 1262–89; Reverend Francis Higginson, *New-Englands Plantation with The Sea Journal and Other Writings* (facsimile; Salem, Mass., 1908), 102; Russell, *Long, Deep Furrow*, 32–5, 40–1, 88; Winthrop, *History of New England*, ed. Savage, I, 39. T. H. Breen argues that the effects of climatic change were minimal; see *Puritans and Adventurers: Change and Persistence in Early America* (New York, 1980), 72–3.

on recently cleared land, whereas English grains generally required a significant amount of soil preparation before they would thrive.[37]

English agricultural techniques (and English crops) gradually took hold in New England, but colonists initially encountered difficulties in employing familiar methods of farming. The greatest challenge lay in the nature of the land itself. Although colonists first planted in areas that had previously been farmed by Indians, the spread of settlement soon brought them into wilder regions, which had to be cleared before they could be cultivated. That task was slow and laborious, particularly since farmers were compelled to pry out the rocks and uproot the tree stumps that hindered their efforts to plow, as they had been accustomed to doing in England. In fact, because the process of clearing fields was so expensive of time and labor, settlers often adopted the Indian practices of planting multiple crops in the same field (i.e., planting beans and squash near the bases of cornstalks to keep down weeds) and relying on the hoe rather than the plow as ways of minimizing their investment of labor when so many other tasks demanded their attention.[38]

The scarcity of labor in New England also induced colonists to modify their previous English agricultural regimen in another way. Particularly during the early decades of settlement when fields were being cleared for arable husbandry, colonists often turned to the raising of livestock as their principal economic activity. Most vessels arriving in New England during the 1630s brought animal as well as human passengers, and

---

[37] Russell, *Long, Deep Furrow*, chs. 2, 5; Darrett B. Rutman, *Husbandmen of Plymouth: Farms and Villages in the Old Colony, 1620–1692* (Boston, 1967), 7–12. For a description of patterns of Indian agriculture, see Cronon, *Changes in the Land*, ch. 3.

[38] Joan Thirsk, "Farming Techniques," in Joan Thirsk, ed., *The Agrarian History of England and Wales*, IV (1500–1640) (Cambridge, 1967), 163–79; Russell, *Long, Deep Furrow*, 16, 21–2, 39–44, 81–2; Rutman, *Husbandmen of Plymouth*, 42–3. John Winthrop, Jr., described the Indian manner of maize husbandry for the Royal Society in 1678; his comments are reprinted in Percy Wells Bidwell and John I. Falconer, *History of Agriculture in the Northern United States 1620–1860* (Washington, D.C., 1925), 10–11.

cattle, sheep, goats, and swine were no less important than their human owners for the success of the colonies. Livestock rearing perfectly suited the needs of settlements short on labor: Goats and swine foraged without supervision in nearby woods, and herds of cattle and flocks of sheep could be managed by comparatively small numbers of men or even children. In addition to providing much of the protein in the colonial diet, these animals – especially cattle – eventually became a critical component of the region's export trade. By the early 1640s, Boston merchants had established a lucrative trade in meat and live animals, directed mainly to the West Indies.[39]

Since most emigrant farmers had originated in England's wood-pasture regions – where inhabitants raised both crops and livestock – New England's pattern of mixed agriculture would not in itself have been unfamiliar. Indeed, their English experience may even have predisposed them to engage in precisely those entrepreneurial activities that helped guarantee both their families' economic security and the prosperity of the New England economy as a whole. Having lived in places where manorial organizations were weak, and therefore unlikely to circumscribe individual economic activity by ancient customary restrictions, the former inhabitants of wood-pasture regions were accustomed to deciding for themselves what to produce and what to sell, and were used to engaging in by-employments to supplement their income from agriculture. Although it is true that the traditional by-employment of England's wood-pasture settlements – clothmaking – scarcely flourished in New England, other opportunities emerged in the colonial setting. That many of these activities would involve production for commercial exchange rather than simply for domestic consumption may also have been related to the settlers' English experience: Most

---

[39] Russell, *Long, Deep Furrow*, 30–8; Rutman, *Husbandmen of Plymouth*, 6, 16–18, 46–9; Rutman, "Governor Winthrop's Garden Crop," *WMQ*, 3rd ser., XX (1963), 404; Bailyn, *New England Merchants*, 89, 101. For a study of the colonial New England diet, see Sarah F. MacMahon, "A Comfortable Subsistence: The Changing Composition of Diet in Rural New England, 1620–1840," *WMQ*, 3rd ser., XLII (1985), 26–65.

emigrants, after all, had lived either in or near market towns and were used to resorting to the marketplace for the purchase and sale of goods.[40]

The extent to which New England farmers engaged in market activity had less to do with their individual preferences for such endeavors than with their proximity to waterways and port towns. One commentator noted that Sudbury's inhabitants complained that their distance from "Mart Towns" made it "burdensome" – not to say expensive – to have to "bring their corne so far by land."[41] But for those settlers living in places such as Boston or Salem, in towns along the Connecticut River, or in any of the small Plymouth Colony ports, access to markets posed little problem. As early as 1633, Boston officials declared Thursday to be the weekly market day, and before long, regular markets were held in more than a dozen other New England towns.[42]

Very few inhabitants produced principally for the market, but virtually every family contrived to find something that it could exchange for money or, more likely, goods (such as sugar or cloth) that could not be made at home. In fact, efforts to establish a domestic textile industry faltered in part because colonists generally found it more expedient to "put away their cattel and corn for cloathing, then to set upon making of cloth."[43] All sorts of New England products found their way to market. Colonists living along the coast sold fish, and once settlers began to raise wheat and other grains in sufficiently large quantities, portions of the harvest could be sold. Farmers also frequently converted the timber they cleared from their farms into boards and shingles that they could sell to merchants. Some settlers, such as

---

[40] On the economy of England's wood-pasture regions, see Joan Thirsk, "The Farming Regions of England," in Thirsk, ed., *AHEW*, IV, 41, 46–9, 54, 67–9, 79–80; David Underdown, *Revel, Riot and Rebellion: Popular Politics and Culture in England 1603–1660* (Oxford, 1985), 4–8. For a description of English market towns and their activities, see Alan Everitt, "The Marketing of Agricultural Produce," in Thirsk, ed., *AHEW*, IV, 466–589.

[41] Johnson, *Wonder-Working Providence*, ed. Jameson, 196.

[42] Russell, *Long, Deep Furrow*, 80, 120.

[43] Johnson, *Wonder-Working Providence*, ed. Jameson, 211.

Henry Dow of Hampton, fashioned wood into barrel staves, which would either be bundled and shipped to West Indian sugar producers or sold to coopers and made into hogsheads to hold other New England goods for export. Of course, many timber products never entered the transatlantic trade at all; Boston's growing population, confined to a narrow peninsula, increasingly required the wood cleared from inland farms to heat their homes and build new structures.[44]

But of all the goods brought to market by New England farmers, the most important were those derived from livestock. Trade in cattle was so brisk that by 1648 the town of Boston petitioned the colonial legislature for permission to hold two fairs a year, one exclusively for the sale of cattle. Some of the demand for livestock and dairy products was domestic: Again, inhabitants of comparatively small port towns such as Boston or Salem lacked sufficient pasturage to maintain large herds, and therefore often bought meat, cheese, and butter from inland farmers. Even more important, however, was the overseas trade in meat and livestock, much of which went to the West Indies and constituted an important sector of the region's growing economy.[45]

Despite its profitability, few colonists engaged in livestock production on a large scale. William Pynchon managed to raise impressive numbers of cattle and hogs in the Connecticut river valley, but in so doing had few equals in entrepreneurship. Only a handful of settlers commanded the resources of a Pynchon, and outside of his domain, there were few areas sufficiently rich in meadow land to support large herds. Moreover, the fate of one ambitious Newbury settler who sought greener pastures elsewhere provided an object lesson to others who might simi-

---

[44] Russell, *Long, Deep Furrow*, 57–67, 112–24; Rutman, "Governor Winthrop's Garden Crop," 396–415; McCusker and Menard, *Economy of British America*, 97–101. When Henry Dow died in 1659, his possessions included 1,000 hogshead staves, valued at £2; his inventory is in the Essex County Registry of Probate, docket no. 8212.

[45] Russell, *Long, Deep Furrow*, 60–4; Rutman, "Governor Winthrop's Garden Crop," 408–12; Bailyn, *New England Merchants*, 89, 101.

larly have found their efforts overwhelmed by unforeseen events. When William Cottle died unexpectedly in 1668, the appraisers of his estate discovered that he owned a sizable stock of cattle in New York and New Jersey, evidently being fattened there for sale. Although this amounted to a significant proportion of Cottle's estate, the appraisers concluded that recovering either the cattle or their cash value was "very hazardable," and thus the unlucky entrepreneur's pregnant widow and four children should not expect to collect anything.[46]

Most New England farmers, then, sold only those cattle that exceeded their domestic needs, rather than engaging in production specifically for the market. As Edward Johnson noted, by the middle of the seventeenth century it had become "the common practice of those that had any store of Cattel, to sell every year a Cow or two, which cloath'd their backs, fil'd their bellies with more varieties then the Country of it self afforded, and put gold and silver in their purses beside."[47] Yet even with small herds, farmers found that their lives were shaped in important ways by the needs of those cattle and that in raising livestock, they could not depend solely on their previous English experience for guidance. For instance, New England farmers, at least initially, grazed their cattle on wild meadows, and not on the cultivated pastures they had known in England. The labor necessary to clear land and plant nutritionally superior grasses was simply beyond the means of most colonists until the second half of the century. As a result, settlers highly prized both the wild meadow within their town's boundaries and their right to graze on the town common. The need for adequate pasturage was so compelling, in fact, that settlers seeking to form new towns often cited as their reason the "want of medowe" in their current homes. Governor William Bradford of Plymouth Colony explicitly blamed the desire for natural pasture for the dis-

---

[46] For Pynchon's activities, see Innes, *Labor in a New Land*, 8–9, 23–4. William Cottle's inventory lists "Debts at New Yorke & New Jarsy & in Cattell there" valued at £140; see *The Probate Records of Essex County, Massachusetts* (1635–1681), II, 129–30.

[47] Johnson, *Wonder-Working Providence*, ed. Jameson, 209.

persal of the population. In 1632, he noted that "no man now thought he could live except he had cattle and a great deal of ground to keep them. . . . By which means they were scattered all over the Bay quickly and the town in which they lived compactly till now [Plymouth] was left very thin and in a short time almost desolate."[48]

The dependence on livestock created problems other than the population dispersal that troubled Governor Bradford. Because the colonists permitted their animals to forage freely, their precious plots of corn and beans often fell prey to hungry swine and cattle. In England in such cases, the laws of trespass allowed the farmer to sue the livestock owner for the crop damage, but colonial conditions dictated a reversal of this practice. Since the animals were so critical to the colonists' survival and their owners had no other efficient way to feed them, the burden fell upon farmers to ensure that their arable fields were adequately fenced. Towns regularly elected fence viewers to see that individual plots were protected in an attempt to reduce the number of disputes that arose over damage by errant beasts.[49]

As time passed and arable husbandry became more productive, the heavy dependence on livestock diminished. More and more fields were cleared, allowing farmers to use plows as well as hoes. Maize continued to be the principal cereal crop, but English grains such as barley, rye, and wheat increasingly appeared in New England fields.[50] Yet even as certain English

---

[48] Bidwell and Falconer, *History of Agriculture*, 19; Russell, *Long, Deep Furrow*, 34; Weeden, *Economic and Social History*, I, 101; Shurtleff, ed., *Mass. Bay Recs.*, I, 210; William Bradford, *Of Plymouth Plantation, 1620–1647*, ed. Samuel Eliot Morison (New York, 1952), 253. For a description of English wood-pasture agriculture, see Thirsk, "The Farming Regions of England," in Thirsk, ed., *AHEW*, IV, 41, 46–9, 54, 67–9, 79–80.

[49] David Thomas Konig, *Law and Society in Puritan Massachusetts: Essex County, 1629–1692* (Chapel Hill, N.C., 1979), 118; Cronon, *Changes in the Land*, 134–7. Cronon notes that swine eventually became such a nuisance that farmers were allowed to kill any pigs caught damaging crops.

[50] Russell, *Long, Deep Furrow*, 40–3, 81–2; Rutman, *Husbandmen of Plymouth*, 17, 33–4, 44–50. There are thirty-two surviving inventories for these emi-

patterns of husbandry were reestablished, farmers found it impossible to reproduce familiar agrarian practices completely. New Englanders may have transplanted English crops to a new land, but they never managed to replicate the system of agricultural labor that they had once known.

Most of the emigrant families had brought servants with them to New England, but once those servants completed their terms, they could not be replaced from the pool of available labor in the new society. Even the occasional hired hand was difficult to obtain, in part because the same economic conditions that had raised the wages of artisans also allowed farm laborers to demand "oppressive" remuneration. The comparatively low productivity of New England farms – and especially the absence of a lucrative cash crop on the order of Chesapeake tobacco – could not support the maintenance of full-time help, and the scarcity and high cost of labor discouraged a widespread system of short-term hiring. The difficulties of bringing in the harvest under such circumstances could be acute: In 1646, the Massachusetts General Court actually instructed town constables to round up idle craftsmen and make them "work by the day for their Neighbours in mowing [and] reaping of corn."[51]

Unable to rely on the seasonal hiring of agricultural labor as they would have done in England, colonists came to rely almost exclusively on their offspring to keep family farms functioning. This practice strengthened the bonds between parents and children, for each needed the other more than ever. If New England sons depended heavily on their fathers to provide them

grants (for the period 1637–83) that list foodstuffs. Two-thirds of the settlers ($N = 21$) possessed Indian corn, half of the inventories listed wheat ($N = 16$), nearly half ($N = 15$) listed barley, and about a third ($N = 12$) listed rye. Although some of these provisions may have been purchased, it is likely that most were produced on the owners' farms.

[51] These involuntary laborers were to be paid, and craftsmen at work at their trades were declared exempt from the provisions of the court order; see William H. Whitmore, ed., *The Colonial Laws of Massachusetts, Reprinted from the Edition of 1660, with the supplements to 1672, Containing Also, The Body of Liberties of 1641* (Boston, 1889), 203.

with the means of establishing their own independent households, their fathers relied no less on them to help with the work
of creating the farms that would one day be theirs.[52]

The effects of this rural labor system impinged not only on
the economy but also on the culture of early New England,
most significantly by strengthening patriarchal control. Fathers
relied so heavily on their sons' labor that they attempted to
prolong the period during which their sons worked for them.
Young boys began with relatively simple chores, such as caring
for livestock, and their responsibilities increased as they grew
to manhood. By the time they reached maturity, sons generally
performed all the necessary tasks of farm work without parental supervision. They continued to work on family farms into
their mid-twenties, and occasionally even after marriage, because their fathers could afford no other source of labor. Fathers
commonly restrained their sons' independence by retaining title to family land until late in their own lives, or even postponing the division of property until their deaths, as a means of
encouraging their sons to settle near – and to continue helping
to improve – the paternal estate. The price paid by sons was
probably more psychological than economic: They were, after
all, working land that they would one day own. Nevertheless,
by postponing their independence for the sake of the family's
security, they behaved in ways unfamiliar to English young
men, for whom youthful mobility – not persistence – was generally the route to economic independence.[53]

[52] Daniel Vickers, "Working the Fields in a Developing Economy: Essex
County, Massachusetts, 1630–1675," in Stephen Innes, ed., *Work and Labor
in Early America* (Chapel Hill, N.C., 1988), 49–69. For the English rural
labor system, see Ann Kussmaul, *Servants in Husbandry in Early Modern
England* (Cambridge, 1981). Less is known about the participation of
women in agricultural work, but one important exploration is Laurel
Thatcher Ulrich, *Good Wives: Image and Reality in the Lives of Women in
Northern New England 1650–1750* (New York, 1982), 13–67.

[53] Vickers, "Working the Fields," in Innes, ed., *Work and Labor in Early America*, 60–2, 68; Greven, *Four Generations*, ch. 4. On the mobility of English
youth, see Peter Spufford, "Population Mobility in Pre-Industrial England," *Genealogist's Magazine*, 17 (1973), 422–4; John Patten, "Patterns of

The enhancement of patriarchal authority was embedded in a cultural context that grew from conditions peculiar to New England. Fathers' efforts to prolong the dependence of their sons constituted an economic strategy rooted in New England's labor shortage and in the fact that the region offered few other alternatives for maturing young men – two conditions unknown in England. The largely unsuccessful attempts by emigrant craftsmen to transplant their trades to the New World (except as part-time work) demonstrated that artisanship provided no remunerative escape from laboring for one's father. Commerce or maritime labor similarly offered no real solution in that the former required more capital than most young men could command, and the latter simply substituted dependence on an employer for dependence on one's father.[54]

Reinforcing the authority of fathers over their sons (and of parents over their offspring in general) was an aspect of the Puritan world view that strongly emphasized the submission of children and other dependents within the family. Puritan lawmakers, drawing upon biblical precedents, went so far as to prescribe the death penalty for "any child . . . above sixteen years old, and of sufficient understanding, [who] shall CURSE, or SMITE their natural FATHER, or MOTHER" without provocation. No matter that this penalty was never enforced: Its existence alone testified to the impressive power of an ideal of obedience that could only have buttressed parents' attempts to keep their children submissive and their sons, in particular, economically dependent. According to such a vision of family government, attempts by sons to establish themselves apart from the paternal household without the father's permission

Migration and Movement of Labour to Three Pre-Industrial East Anglian Towns," *Journal of Historical Geography,* 2, (1976), 111–29.

54 Bailyn, *New England Merchants,* 31–3, 35–7, 82; Daniel Vickers, "Work and Life on the Fishing Periphery of Essex County, Massachusetts, 1630–1675," in David D. Hall and David Grayson Allen, eds., *Seventeenth-Century New England* (Boston, 1984), 83–117; Daniel Vickers, "Nantucket Whalemen in the Deep-Sea Fishery: The Changing Anatomy of an Early American Labor Force," *Journal of American History* 72, No. 2 (1985), 277–96.

smacked not of youthful independence but of grossly impious insubordination.[55]

Fortunately for New England society, the potential for intergenerational antagonism inherent in the growth of patriarchal authority was never realized. Few sons balked at their fathers' control, principally because most expected to become freeholders and patriarchs themselves and eventually to exercise a similar control over their own children. In fact, colonial economic conditions, including the tightly knit bonds between families and their land, ensured that most sons would inherit the status and livings of their fathers. When emigrant fathers chose to settle in towns where they could become proprietors, they deliberately intended to acquire enough land to settle their sons nearby. Their success in passing on their economic status to the next generation meant that the relatively homogeneous social structure distinctive to colonial New England was not simply an artifact of the selective process of the Great Migration of the 1630s, but instead persisted throughout most of the seventeenth century.

If the colonial economy afforded few ways to gain great wealth, it offered even fewer ways to retain it. At the same time, the policy of providing free land to inhabitants of towns ensured that few New Englanders (barring physical or mental handicap or sheer incompetence) would live in poverty. The world of seventeenth-century New England, fashioned by the collective efforts of farmers, artisans, and many artisans-turned-farmers, displayed – in sharp contrast to the stratified society of the home country – a remarkably limited degree of social differentiation. The visible manifestation of this important fact is clearly revealed in the material conditions of New England life. Most settlers enjoyed a modest style of life that closely resembled that of their neighbors and that constituted the competency to which they aspired.

[55] Whitmore, ed., *Colonial Laws of Massachusetts*, 129; Philip Greven, *The Protestant Temperament: Patterns of Child-Rearing, Religious Experience, and the Self in Early America* (New York, 1977), 32–55; John Demos, *A Little Commonwealth: Family Life in Plymouth Colony* (New York, 1970), 100–6.

IV

Competency signified more than simply an economic status; it also implied the political dimension of household independence. The bedrock of that independence, and therefore of competency, was landownership. In seventeenth-century New England, landownership among adult white males was virtually universal. Acceptance as a member of a town in the first generation of settlement was synonymous with landownership; in Andover, for instance, settlers resolved to "give every Inhabitant whome they received as a Townsman an house lott proportionable to his estate, . . . with suteable accomodations thereunto of meadow, and all other divisions of upland & plouging ground[.]" The amounts of real property any man held would vary over the course of his life as he accumulated land through middle age and then gradually disposed of it to his children as he reached old age. But throughout their working lives, the vast majority of settlers owned enough land to support their families. Edward Johnson noted that even "the poorest person . . . hath a house and land of his own, and bread of his own growing, if not some cattel[.]" Most settlers owned somewhat more.[56]

The critical importance of land in the family economy is demonstrated by the fact that, for two out of three settlers, real property (housing and land) comprised over half the total value of their estates.[57] Much of this land remained uncultivated by

[56] Quotation from Andover records is in Greven, *Four Generations*, 45; Johnson, *Wonder-Working Providence*, ed. Jameson, 210. For a detailed description of the fluctuating amounts of land owned over the course of the life cycle, see Jackson Turner Main, *Society and Economy in Colonial Connecticut* (Princeton, N.J., 1985), ch. 6.

[57] Thirty-eight of fifty-seven emigrant household heads with adequate probate information (66.7 percent) held estates in which real property constituted more than half the total value. Since housing was almost always valued along with land, it is impossible to separate the value of buildings from that of the land itself. For inhabitants of port towns such as Boston, Charlestown, or Salem, the proportionate value of land in probate inventories was somewhat less. Several of these men engaged in commercial

the first generation of colonists, but its value as an asset remained undiminished since sons would inherit and farm land unimproved by their fathers. In fact, although New England society displayed little social differentiation among its inhabitants, what mainly distinguished more prosperous settlers from their neighbors was not their more genteel style of life but simply the greater amount of land that they owned.[58]

Most colonial farmers enjoyed a standard of living approximately comparable to that of an English yeoman. In addition to owning a house and land, they generally possessed enough livestock, farm equipment, and household goods to provide a comfortable existence. The estate of John Pers, a Watertown farmer and part-time weaver, typified that of most first-generation New England settlers. Pers died in 1661, at the age of seventy-three, and left an estate worth just over £285.[59] About half the value of Pers's estate (£128 10s.) consisted of his house and lands in Watertown. He also owned a modest herd of livestock – two oxen, five head of cattle, one mare, two sheep, and six pigs. His barn

ventures and thus owned significant amounts of capital (such as Nicholas Busby's Boston shop goods) absent from the estates of other settlers. What little land they did own, however, was often worth more than property in rural communities.

58 Complete inventories exist for fifty-seven emigrant household heads. Of the eleven with estates valued at more than £500 (twice the median estate size for the total group), six held estates in which real property (housing and land) constituted 75 percent or more of the total estate value. For the forty-six men with estates worth less than £500, only twelve held estates in which real property constituted 75 percent or more of the total value.

59 This figure is close to the median estate size – £261 – for the emigrants in this study with adequate probate information. It also corresponds roughly to the average estate sizes obtained by Terry Anderson from a random sample of New England inventories from the second half of the seventeenth century; see his "Wealth Estimates for the New England Colonies, 1650–1709," *Explorations in Economic History,* 12 (1975), table 2, 156. Connecticut settlers may have been, on average, somewhat wealthier than their Massachusetts neighbors. Jackson Turner Main has calculated mean values of probated estates in seventeenth-century New Haven, Fairfield, and Hartford counties ranging from £310 to £377; see *Society and Economy in Colonial Connecticut,* Table 3.1, 66. I have not used the mean estate size in my sample of emigrants because the presence of four very large estates, valued at over £1,000, skews the mean upward to nearly £400.

contained the usual agricultural implements, including a cart and tumbrel, a plow, ox yokes, and chains. Pers also maintained a small shop, where he kept his loom and other weaving equipment, as well as a few hoes and "lumber." At the time of his death, he employed a single servant whose contract had four years to run; since the seven Pers children were grown and living away from home, their aging father needed an extra hand to help run the family farm.[60]

The remainder of Pers's estate consisted of personal property arranged within a modest house typical of seventeenth-century New England dwellings. When first constructed, his two-story house contained two rooms, one above the other, but subsequent additions doubled the building's size to accommodate the large Pers family. In addition to a leanto attached to the rear of the dwelling, another two-story wing was added, so that the house eventually contained five rooms.[61] Like most New England families of modest means, the Pers family made little attempt to set aside certain rooms for specialized functions. The main ground-floor room served as the kitchen and contained an assortment of brass and iron cookware, pewter dishes, and fireplace implements, but it was also the place where Pers kept

[60] Pers's inventory is in the Middlesex County Probate Records, docket no. 17493. Since, in his will, he bequeathed all of his property to his wife (on the condition that she pay small sums of cash to their children one year after his death), it seems likely that Pers had already helped to set his children up on their own farms prior to his death. Pers's will is reprinted in Peirce, *Peirce Genealogy*, 19; other biographical information is on 17–18. See also Mary Lovering Holman, *Ancestry of Colonel John Harrington Stevens and His Wife Frances Helen Miller* (privately printed, 1948), 216–19; *Watertown Records*, I, 63, 111, 143.

[61] Pers's inventory lists a "new chamber," "the old house," an "uper old chamber," and an "upper new chamber," in addition to the leanto. Although "the old house" may in fact have contained two rooms, the fact that there is only one "uper old chamber" suggests that the lower room was probably a single large space functioning mainly – given the items listed in it – as a kitchen. Other New England house plans, derived from probate inventories and surviving dwellings, are discussed in Cummings, *Framed Houses*, ch. 3. For descriptions of English yeomen's houses, which often also contained four or five rooms, see M. W. Barley, "Rural Housing in England," in Thirsk, ed., *AHEW*, IV, 734–59.

his "fouling peece" and a variety of hatchets, saws, and axes. The other ground-floor chamber evidently served as the "best bedroom," since it held Pers's most valuable feather bed and bedstead, along with the usual "furnishings" of sheets, blankets, bolster, and pillows. But the room also contained two other beds (one a trundle bed), two tables, two chairs, a cupboard, a trunk, a chest, and a box. As the only room in the house with curtains, and the repository of the looking glass and treble viol that had probably been transported from England, the room seemed to have served as both parlor and best bedroom. Yet it also contained a considerable amount of cloth, presumably woven by Pers, as well as 170 skeins of cotton yarn, 14 cheeses, butter, and soap, further indicating that, in the cramped space of these early New England houses, no room could escape being used for storage. The two second-story chambers likewise contained a jumble of goods, including beds, a loom, stores of Indian corn, old lumber, and "3 old sacks."[62]

The contents of Pers's house and barn, in short, bespoke a modest standard of living. Though he owned few luxuries, Pers had enough furniture, linen, kitchen implements, agricultural tools, and weaving equipment to provide a certain rude comfort. Stored in his house and barn were sufficient supplies of Indian corn, "English grain," cheese, butter, apples, and beer to ensure that his family would have plenty to eat. Like most of his New England neighbors, Pers had very little cash in the house; at the time of his death, he possessed a total of two shillings in wampum ("peag") and silver. Only about a third of emigrant household heads possessed any money at the times of their deaths, and the amounts were invariably small – usually less than £5. In fact, William Paddy, a Boston merchant whose total estate was valued at over £2,700, possessed cash assets of only £161 6s. 8d. – in wampum, not silver. Little currency circulated within the colonial economy, and particularly outside of

---

[62] On the lack of specialized use of rooms, see also Demos, *A Little Commonwealth*, ch. 2.

Boston, colonists generally relied on a complex system of exchanging goods and labor to obtain what they did not produce for themselves.[63]

This system of exchange passed goods and services from neighbor to neighbor in communities that evinced a roughly equivalent style of life, made up of families with similar needs to fill and similar kinds of help to offer. Most New Englanders, like the Pers family, enjoyed a modest standard of living that substantially mirrored that of their fellow colonists. Upon entering the house of Deacon Richard Knight of Newbury, for instance, one would encounter objects nearly identical to those that filled the Pers dwelling. Rooms bulged with beds and bedding, tables and chairs, linen and kitchen equipment, cheeses and Indian corn, sacks, and the ubiquitous "old lumber." Knight's barn likewise contained agricultural implements, a cart, a plow, and stores of grain, and his livestock included horses, cattle, sheep, and swine. Nothing in this inventory of possessions, however, would give any indication that Deacon Knight's estate was, in fact, worth nearly three times that of John Pers. For Knight's greatest asset was not his personal but his real estate: His holdings in "orchards, upland & meadow" dwarfed those of Pers in quantity and value.[64]

Knight's possessions gave little indication of his comparative affluence because he, like most New Englanders, avoided using wealth for the sake of display. Prosperous colonists, instead of constructing grand houses and adorning them with expensive furnishings, tended to invest in land to pass on to their children and often used surplus cash or goods to enhance their status as creditors to their neighbors. Yet even with this

[63] The large quantity of foodstuffs listed in Pers's inventory is due to the fact that his estate was assessed in September, shortly after the harvest. Of the sixty-nine emigrant household heads whose inventories listed personal property, only 26 (37.7 percent) possessed money. Sixteen of the twenty-six with money (61.5 percent) had less than £5. William Paddy's inventory is in the Suffolk County Probate Records, docket no. 189.

[64] Knight died in 1683 at the age of eighty; his inventory is in the Essex County Probate Records, docket no. 16014.

self-imposed restraint on the display of wealth, no one would have mistaken New England for an egalitarian society. Townsmen knew who among their number enjoyed the greatest prosperity and were periodically reminded of their relative economic standing. Every Sabbath morning, when they entered their meetinghouses, New Englanders sat in pews arranged according to their social rank. Whenever towns parceled out previously undivided lands, inhabitants with the largest initial grants received the largest shares of the new land, since one's claim in subsequent divisions corresponded to the extent of one's original holdings. Inhabitants regularly recognized the status of their wealthier neighbors by electing them to the most important town offices. Even so, the visible distinctions between wealthy and poor were substantially understated by the region's material culture.[65]

The simplified and relatively homogeneous material conditions of New England life were not simply a function of the hardships of life in a "wilderness," where there were few luxuries to buy and little money with which to buy them. Almost from the beginning of New England settlement, merchants imported cloth, glass, and metal goods from England, along with such luxuries as Spanish and Canary wines. Colonists could afford to pay for at least some of these items by selling whatever surpluses their farms yielded.[66] Thus their preference for limiting their consumption of luxuries was largely a matter of choice, not necessity. It grew in part from a judicious assessment of long-run benefits: Investments in land and its improvement would help one's children far better than bequeathing them fine imported silver or handsome fabrics. English colonists elsewhere in the New World, faced with similar conditions, also chose investment over consumption. In New England, however, these practical considerations were reinforced

---

[65] For the connection between wealth and political office, see T. H. Breen, *The Character of the Good Ruler: Puritan Political Ideas in New England, 1630–1730* (New Haven, Conn., 1970), 68, 219–20.

[66] Bailyn, *New England Merchants*, 83; Rutman, "Governor Winthrop's Garden Crop," 396–415.

by a strong, if somewhat ambiguous, Puritan heritage that enjoined believers to work hard but not to waste their earnings on frivolities. Conspicuous consumption invited covetousness, a sin that, by definition, distracted believers from their duty to maintain a proper focus on their spiritual, rather than material, estates.[67]

The principal exception to the rule of moderation occurred in Boston, where commercial opportunities allowed some families to acquire considerable wealth and to publicize their fortunes with extravagant possessions. Boston's merchants were by necessity inveterate risk takers, enjoying easy access to imported commodities with which – if their risks paid off – they adorned their persons and furnished their houses, and it was therefore mainly in the capital that one could find a marked disparity in standards of living. Consider, for instance, the sumptuousness of William Paddy's surroundings in comparison to the average-sized estate of John Pers and the substantial holdings of Richard Knight. A prosperous Boston merchant (though by no means one of the town's richest men), Paddy lived in an eight-room dwelling comparable in size to that of Governor John Winthrop. The entrance hall was clearly arranged to capture visitors' attention, with its eleven "Rusha lethr" chairs and livery cupboard, its "streked" carpet and matching window curtains. In all, Paddy owned twenty chairs, more than all the inhabitants of some small rural towns together might have been able to muster. Paddy's chairs, moreover, were not simple wooden models but ornate leather and Turkey work (embroidered) pieces. Around his fireplaces, the andirons and other implements were trimmed with brass. All seven of his beds – even his children's trundle

---

[67] Gloria Main found a similar preference for investment over consumption among Maryland's early settlers; see *Tobacco Colony: Life in Early Maryland, 1650–1720* (Princeton, N.J., 1982). For a discussion of Puritan attitudes toward wealth, see Stephen Foster, *Their Solitary Way: The Puritan Social Ethic in the First Century of Settlement in New England* (New Haven, Conn., 1971), ch. 4. Similarly ambiguous attitudes prevailed among English Puritans; see, for instance, Paul S. Seaver, *Wallington's World: A Puritan Artisan in Seventeenth-Century London* (Stanford, Calif., 1985), ch. 5.

beds – had feather mattresses, and most were covered with "pintadoe" or imported chintz quilts. The walls of the house were adorned with mirrors and "hanging candlesticks," and Paddy's supply of linen (33 pairs of sheets, 104 napkins, 22 towels, 16 tablecloths) would have sufficed for more than a dozen families of average means. But the merchant's financial success was never more noticeable than when he strolled through the streets of Boston, clad in his "sadcallr Broadcloth sewte," "Red wastcot," and "new blacke stuff Cloake" while attended by his "neager man servant."[68]

An English gentleman might have sniffed at the amount and character of Paddy's household furnishings, but the merchant's neighbors – not to mention farmers from outlying towns – would surely have gaped at the luxury of his surroundings. Not all would necessarily have envied him, however, for many settlers would have recognized the challenge that such material wealth posed to the Puritan ideal of living in the world without being of it. Many Boston merchants remained conscientious Puritans despite their prosperity, but they did so only at the price of a constant struggle against the seductions of worldliness. No better example of this struggle exists than Robert Keayne, a wealthy Boston merchant convicted in 1639 of the crime of selling goods at an excessive rate and simultaneously admonished by the Boston church for the same act as a sin that called into question his spiritual state. Tormented for the rest of his days by this humiliation, Keayne transformed his last will and testament into a lengthy defense of both his business practices and his piety. That Keayne cared so deeply about his double vindication testified to his thorough immersion in Puritan culture. Protesting his innocence of the crime of profiteering was only half the task; he knew that he must also respond to

[68] Paddy's inventory is in the Suffolk County Probate Records, docket no. 189. John Winthrop's inventory indicates that the governor lived in a two-story, nine-room dwelling; see *Winthrop Papers*, 5 vols. (Boston, 1929–47), V, 333–6. For evidence that the presence of chairs in a house indicated a family's comparative prosperity, see Demos, *A Little Commonwealth*, 43; Main, *Tobacco Colony*, 169, 242, 249–51.

the church's judgment against him, insisting, in effect, that he was not simply an honest merchant but a Christian one.[69]

Keayne's difficulties stemmed in part from his considerable wealth – his estate was valued at £4,000 – and in part from the manner in which he had earned it. Commercial activity was by its very nature speculative, and could on occasion produce sums of wealth unattainable by farmers plowing New England's rocky soil. At the same time, it afforded greater opportunity (and, perhaps, temptation) to go beyond the bounds of what many believed to be proper economic behavior. This was particularly worrisome in New England, where a relatively small group of merchants, located in a few port towns, controlled the flow of imports to the majority of inhabitants living in the large number of country towns. New England Puritans by no means deplored or discouraged mercantile activity – they could hardly afford to do so – but they recognized the special dangers it posed to righteous living.[70] For most settlers, however, these were dangers with which others would have to wrestle, since their labors on their farms produced at best small surpluses scarcely conducive to indulging in either greed or display. And for those few settlers at the bottom of the economic ladder, the daily struggle for a decent subsistence overwhelmed any concerns about how best to spend the surplus they did not have.

William Gault, a shoemaker from Salem, probably devoted most of his energies to making ends meet and yet never rose

[69] Bernard Bailyn, ed., *The Apologia of Robert Keayne: The Self-Portrait of a Puritan Merchant* (New York, 1965); Bailyn, *New England Merchants*, 41–4. For another portrait of a Puritan merchant, see David Hall's description of Samuel Sewall's mental world in *Worlds of Wonder, Days of Judgment: Popular Religious Belief in Early New England* (New York, 1989), ch. 5. In her meticulous study of the towns of Marblehead and Gloucester, Christine Heyrman describes the process by which commercial activity eventually harmonized with Puritan culture; see *Commerce and Culture: The Maritime Communities of Colonial Massachusetts, 1690–1750* (New York, 1984).

[70] Bailyn, ed., *Apologia*, 82; Foster, *Their Solitary Way*, 114–20. These complex attitudes toward commercial activity and wealth persisted into the eighteenth century; see J. E. Crowley, *This Sheba, Self: The Conceptualization of Economic Life in Eighteenth-Century America* (Baltimore, 1974).

above economic mediocrity. When he died in 1660 at the age of fifty-two, he left his widow and three daughters with an estate of only £49, encumbered by £21 in debts. Gault's debts, ranging from 5s. to £3 12s., were all owed to men more prominent than himself. Five of his creditors – William Browne, George Corwin, John Gedney (a fellow passenger on the *Mary Anne* twenty-three years earlier), Philip Cromwell, and Edmund Batter – were prosperous merchants and leading political figures in Salem. Gault probably relied on these men for imported goods and provisions, although, since all of them except Cromwell managed taverns, his debts may also have reflected consumption patterns of a different sort.

Whatever the reason for his lack of success, William Gault clearly belonged near the bottom of Salem society. Even so, he owned a small plot of land and a house furnished in a manner similar to that of other New Englanders. The Gault family, like so many others, possessed furniture, adequate linen, kitchen utensils, tools, and a few additional items, in this case a bible and "other small bookes." The quantities may have been smaller and quality somewhat cruder (for instance, the family's napkins were "ould Course" ones), but this listing of goods indicates that even New England's poorer families were, by most measures, comparatively well off.[71] The prospects for Mary Gault and her three teenage daughters were quite uncertain, of course, but other widows managed to eke out hardscrabble lives, carefully balancing limited expenditures against equally limited resources. The Gaults' Salem neighbor, Emme Mason, who had emigrated as a widow to be with her children

[71] For biographical information on Gault, see Perley, *History of Salem*, II, 30–1. His inventory is printed in *Probate Records of Essex County*, I, 316–17. Gault's two other creditors were a Mr. Bridgham of Boston, who may have been a merchant, and John Porter, Jr., the oldest son of a prominent Salem figure, who was a mariner of about the same age as Gault. Since Gault's landholdings amounted to a houselot and only sixteen poles of land, and the shoemaker owned no livestock, it is possible that his debts represent purchases of provisions, since he could not have produced his own food. For information on Gault's Salem creditors, see Perley, *History of Salem*, II, 4, 8, 9, 37–9, 161, 183–4, 212, 352–3, 360–2, 365–6, 401.

who had arrived earlier, died in 1646 with an estate worth about £25. Her property consisted of a house on a one-acre lot, a few pieces of furniture, linen, household utensils, clothing, some books, and "one smalle kow." Mason's life could only have been a hard one. But it would have seemed unquestionably attractive to the thousands of landless, wandering poor who constituted the least fortunate subjects of the realm that the New Englanders had left behind.[72]

V

In short, in its first generation of settlement, New England had as few poor people as it did rich inhabitants. Town poor rates remained minimal throughout much of the seventeenth century; the region's few unfortunates could be adequately helped by private charity and small public outlays. So long as the principal means of subsistence in the agricultural economy – land – remained available, most settlers managed to support their families in relative comfort. Those without the resources to develop farms of their own relied on the region's labor shortage to enhance their ability to gain those resources by working for others. In the first generation, this usually meant working for neighbors or a community's better-off members, whereas by the second generation it generally entailed laboring for one's father. By that point, once access to labor mainly depended on family circumstances – that is, on the control of sons' labor – colonists without male heirs found themselves at a distinct disadvantage. What they could not command by virtue of paternal authority had either to be forgone or purchased, at a high price, in the restricted labor market. Had William Gault fathered three sons instead of three daughters, for example, it is likely that his financial straits (and, eventually, those of his widow) would not have been quite so severe. Nevertheless, throughout much of

---

72 Mason's inventory is in Dow, ed., *Records and Files of the Quarterly Courts of Essex County*, I, 104–5. On poverty in seventeenth-century England, see Wrightson, *English Society*, 141–2.

this period, poverty was the condition primarily of those whom contemporaries called "impotent" – widows, orphans, or people incapacitated by a physical or mental handicap. Problems of impoverishment would increase toward the end of the century as war and commercial depression disrupted the region's economy. But for most of its first century, New England escaped the effects of what was probably England's most intractable social problem of the period.[73]

By the end of their lives, then, most participants in the Great Migration had obtained the competency to which they had aspired. Even those who had emigrated as servants generally acquired enough property to provide a comfortable subsistence.[74] Most adult white males owned land – freehold property – that guaranteed their economic security and personal independence. Landownership and a willingness to take an oath of fidelity or allegiance sufficed to admit inhabitants of Plymouth, Connecticut, and Rhode Island to the colony franchise, whereas Massachusetts and New Haven further stipulated that freemanship be limited to church members. For most colonists, therefore, eco-

---

[73] Foster, *Their Solitary Way*, 134–52; Jack P. Greene, *Pursuits of Happiness: The Social Development of Early Modern British Colonies and the Formation of American Culture* (Chapel Hill, N.C., 1988), 72–4.

[74] Probate information has survived for eighteen of the thirty-nine traceable male servants. The median value of their estates (£162) was only about three-fifths that of emigrant household heads, although more than half of them (N = 10) were clustered in the £100–£300 range, and two former servants eventually accumulated estates worth over £1,000. The lower figure for median estate size may simply reflect the fact that former servants lacked the capital and skills available to older emigrants as they started their farms. It may also be due to a peculiar pattern of mortality among the servants. Over half of all the emigrant household heads were aged sixty to seventy-nine at the time of their death, whereas only 41.2 percent of servant emigrants (seven of seventeen with estate and mortality data) were in that age group. Nearly a quarter of the servant emigrants (four) died under the age of fifty (compared to only 8 percent of the emigrant household heads) before they had reached their full economic potential, whereas nearly a third (five) were in their eighties, an age when they might well have distributed much of their property to their heirs. The distribution of ages at death for emigrant household heads is much more even from sixty to eighty-nine years.

nomic status proved no bar to political participation at the town and colony levels. Although many eligible settlers apparently declined to exercise the responsibilities and rights of the franchise, that was at least their *choice:* an option unknown to the vast majority of their countrymen in Old England, and one that many of them would have been unlikely ever to have enjoyed had they remained.[75]

The colonists' efforts produced not only the prosperous farms that provided economic security and the basis for political participation, but also a broadly shared, comfortable style of life. Subsistence crises were unknown in New England after the first few years of settlement: Even the poorest inhabitants had enough to eat, as well as roofs over their heads, clothing on their backs, and furniture in their houses. Thus the reality of New England economic conditions fortuitously – or, as contemporaries would have argued, providentially – matched the New Englanders' ideal of competency. Settlers lived independent and relatively prosperous lives, achieved at the price of hard – and godly – work. Most colonists had enough of this world's goods to free them from constant and distracting worries about the source of their next meal, yet few attained an affluence capable of eroding their spiritual purpose with opportunities for greed and pride.

Perhaps no better evidence of the settlers' careful balancing of spiritual and temporal concerns exists than one distinctive aspect of their patterns of consumption. Whenever family finances permitted the purchase of nonessential items, New Englanders overwhelmingly chose to add neither silverware, nor fine pottery, nor other household adornments to their possessions, but to buy books, principally religious books. Puritanism, of course, emphasized the critical importance of the lay study of Scripture, and bibles were nearly ubiquitous in New

---

[75] Charles M. Andrews, *The Colonial Period of American History,* 4 vols. (New Haven, Conn., 1936; reprinted 1977), II, 27, 104–6; George D. Langdon, Jr., *Pilgrim Colony: A History of New Plymouth, 1620–1691* (New Haven, Conn., 1966), 80–5; Foster, *Their Solitary Way,* 173–9. These qualifications refer to suffrage in these colonies during their first decades of settlement; requirements changed with the adoption of later charters.

England homes. But many households contained more than
the family bible; their small libraries often included well-known
Protestant religious tracts, devotional manuals, and printed sermons by English and New England divines. Michael Metcalf,
Comfort Starr, and Nathaniel Tilden, for instance, all owned
copies of John Foxe's *Book of Martyrs*, as well as other religious
titles – in Tilden's case, as part of a collection of over thirty
volumes. Nicholas Busby, the Boston shopkeeper and part-time
weaver, owned several "bookes of Divinitie, vizt. Mr. Perkings,
Mr. Willet sinops and Comentary on the Romains, & Mr.
Hieroms two bookes." Thomas Hayward of Bridgewater possessed (and presumably studied) "Mr. Sheppards book upon
the parable of the ten virgins & Mr. Sheppard upon the sincere
Convert, Mr. Ralph Allen of the riches of the covenant of grace,
also his victory over the world: & doctor pressons of gods
alsufficiency & severall other sermons Annexed there unto &
Mr. Dod upon the Commandements & Mr Coopers book of
Jacobs wrestling with God[,] Mr. Byfield his marrow & his principles," along with a bible and "some other smale books" – an
impressive library indeed for a farmer of modest means.[76]

In fact, although book ownership was somewhat more preva-
lent among more prosperous households, New Englanders of

---

[76] Probate inventories have survived for seventy emigrant household heads;
of these inventories, fully fifty-two (74.3 percent) list books. This figure is
roughly comparable to those calculated by David Hall and Gloria Main.
See Hall, *Worlds of Wonder*, 247–9; Gloria L. Main, "The Standard of Living
in Southern New England, 1640–1773, *WMQ*, 3rd ser., XLV (1988), 124–34.
Scholars have recently noted that book ownership was considerably more
widespread among seventeenth-century New Englanders than among
their Chesapeake contemporaries; see Lois Green Carr and Lorena S.
Walsh, "The Standard of Living in the Colonial Chesapeake," *WMQ*, 3rd
ser., XLV (1988), 145, 148; Main, *Tobacco Colony*, 169, 242, 256. On the
importance of religious reading as part of lay devotion, see Hall, *Worlds of
Wonder*, ch. 1; Charles E. Hambrick-Stowe, *The Practice of Piety: Puritan
Devotional Disciplines in Seventeenth-Century New England* (Chapel Hill,
N.C., 1982), 143–50, 157–61. Busby's and Starr's inventories are in the
Suffolk County Probate Records, dockets no. 165 and 233, respectively;
Metcalf's is also in the Suffolk records, Vol. 4, 214–15. Tilden's inventory is
printed in *Mayflower Descendant*, 3 (1901), 222–3. For Hayward, see Plym-
outh County Probate Records, Vol. 4, Pt. 1, 84.

all economic circumstances purchased books. William Paddy possessed "severall Bookes" worth over £11, but William Gault also owned a "bible with other small bookes," and the widow Emme Mason had a library of fourteen volumes, including a bible, a book of sermons, and "one salme booke." Valued at more than £1, Mason's library comprised a far greater proportion of her entire property than did Paddy's books as part of his estate.[77] To Puritans, however, the decision to purchase a book (almost always a religious title) was not so much a rational economic preference as a devotional choice, involving the proper application of worldly means to spiritual improvement. As such, it demonstrated yet again the power of the Puritan world view to influence the seemingly mundane activities of the believers.

The Puritan world view did not distinguish between secular and spiritual affairs so much as interweave them. Religious significance infused all temporal events, and economic activity was no exception. If the Lord ordained all that happened on earth, then the colonists' prosperity could be no accident. Thus the settlers' widespread achievement of their competencies – the secular state that "sorted best" with piety – might easily be seen as a sign of divine approbation, a blessing bestowed on their society in return for their steadfast commitment to godly living. This consistency between the ideological and the economic underpinnings of New England society, in fact, strongly reinforced the Puritan regime beyond the first generation of settlement. Individual competency became not only a reward for past faithfulness, but also a divine gift vouchsafed in return for continuing to live faithfully within the covenant of grace.

The distinctiveness of the New Englanders' settlement experience derived precisely from this conjunction of their spiritual and secular lives. From the start, their religious motivation distinguished them from other English emigrants to the New World, but the persistence of that religious vision depended

---

[77] Hall and Main likewise found book ownership to be more frequent in more prosperous households; see the sources cited in the previous footnote.

upon the rapid evolution of a society that would nurture it. New England was a most congenial location for the establishment of Puritan communities, for its natural resources – mainly stony land and abundant meadows – could be transformed, with hard labor, into the means for modest livings, but rarely into the achievement of (or even hope for) great wealth. Only a few Boston or Salem merchants wrestled with the temptations that affluence afforded; no sugar, tobacco, or other profitable cash crop appeared that might similarly challenge the spiritual commitment of the mass of rural dwellers throughout the region. New Englanders, after all, did not strive *not* to rise above a modest standard of living in order to ensure that their spiritual goals survived unthreatened by secular success. The material circumstances of their lives, however, particularly during the first generation, simply did not encourage worldliness. It requires no derogation of the genuineness of the Puritans' spiritual commitment to suggest that their ability to uphold their ideals depended in good part on the fact that they settled in an area that would not easily undermine them.[78]

[78] Compare, for instance, the history of early New England with an account of the attempt to establish a Puritan colony in the West Indies; see Karen Ordahl Kupperman, "Errand to the Indies: Puritan Colonization from Providence Island through the Western Design," *WMQ,* 3rd ser., XLV (1988), 70–99.

5
Legacy

At the age of seventy-seven, Edmund Batter could look back on a long and productive life. He had emigrated to Massachusetts on the *James* with his wife, Sarah, a half-century earlier and settled in the port town of Salem. Although trained as a maltster, he had turned to a career in commerce and succeeded handsomely, amassing an estate worth over £1,000. An impressive political career had complemented his financial success: He had served in an array of Salem town offices and repeatedly represented his community in the General Court. A member of the Salem church since his first year in town, he had been a staunch defender of Puritan orthodoxy. When Quakers first entered Salem in the 1650s, Batter strove to silence them, occasionally by the most direct means. At one memorable town meeting in 1658, Batter grabbed one of the offenders by the hair and stuffed a glove and a handkerchief into his mouth.

Now, however, in the February chill of 1685, Batter turned from public to private matters, setting his worldly affairs in order before the Lord called his "precious soul" to judgment. Batter needed to consider the welfare of the woman who would soon become his widow, as well as of their four children, all of whom were minors. Batter knew that his economic success would carry them through the crisis of his death and stipulated the customary division of his estate. His widow, Mary, would receive a third of the property and his children would share the remainder, with his older son and namesake receiving a double portion. But Batter also felt compelled to use his will to express his abiding concern for the moral as well as material well-being of his children. He enjoined his widow to raise their two sons and two daughters "in the feare of god and good nurture" and especially stressed that, should Edmund, Jr., "be thought fitt to enter the Colledge," a portion of his inheritance should be invested in a Harvard education. Finally, this elderly father, knowing that he would not live to see his children reach adulthood, recorded his hope that, if the Lord were willing, his children would prove to "be serviceable to both god & man in their generation."[1]

To be serviceable in their generation: Edmund Batter's desire for his children's usefulness echoed similar sentiments being expressed throughout New England at the time when he was composing his last testament. Beginning in the 1660s and lasting throughout the 1680s, the principal interpreters of New England culture – the ministers – repeatedly focused their preaching on the "serviceability" of what they usually termed the "rising generation." Batter's rather terse expression of concern for his children implied two propositions that were made explicit in the sermons of the period. First, the interjection of his hopes into a legal document usually devoted to technical matters of property transfer suggested not simply his desire that his heirs would be "serviceable" but also his fear that they might not be. And second, given Batter's own civic achievements and his evidently irascible temperament, one might infer a second, unwritten clause as well: that is, that Batter's children should be as serviceable in their generation as he had been in his own.

New England's ministers were less reticent in their treatment of these themes and employed a special genre of sermon – the jeremiad – to explicate and deplore the failure of the second generation to uphold the standards of piety and competence their predecessors had established. Yet the preachers' often scathing critique appeared even as the second generation assumed control of their towns and churches and successfully preserved the godly society that their parents had worked so hard to construct. Moreover, they did so in the face of far more

---

[1] Sidney Perley, *The History of Salem, Massachusetts*, 3 vols. (Salem, Mass., 1924), I, 198, 293–4; II, 4, 245–8; Christine A. Young, *From "Good Order" to Glorious Revolution: Salem, Massachusetts, 1628–1689* (Ann Arbor, Mich., 1980), 45, 50–1, 83; Jonathan M. Chu, *Neighbors, Friends, or Madmen: The Puritan Adjustment to Quakerism in Seventeenth-Century Massachusetts Bay* (Westport, Conn., 1985), 62–3, 69, 92, 131, 135. Batter's will and estate administration are in the Essex County Probate Records, docket no. 2137, Vol. 302, 147; Vol. 305, 119. Sarah, Edmund Batter's first wife, died in 1669; the following year he married Mary Gookin.

serious external challenges to New England than any that the first generation had ever had to confront.[2]

And yet the ministers were not simply inventing a problem to give themselves something to complain about. They had genuine doubts about the ability of New England to succeed in a world that, so far as they could see, was changing for the worse. But what gave real force to their concerns about the concatenation of events threatening New England and the ability of the members of the second generation to preserve their spiritual inheritance was not only the events themselves but also a distinctive, indeed unparalleled, feature of their society. For seventeenth-century New England was a place where the normally metaphorical concept of "generation" had a concrete reality, a precision of meaning that magnified the ministers' hortatory use of the term. The colonists' own generational identity derived from their connection with the original migration from England. The nature of that connection – whether settlers could claim a personal experience of expatriation or only a genealogical link – virtually guaranteed that the second generation would bear the brunt of their parents' anxieties and adopt those concerns as their own.

I

One of the many signs of decline noted by ministers in the second half of the seventeenth century was the increasing fre-

---

[2] The literature on the Puritan jeremiad is vast. The starting point is the work of Perry Miller, expressed most succinctly in "Errand into the Wilderness" in his collection *Errand Into the Wilderness* (Cambridge, Mass., 1956), 1–15; see also his "Declension in a Bible Commonwealth" in *Nature's Nation* (Cambridge, Mass., 1967), 14–49, and *The New England Mind: From Colony to Province* (Boston, 1953), 19–146. Other works dealing with the subject include Sacvan Bercovitch, *The American Jeremiad* (Madison, Wis., 1978); Emory Elliott, *Power and the Pulpit in Puritan New England* (Princeton, N.J., 1975); Harry S. Stout, *The New England Soul: Preaching and Religious Culture in Colonial New England* (New York, 1986), ch. 4; Andrew Delbanco, *The Puritan Ordeal* (Cambridge, Mass., 1989), ch. 7; Theodore Dwight Bozeman, *To Live Ancient Lives: The Primitivist Dimension in Puritanism* (Chapel Hill, N.C., 1988), chs. 9, 10.

quency of deaths of leaders of the founding generation. "Alas! our Nehemiahs are gone," lamented Increase Mather in 1679. "[O]ur Pauls are likewise departed from amongst us, in which respect we may fear corruption in Religion will follow."[3] Why Mather responded in this way is by no means intuitively obvious. Even among the godliest of parents, mortality was inevitable, and the circumstances of the founders' deaths might have furnished consolation for their grieving descendants. The fact that so many of the founders lived remarkably long lives might as easily have been interpreted as a sign of God's benediction. One first-generation leader, William Bradford, clearly understood their deaths in this way and wrote about them with none of the anxiety of the second-generation preacher Increase Mather. Bradford marveled that "notwithstanding the many changes and hardships that these people went through, and the many enemies they had and difficulties they met withal, . . . so many of them should live to very old age!" Far from dwelling on their deaths as indicative of decline, their longevity was, to Bradford, a "marvelous providence of God!" The Plymouth governor himself would live to the age of sixty-seven, and surprising numbers of magistrates and church leaders among his contemporaries also reached their sixties and seventies.[4]

The remarkable longevity of New England's leaders was matched in the general population. Many settlers enjoyed threescore and ten years or more of life, and fully one out of five of the colonists in this study lived to surpass eighty years of age. Women, who repeatedly faced the physical dangers of childbirth, fared less well than men, but those who survived their childbearing years could also look forward to an extended old

---

[3] Increase Mather, *A Call from Heaven to the Present and Succeeding Generations* . . . (Boston, 1679), 66.

[4] William Bradford, *Of Plymouth Plantation, 1620–1647*, ed. Samuel Eliot Morison (New York, 1952), 328. Ages at death for other first-generation leaders include John Winthrop (sixty), Roger Williams (eighty), Richard Mather (seventy-three), John Cotton (sixty-eight), John Wilson (seventy-nine), and Thomas Hooker (sixty-one).

age.[5] In fact, the settlers, male and female, had strikingly longer life spans than their nonmigrating English counterparts.[6]

The colonists' longevity probably stemmed from interrelated environmental factors – dispersed settlement, lack of epidemic disease (at least during the first decades of settlement), clean air and water, and perhaps a better diet – and the selective nature of the migration itself. Few sickly people would have been likely to cross the Atlantic, and fewer still of those who took the risk (or who, like the Reverend Francis Higginson's young daughter, had it imposed on them) would have been likely to survive. Thus the population that began to reproduce in New England was for the most part unusually fit, having already survived the hazards of infectious disease, and thus brought a healthy immune response, along with the rest of their possessions, from the home country. Their children still had to face the threat of childhood diseases and other infections on New England soil, and although the survivors among them would

[5] See Table 8 in the Appendix. These figures are roughly comparable to those derived from community studies; see Philip J. Greven, Jr., *Four Generations: Population, Land, and Family in Colonial Andover, Massachusetts* (Ithaca, N.Y., 1970), 26; John Demos, *A Little Commonwealth: Family Life in Plymouth Colony* (New York, 1970), 193. Age at death seems to have varied according to age at the time of migration. Men in their thirties and forties when they left England tended to live longer than either younger or older male emigrants. For women, those who were in their forties when they emigrated lived on average another thirty-five years, surpassing the experience of males in the same age group. But those who came to New England during their child-bearing years fared less well. (See Table 9 in the Appendix.)

[6] English men and women who were born during the second half of the sixteenth century and who survived to age 30 lived on average 29.2 (men) and 30.2 (women) years longer. The figures for New England emigrants born before 1600 (thirty-five men and thirteen women) are quite different. Emigrant men survived on average for 38.6 years more and women for 39.0 years – nearly a decade longer than the English sample. Similarly, the expectation of life for English men and women born between 1600 and 1649 and surviving to age 30 was 29.8 and 29.6 years, respectively. For emigrants born in the first half of the seventeenth century and surviving to age 30, however, the comparable figures were 40.5 for men ($N = 50$) and 32.3 for women ($N = 21$). The English figures were derived from reconstitutions of twelve parishes; see E. A. Wrigley and R. S. Schofield, *The Population History of England, 1541–1871: A Reconstruction* (London, 1981), 250.

also enjoy long lives, as a group they would experience greater morbidity than those who had emigrated as adults. Good Puritans, of course, assumed that there were "more than ordinary and above natural reason[s]" for great longevity. Always seeking evidence of God's providence, some, like William Bradford, reached an optimistic conclusion. Others, a comparatively larger group including Increase Mather, dwelled on the deaths as much as the lives of the founders and discerned in them an altogether more ominous message.[7]

Another prominent feature of New England life, one no less susceptible of interpretation as a sign of God's favor than the founders' longevity, was the fact that they had reared such remarkably large and healthy families. Even though the ocean crossing often occurred in the middle of parents' reproductive lives, most couples eventually produced seven or more children – a slightly higher rate than that of the nonmigrating English population.[8] Moreover, childhood mortality apparently posed less of a threat to colonial children than to those in the home country. During the first half of the seventeenth century, only three out of four English-born children survived to the age of ten, whereas in New England, closer to four out of five would reach adulthood. So the colonists not only produced somewhat larger families, but also saw more of their children survive to produce families of their own.[9]

---

[7] Greven found a lower life expectancy for second-generation Andover inhabitants; see *Four Generations*, 26–7. The quotation is from Bradford, *Of Plymouth Plantation*, ed. Morison, 328.

[8] The average number of children per family was 7.74 ($N = 39$); see Table 10 in the Appendix. The average figure is comparable to those calculated by Greven for first-generation Andover families (8.3 children) and by Demos for first-generation Plymouth settlers (7.8 children); see *Four Generations*, 30; *A Little Commonwealth*, 192. English women born during the first half of the seventeenth century had, on average, 7.03 children, approximately one less than New England mothers; Wrigley and Schofield, *Population History of England*, 249.

[9] For childhood mortality in England, see Wrigley and Schofield, *Population History of England*, 254. The New England figures are from an analysis of twenty-one first-generation families for whom there is complete demographic information. These families produced a total of 170 children, of

As a result of these favorable demographic circumstances, New England witnessed a staggering rate of population growth during the lifetime of the first generation. During the single decade between 1640 and 1650, the population increased by 66 percent: an expansion in numbers attributable almost entirely to natural increase, since immigration virtually ceased with the outbreak of the English Civil War.[10] The colonists, of course, perceived these developments from a personal perspective as they raised their numerous children and watched their communities grow. The longevity of parents provided stable family environments, quite unlike those in the Chesapeake colonies, where, for much of the seventeenth century, malaria and other diseases carried off many parents and children, leaving survivors to grow up in mixed households headed by stepparents, collateral relatives, or friends.[11]

whom 137 (80.6 percent) reached adulthood (defined as age twenty-one or marriage). Greven found that first-generation Andover families produced an average of 8.3 children, 7.2 of whom survived to age twenty-one; see *Four Generations*, 30. Demos similarly calculated that of an average 7.8 children born to Plymouth families, 7.2 lived to age twenty-one; see *A Little Commonwealth*, 192. The average figures for the twenty-one emigrant families, however, are somewhat different: The emigrants produced an average of 8.1 children, 6.5 of whom survived to adulthood. This discrepancy is probably due to the fact that twenty of the twenty-one couples began their families in England, with its higher infant mortality rate. In fact, the two families with the worst demographic experience, the Tildens and the Busbys – each of whom produced 12 children, with 7 surviving to adulthood – produced all of their children in England. When these two families are omitted from the calculations, the results for the other nineteen (an average of 7.7 children produced and 6.5 surviving to adulthood) more closely resemble the figures from Andover and Plymouth. A further consideration is that the emigrant sample is derived from a variety of towns, and this may suggest different rates of childhood mortality in different areas of New England.

10 Henry A. Gemery, "Emigration From the British Isles to the New World, 1630–1700: Inferences from Colonial Populations," *Research in Economic History*, V (1980), 212.

11 See, for instance, Lorena S. Walsh, " 'Till Death Us Do Part': Marriage and Family in Seventeenth-Century Maryland," and Darrett B. Rutman and Anita H. Rutman, " 'Now-Wives and Sons-in-Law': Parental Death in a Seventeenth-Century Virginia County," both in Thad W. Tate and David L. Ammerman, *The Chesapeake in the Seventeenth Century: Essays on Anglo-American Society and Politics* (New York, 1979).

As second-generation New Englanders married and formed their own families, they established the kinship connections that had largely been missing in the emigrant society of the region's early years. Because the original emigrant population was mainly composed of nuclear families, the principal kinship links among New Englanders during the first years after the migration ended were those between parents and children; for the most part, other extended kin had been left behind in England. But as the years passed, settlers could claim as relatives a larger and larger circle of inhabitants in their own and neighboring communities. The increasingly elaborate web of kin relationships connected people across generations as well as within them, since so many founders lived to see their grandchildren. In their wills, first-generation settlers regularly remembered their children's offspring, often bequeathing them small parcels of land, money, or cattle to be maintained by the parents until the child reached his or her majority. Some bequests were more personal and testified to strong emotional ties between grandparents and grandchildren. Michael Metcalf, for instance, left his "Largest gray Horsmans Coate" to a grandson, and Robert Page directed that his grandson and namesake receive "thatt Chest which I brought outt of old England," an item with perhaps as much sentimental as material value. Thomas Besbeech of Sudbury not only bequeathed a large portion of his estate to his "grandchild & adopted son Thomas Besbeech (alias) Thomas Browne" but also lived long enough to see his grandson's three daughters born – and left five shillings to each of them.[12]

This elaboration of kinship connections occurred across a widening geographical area; with the marriage of their children, settlers acquired relatives not only in their own towns but also in nearby communities. Sons often remained in their home towns, having either found spouses there or married women

[12] Fifty-five percent of first-generation settlers' wills mention grandchildren (thirty-six of sixty-five). Metcalf's will is in the Suffolk County Probate Records, I, 497–500; Page's is in the Essex County Probate Records, docket no. 20371; and Besbeech's is in the Middlesex County Probate Records, docket no. 1476.

from neighboring communities. For daughters, marriage more frequently required a move away from home. Four of Edward Johnson's five sons remained in Woburn, where their father had settled in 1640, but both of Johnson's daughters moved away, to Boston and to Cambridge, when they married. Similarly, in Michael Metcalf's family, two of three sons stayed in Dedham, whereas the third settled in Medfield – without actually having to move from his home town, since Medfield was carved out of Dedham land in 1651. Four Metcalf daughters found spouses in Dedham, but two of their sisters moved to Reading and Rehoboth when they married. Elizabeth and Jane Metcalf were unusual in traveling more than twenty miles from home; most daughters ended up living within ten miles of their parents.[13]

Both Edward Johnson and Michael Metcalf were town proprietors, and this fact largely determined the settlement patterns of their sons. Their experience, like that of many other New England families, illustrated the success of the first generation's strategy of settling in new towns with open proprietorships. Sons remained in their hometowns because their fathers had acquired enough land – from initial grants and subsequent divi-

[13] Alfred Johnson, *History and Genealogy of One Line of Descent from Captain Edward Johnson Together with His English Ancestry 1500–1914* (Boston, 1914), 59–63; Johnson's son George returned to England in the 1650s and eventually settled in Maryland. For the Metcalfs, see Isaac Stevens Metcalf, *Metcalf Genealogy* (Cleveland, Ohio, 1898), 8–20. My discussion of marital migration is based on impressionistic evidence drawn from genealogical materials for first-generation families. Nevertheless, my observations match the results of other scholars who have also concluded that, during the seventeenth century, women were more exogamous than men. See Linda Auwers Bissell, "From One Generation to Another: Mobility in Seventeenth-Century Windsor, Connecticut," *William and Mary Quarterly*, 3rd ser., XXXI (1974), 87, 94; Greven, *Four Generations*, 211. Susan Norton's figures for eighteenth-century Essex County, Massachusetts, show the reverse, with more men than women marrying outside of their home town; the change over time may be due to population increase within the Essex towns, which allowed more women to find spouses close by; see Susan L. Norton, "Marital Migration in Essex County, Massachusetts, in the Colonial and Early Federal Period," *Journal of Marriage and the Family*, 35 (1973), 409–11.

sions of town land – to provide them with viable farms. And although most fathers favored one son with a larger share of the paternal estate, most could provide all of their sons with some land and all of their daughters with money or movable property. Proprietary status also allowed settlers to bequeathe rights to land they would not technically own until their towns agreed to apportion undivided reserves. In 1680, for instance, Anthony Morse of Newbury left his son Benjamin "the on[e] half of all comon lands when devided." Often such grants of unimproved land that towns had not yet, or had only recently, divided went to grandsons, as when Robert Page left "one Hundred Acres of land Granted to mee in the west partt of Hampton bounds Called the new plantation" to his grandson John Page. First-generation settlers doubtless assumed that their descendants would have plenty of time to improve these lands by the time their grandchildren reached adulthood.[14]

Although fathers often waited until near the time of their own deaths to confirm by will their sons' legal title to family land, they frequently encouraged their sons to marry and establish independent households decades earlier. Many fathers referred to property already possessed by their sons when they wrote their wills. Walter Haynes of Sudbury, for instance, mentioned that he "did give and doe now give" a piece of meadow to his son John, obviously confirming a grant made earlier. Richard Leeds of Dorchester similarly bequeathed to his son Benjamin the house in which the son already lived, as well as the "Lands which my said son Benjamin is possessed off." John Emery followed the same pattern when he left a considerable amount of property to his son Jonathan, "the one half whereof I have formerly given him and doe now Confirm to the said Jonathan."[15]

---

[14] This summary is based on an examination of probate materials for sixty-five first-generation household heads. For Morse's and Page's wills, see Essex County Probate Records, docket nos. 18903 and 20371, respectively. On the persistence of second-generation sons, see also Bissell, "From One Generation to Another," 86–8; Greven, *Four Generations*, 39–40, 65–7.

[15] Of the sixty-five wills of emigrant household heads, twelve (18.5 percent) make explicit reference to property already given to sons. However, this

186

Such informal transfers of property, which probably had occurred at the time of the sons' marriages, testified to the fact that sons who had been working alongside their fathers since they were old enough to be of help had more than simply a hereditary claim to their fathers' estates. Indeed, although they would not have used the word to describe it, their equity, based on their contribution of labor, was virtually equal to that of their fathers. No settler realized this fact more clearly than did Abraham Toppan of Newbury, because certain unfortunate developments frustrated his attempts to repay fairly the particular help of two of his sons. The resulting protracted family dispute revealed the extent to which sons believed that it was their effort, no less than their fathers' wishes, that established their claims to inheritance.

Ironically, Toppan's problems stemmed from his overriding concern to see all of his children well provided for. Five of his seven children evidently were content with their father's provisions for their welfare. So was his oldest son, Peter – until he learned of the particulars of Abraham's will. At the time of Peter's marriage in 1661, Abraham Toppan had given his son one-half of his Newbury property, with the understanding that Peter would receive the other half after the death of his parents. Nine years later, however, as Abraham Toppan composed his will, he altered this plan in order to provide for his third son, Jacob. Because Jacob had stayed at home with his parents and

practice was probably much more widespread. In many wills, only token bequests of small amounts of land or money were made to children who were married and raising families of their own. These children almost certainly received property from their parents in order to set up their households, even though such transactions are not mentioned in their fathers' wills. For Walter Haynes, see Middlesex County Probate Records, docket no. 10939; for Leeds, Suffolk County Probate Records, docket no. 2015; for Emery, Essex County Probate Records, docket no. 8976, Vol. 302, 100–2. In *Four Generations*, Greven argues that real independence for sons came only when they received title to their lands, which usually occurred at the times of their fathers' deaths; see 83. My sense from the genealogical and local historical evidence is that the sons' receiving title to land they already lived on and worked may have been more of a formality than Greven suggests.

was about to be married, Abraham thought that the "good service by him done for the benefit of my whole family And more Especially in my Elder years" justified a change in plan. He accordingly asked Peter to relinquish his claim to the remaining half of the estate so that it could go to his younger brother. The elder Toppan believed that this would cause no real hardship for Peter, since he was "through Gods blessing on his labours And the Estate he received from mee And raysed betwixt us, . . . well provided of howsing and otherwise." Moreover, in return for acceding to his father's request, Peter would receive from Jacob the sum of £20, to be paid either in corn or cattle.

But Peter Toppan was unconvinced by his father's assessment of equitability and, seven months after Abraham's death, sued his mother and Jacob (as executors of the will) in order to retrieve what he believed was his rightful inheritance. In the court proceedings that followed, Peter produced the 1661 deed that indicated that he was eventually to receive all of his father's Newbury property. He also produced at least one witness to supplement the legal argument by turning Abraham's reasoning against him. John Knight, a neighbor, noted that Peter had contributed his labor to the paternal estate no less faithfully than Jacob. "Peetar have bin vary dutiful too his father and vary carfull of his bisnis," Knight testified, especially "at harvest time: his meedow liing neer min: I have often wrought with him: and I have observed his diligenc," as the son was "willing to Improv all sesons for his fathers good." "It is well knouen," Knight concluded, that "the care of Improvment of the estat lay much upon peetar."

In the end, however, the court supported Jacob, convinced by Abraham's testamentary contention that the labor of both of his sons deserved due compensation, particularly since Peter did not really need the additional property. The Toppan case thus illustrated an inheritance plan gone awry, but its resolution reaffirmed an important principle governing the relations between first-generation fathers and their sons. The relationship between fathers and sons, particularly in legal and familial terms, rested upon formal recognition of patriarchal authority and filial obedience, assuming paternal generosity as well as filial dependence. Yet New England culture and society, especially in the formative years when fathers so needed the labor of their sons, tempered the theoretically unequal nature of the relationship with a healthy recognition of the need for reciprocity in the face of what was in fact a mutual dependence.[16]

As he contemplated his children's inheritances, Toppan evidently reasoned from a related set of concerns. His efforts on behalf of Jacob and his satisfaction with Peter's condition both grew from a determination to see that his children continued to enjoy the competency that the whole family had worked so hard to achieve. As Abraham saw it, Peter was already "well provided" for: He had his competency, whereas Jacob as yet did not. Toppan clearly understood it to be a father's duty to help all of his children achieve the modest prosperity that would ensure their personal independence. Like all Puritans, Toppan knew that the Lord merely lent him the "good things of this world" for his "Care and Management during my pilgrimage in this present life." The responsibilities of stewardship included the proper dispersal of his worldly estate as his life drew to a close. All fathers, in effect, were charged with transferring the goods God had entrusted to them to sons whom they expected to carry on the "improvement" of estates that had spiritual as well as financial dimensions.[17]

Fathers like Abraham Toppan paid particular care to the division of their estates precisely because they appreciated the dou-

[16] Peter P. Good, *The Family Records of James and Nancy Dunham Toppan, of the Fourth Generation . . .* (Liberty, Ind., 1884), 12–13; *The Probate Records of Essex County, Massachusetts (1635–1681)*, 3 vols. (Salem, Mass., 1916–20), II, 328–32; George F. Dow, ed., *Records and Files of the Quarterly Courts of Essex County, Massachusetts*, 8 vols. (Salem, Mass., 1911–21), V, 176–8. On relations between parents and children, see Demos, *A Little Commonwealth*, ch. 6; Edmund Morgan, *The Puritan Family: Religion and Domestic Relations in Seventeenth-Century New England* (New York, 1944; reprinted 1966), ch. 3.
[17] The quotation is from the preamble to Toppan's will; see *Probate Records of Essex County*, II, 328. Similar sentiments are expressed in many of the first-generation settlers' wills.

ble meaning of inheritance. In a land desperately short of labor and capital, economically viable family farms had become the bedrock of the whole New England way of life. If Jacob Toppan had been denied his share of the paternal estate, he would have faced a life of economic hardship that would inevitably have impinged upon his ability to raise a family and to be a useful member of his community and church. There were few avenues to prosperity that lay outside of the system of property transfer from one generation to the next. Prosperity was not a necessary condition for piety, of course, but the spiritual duties of a good Puritan – in terms of both personal devotion and membership in the congregation – required time, something that was always scarce in a hardscrabble agricultural society but that was especially dear to those worried about where the next meal would come from. Poverty also posed a particular challenge in New England, where the covenantal model of community relations implied a high degree of comparative equality in social relations. Individuals, of course, did not enjoy equal status in this society: Children deferred to adults, women deferred to men, and men knew precisely where they stood in their community's economic hierarchy. But *families* were the principal constituents of the community, and as such were expected to maintain (in ascending order of importance) their economic viability, internal harmony, and religious piety – in other words, to sustain their ability to fulfill the many responsibilities that attended membership in the social covenant. In this sense, then, the New England way of life functioned best when its families shared a roughly equal ability to shoulder their communal duties. No wonder that the two groups of people most frequently ostracized from New England society were religious dissidents and the poor – people either unwilling to fulfill or incapable of fulfilling their social responsibilities.

Fortunately for the future stability of New England society, most first-generation fathers could help their sons maintain their families' economic standing. In bequeathing them viable farms, of course, the fathers by no means equipped their children for lives of greater ease than they had themselves lived.

190

Sons and daughters labored as hard on their own farms as they had on their parents' lands, and in most families the economic condition of the younger generation did not dramatically exceed that of their parents.[18] However difficult the founders' task of establishing a remarkably stable society had been, the responsibility of their descendants for maintaining that society proved equally demanding of energy and emotion. In this work, the role of New England's second generation was particularly critical, for they were the first to effect the transfer of power and authority from their elders. The transition was by no means easy, for a series of catastrophes seriously threatened the second generation's efforts to preserve their cultural inheritance and prevented their appreciation of precisely those demographic and economic achievements that might otherwise have inspired a cautious optimism. Political upheaval, economic distress, and religious conflict all arose at precisely the time when the new generation assumed control of New England society. All of these threatened the stability and even the continued existence of that society, but even more ominous was the way in which they combined to create a severe psychological strain that challenged the rising generation's ability to deal effectively with them.

II

The succession of crises began just as members of the founding generation began to die off in substantial numbers – a coincidence not lost on their successors.[19] Disaster seemed to strike at every aspect of life. Periodically throughout the 1660s, agriculture – the mainstay of the New England economy – suffered serious setbacks. Severe droughts occurred in 1662 and 1666, and the cultivation of wheat, which once seemed destined to be a valuable export crop, all but disappeared in the

---

[18] Gloria L. Main, "The Standard of Living in Southern New England, 1640–1773," *WMQ*, 3rd ser., XLV (1988), 124–34.
[19] The median date of death for the first-generation settlers in this study was 1670.

wake of black stem rust and an invasion by an "Army of Cater-pillars." In 1666, while London reeled from the twin disasters of plague and fire, parts of New England endured no less threatening visitations of fire and smallpox. And if terrestrial crises were not enough, colonists also observed an "avenging comet" in 1664 and a peculiar display of "zodiacal" light three years later – celestial signs that, they believed, clearly por-tended doom.[20]

Religious controversy, never absent from New England life, erupted with great vigor in the second half of the seventeenth century. Legions of dissenters seemed as relentless as the wheat-eating armies of caterpillars in their repeated attacks on Puritan orthodoxy. "Anabaptists" and Quakers questioned ba-sic tenets concerning the efficacy of infant baptism, the role of revelation and free grace in the process of salvation, the func-tion of church ordinances, and the authority of ministers as interpreters of God's will. Quakers in particular supplemented their spiritual arguments with dramatic displays of dissent. Some, such as John Small and John and Elizabeth Kitchin – all of Salem – refused to attend their local church. Others dis-rupted Sabbath services or took to the road to proselytize, ac-tions that led to corporal punishment for several offenders and execution for those few who refused to abide by earlier sen-tences of banishment.[21]

But the main source of religious turmoil after midcentury came not from these dissenters, threatening though their ap-pearance seemed to civil and ecclesiastical authorities. It arose

[20] These various crises are listed in Stout, *New England Soul*, 75. On agricul-tural difficulties, see also Howard S. Russell, *A Long, Deep Furrow: Three Centuries of Farming in New England* (Hanover, N.H., 1976), 42, 132–3.

[21] The Kitchins and John Small were among the six emigrant families in this study who can be identified from court records as Quakers. On religious dissent in this period, see Philip F. Gura, *A Glimpse of Sion's Glory: Puritan Radicalism in New England, 1620–1660* (Middletown, Conn., 1984), chs. 4, 5; and Chu, *Neighbors, Friends, or Madmen*. Chu makes the important distinc-tion between the more radical emigrant Quakers from England, who di-rectly challenged Bay Colony authority, and resident converts who, if peaceable, were allowed to retain membership in their communities.

instead from a debate within the religious establishment itself, at the heart of which lay the success or failure of the New England experiment in congregational Puritanism. The focus of this debate was the definition of church membership. In their zeal to ensure that New England's first churches included only visible saints, the founders had insisted that prospective members not only lead godly lives and exhibit a clear understanding of the main tenets of their Christian faith, but also demonstrate that they had experienced true evidence of the workings of God's grace in their souls. Only those who gave a convincing account of such a conversion experience could be admitted to full church membership. Others, such as the founders' children, could be baptized by virtue of their parents' membership but were excluded from participating in the Lord's Supper until they too could give evidence of conversion. Clerical leaders assumed that most of these individuals would eventually attain full membership but did not anticipate a vexing problem that arose in the meantime.

By midcentury, many of the founders' children, who had not yet become full members themselves, had begun to have children of their own, and the system of church membership devised in the 1630s provided no way to deal with this new third generation. Because their parents were not full members, the children could not be baptized and therefore remained outside the purview of the church. Ministers foresaw the none-too-distant day when the majority of New England's inhabitants would be excluded from the church and contrived a plan to stave off such a dire threat to godliness. The divines' solution proved to be a pragmatic compromise between a desire for congregational purity and the need to preserve the churches' authority over the inhabitants. A synod meeting at Cambridge in 1662 proposed to allow third-generation children to be baptized if their parents had been baptized and were living sober Christian lives. But the laity, to whom this so-called Halfway Covenant was submitted for approval, overwhelmingly rejected what they saw as a dangerous departure from the standards instituted by the founders – even though more than a few first-generation ministers attended the synod and supported the plan. Thus what had been intended to be a solution to the problem of declining church membership instead became an engine of conflict dividing the clergy from the very congregations that they strove to serve.[22]

Ironically, what eventually helped congregations put aside their differences over membership was yet another crisis: a catastrophe that threatened New England's very existence. In 1675, exasperated by ceaseless English encroachments on their territory, a confederation of New England Indian tribes responded with violence of their own. Led by Metacom, a Wampanoag known to the English as King Philip, the Indians destroyed twelve towns and attacked forty more, killing nearly 2,000 settlers. The English retaliated by destroying many Indian villages and killing even more of their enemies. Within a year the war was over, but the settlers tempered their celebrations of victory with an acknowledgment that the devastating conflict offered irrefutable proof of divine displeasure. As such, it demanded scrupulous examination of individual souls and collective behavior in order to discern the causes for such an awful chastisement.[23]

Nothing in the Puritans' world happened by accident. Because all events, good or bad, offered temporal evidence of God's judgment, settlers ignored signs of divine disfavor at their peril. The decades of the 1660s and 1670s, replete with outbreaks of natural catastrophe, religious strife, and war, provided more than enough grounds for questioning the state of

[22] The best treatment of the Halfway Covenant is Robert G. Pope, *The Half-Way Covenant: Church Membership in Puritan New England* (Princeton, N.J., 1969). For the original scheme of church membership, see Edmund S. Morgan, *Visible Saints: The History of a Puritan Idea* (New York, 1963).

[23] The classic treatment of this conflict is Douglas Edward Leach, *Flintlock and Tomahawk: New England in King Philip's War* (New York, 1958). A different treatment, much harsher on the colonists' role in instigating conflict, is Francis Jennings, *The Invasion of America: Indians, Colonialism, and the Cant of Conquest* (Chapel Hill, N.C., 1975), chs. 17, 18. On the role of the war in ending religious strife over the Halfway Covenant, see Pope, *The Half-Way Covenant*, 186–9.

New England's soul. For the doctrine of God's providence taught the settlers to consider the events of their time not as random occurrences but as a connected chain, and required that they look within their own hearts to find the cause of God's rebukes. To Puritans steeped in providentialism, the Indians were less the cause of King Philip's War than they were God's instruments for teaching the colonists a lesson. Because New England's real problems lay not with the Quakers or the Indians or the caterpillars, but with God's covenanted people themselves, the price of ignoring His judgments would be the sundering of the contract that had defined New Englanders as God's special people, His saving remnant in a corrupt world.[24]

In sermon after sermon, ministers explicated recent ominous events, always concluding with the same message to a backsliding people in need of changing their views. Identical warnings issued from scores of pulpits: Not only did the clergy refer to the same set of events but, since virtually all of them had learned their profession at Harvard College, they also drew upon a common understanding of how that warning should be expressed and what the proper response should be. Together the preachers exhorted New Englanders collectively to undertake the processes of self-examination that were the accustomed duty of each individual believer in search of evidence of personal salvation. In 1679, the ministers assembled in a synod to draw up what was in effect a bill of indictment against a dangerously complacent people.[25]

Significantly, the ministers addressed their admonition primarily to New England's young people. Their list of colonial failings fell into two broad categories. On the one hand, this new generation of settlers had grown too fond of merely tempo-

---

[24] A brief but vivid discussion of providentialism can be found in David D. Hall, *Worlds of Wonder, Days of Judgment: Popular Religious Belief in Early New England* (New York, 1989), 77–80. The doctrine was not, of course, exclusive to Puritan theology, but it was emphasized by Calvin and his followers. See also Keith Thomas, *Religion and the Decline of Magic* (London, 1971), ch. 4.

[25] On the role of Harvard College in defining the style and content of second-generation ministers' preaching, see Stout, *New England Soul*, 56–7, 88–96.

ral things, advertising their misplaced affections through greed, extravagant apparel, pride, intemperance, contentiousness, and lying – misbehavior especially apparent in matters where profit was concerned. On the other hand, ministers worried about the erosion of personal piety that underlay this worldliness. Sabbath breaking, disrespect for civil and religious leaders, and the breakdown of family government all seemed to be symptoms indicating a serious sickness of the soul. Thus in their prescription for reform to help New England regain its spiritual health, preachers strove not simply to deal with outward behavior but also to restore the inner condition of piety without which real improvement would be impossible.[26]

The clergy's critique was potent indeed, in large part because it incorporated elements of Puritan thought and culture with which their hearers were exceedingly familiar. Concerns about worldliness had figured in the first generation's deliberations about emigration; Thomas Dudley was by no means the only early leader who warned that anyone who sailed for material gain "comits an errour of which he will soon repent him." That concern did not diminish with time, for as settlers labored for a competency, they were reminded that only a fine line separated honest labor from an untoward search for excessive gain. The Reverend Eleazar Mather thus struck a resonant chord with his assertion that "when the abounding of temporal blessings is accompanied with the abounding of sin," the Lord was preparing to abandon his wayward people.[27]

---

[26] Stout, *New England Soul*, 96–9. Perry Miller has written extensively on the Reforming Synod of 1679 (see his *The New England Mind: From Colony to Province* [Boston, 1953], ch. 2), but, as Stout points out, he overemphasized the ministers' interest in the reform of outward behavior.

[27] "Gov. Thomas Dudley's Letter to the Countess of Lincoln, March, 1631," in Peter Force, ed., *Tracts and Other Papers Relating Principally to the Origin, Settlement, and Progress of the Colonies in North America, From the Discovery of the Country to the Year 1776*, 4 vols. (Washington, D.C., 1838), II, 12; on this point, see also Bradford, *Of Plymouth Plantation*, ed. Morison, 333; Eleazar Mather, *A Serious Exhortation to the Present and Succeeding Generation in New England, Earnestly calling upon all to Endeavour that the Lords Gracious Presence may be continued with Posterity* (Cambridge, Mass., 1671), 9–10.

The ministers' description of New England's decline from an earlier state of grace, always coupled with encouragement to strive to return to their former condition, likewise constituted a variation on a familiar theme. In their jeremiads, the preachers applied the model of the individual's progress toward salvation to New England as a whole. Every believer passed through stages of complacency, recognition of sin, despair, prayer and reformation, hope, and assurance – often several times over – as he or she followed the path toward piety described by ministers. During the 1670s, preachers of jeremiads suggested that New England as a *corporate* entity had reached that critical point where acknowledgment of error might lead either to a healthy recognition of its complete dependence on God or to a continued pursuit of sinful ways, ending in damnation. The analogy between the individual's path to salvation and New England's corporate fate – and its implications – could not have been lost on an audience trained to habits of both introspection and covenantal allegiance.[28]

What was striking about these jeremiads was less the novelty of their message than the frequency and urgency with which that message was delivered. From New England's earliest days, preachers had castigated their congregations for the errors of their ways and issued calls for communal reformation.[29] But beginning in the 1660s, their lamentations grew more frequent and more strident, and they were triggered not merely by the finely tuned operations of the Puritan conscience, but by what seemed the irrefutable evidence of decline drawn from current events. But what really made these later jeremiads pierce the

---

[28] Charles Lloyd Cohen provides a sensitive analysis of the stages in the Puritan's progress toward an assurance of salvation in *God's Caress: The Psychology of Puritan Religious Experience* (New York, 1986). Among the many discussions of the content of jeremiads, see Miller, *The New England Mind: From Colony to Province*, ch. 2; Elliott, *Power and the Pulpit*, ch. 3; Bercovitch, *American Jeremiad*; Stout, *New England Soul*, 62–4, 75–7. On the role of introspection in Puritan devotion, see also Charles E. Hambrick-Stowe, *The Practice of Piety: Puritan Devotional Disciplines in Seventeenth-Century New England* (Chapel Hill, N.C., 1982), esp. ch. 6.

[29] Bercovitch, *American Jeremiad*, 6–7; Bozeman, *To Live Ancient Lives*, 309.

hearts of their audiences in a new and far more potent way was not their providentialist interpretation of recent catastrophes so much as it was the predominant image of *generational* decline that informed the sermons' structure of causation.

When preachers addressed the "present" or "rising" generation, they did not employ the term merely as a synonym for the people of their congregations. Nor, fond as they were of biblical typology, did they mean simply to echo scriptural references to the generations of Israel. Instead they deliberately intended to distinguish between two clearly divided biological generations present in their audience. The ministers recognized the years around 1660, when the founders were dying off in increasing numbers, as a genealogical watershed that corresponded only too closely with the providentialist watershed of New England's time of troubles. As Increase Mather bluntly put it, "the first Generation of Christians in New-England, is in a manner gone off the Stage, and there is another and more sinful Generation risen up in their stead."[30]

The pervasive realization that New England society and history were bifurcated by generation gave the jeremiads an organizing principle with which the ministers could explain recent events. The Lord was not so much angry with New England as He was displeased with the worldliness, the apostasy, of its rising generation. The task of the founders had been largely creative, involving the formation of due government for churches and towns, and the Lord had blessed their efforts. But their successors were so obviously incurring divine disfavor that the only reasonable conclusion to be drawn was that they were failing in their mission of preservation and commemoration. Thus the ministers' exhortations to each generation differed, as befitted their unequal roles in precipitating the current crises. The older generation, according to the Reverend Eleazar Mather, needed to "Labour to keep God still with you, even as in dayes of old," to keep alive its "right New-England Spirit," which would wither without constant attention. But their hard-hearted successors,

[30] Mather, *A Call from Heaven to the Present and Succeeding Generations*, 61.

brought up with every spiritual advantage in a godly society "and yet not wrought upon," had no pious past of their own. The younger generation's iniquity tested the Lord's patience and thereby endangered the very covenant that had bound their fathers to Him. "He that hath been with them [the first generation], may leave us," warned Mather, "he that hath been a Saviour in former Generations, may become a wayfaring man[.]"[31]

When he expressed his fear that God "may leave us," Eleazar Mather identified himself as a member of the backsliding second generation. In fact, most of the preachers of jeremiads were the sons of founders, and indeed were often the children of New England's most eminent divines. There is an unmistakably personal note of anxiety in the writings of Increase Mather, Eleazar Mather, Thomas Shepard, Jr., and others who worried that they did not meet the standards of their forebears. But their resort to the generational theme was no simple extrapolation from personal experience; rather, these ministers understood all too well that, in New England as nowhere else, generational affiliation constituted a critically important component of individual identity.

The centrality of generational identity in New England culture, of course, resulted from the unique character of the Great Migration, with its clear division of the emigrant population into distinct generational groups. Most of the adults (who made up a majority of the emigrants) had been born within a fairly narrow span of time, three out of four between 1600 and 1619. Besides the fact of migration, then, adult emigrants shared a common experience of youth during England's most troubled decades prior to the Civil War, which, along with expatriation itself, could only have helped to foster a strong sense of genera-

---

[31] Eleazar Mather, *A Serious Exhortation to the Present and Succeeding Generation in New England*, 14, 27, 6. On the general theme of generational decline, see Elliott, *Power and the Pulpit*, ch. 3. Theodore Dwight Bozeman has recently argued that second-generation spokesmen eventually came to regard the founding era as second in importance only to biblical times in its establishment of a pure Christianity unadulterated by human invention; see *To Live Ancient Lives*, ch. 10.

tional affiliation among them. But their children – the oldest born during the 1620s in England and the youngest later in New England – shared an entirely different experience of settlement, which in turn shaped their sense of themselves as a group in an entirely different way. These sharp lines of generational division, present in the original emigrant population, remained distinct throughout the seventeenth century because so little subsequent immigration occurred (as in the Chesapeake or the West Indies) to blur them.[32]

The key factor here, of course, is experiential more than simply demographic, and the defining experience was voluntary participation in the Great Migration. New England's first generation comprised a cohort of people whose youths had been spent in England when Puritanism seemed threatened as never before and whose early adulthood was shaped by their radical response to that threat: voluntary exile from their homeland. Their transatlantic voyages marked the critical division in their lives – a division absent from the experience of their descendants, who either emigrated as dependents or who were born in New England. The Reverend Eleazar Mather, preaching some thirty years after the Migration had ended, employed maritime metaphors only when addressing the elders in his audience, for in so doing he helped them to recall the critical experience that united them as a generation. "Me thinks I see them [the second generation] like a company of Children in a Boat that is driven out to Sea," he proclaimed, "may be it may come to shore, but [it is] in greater danger to sink or drown then otherwise." He went on to ask his congregation, "What think you of a Vessel at Sea that springs a leak, and takes in water apace, and Marriners some dead, many sick, a few left to keep [the] Pump going, Are they not in danger to sink and perish in the waters? Is it not so here?" Such imagery served

[32] The demographic data are based on dates of birth for 414 emigrants, 260 of whom are defined as adults (born before 1620). Of those 260, 42.3 percent ($N = 110$) were born between 1610 and 1619, and 31.9 percent ($N = 83$) were born between 1600 and 1609, for a total of 74.2 percent ($N = 193$) born between 1600 and 1619.

not only to join the older generation in a common bond of memory but also to exclude the other half of the audience, who had not chosen to sail dangerous seas for the good of their souls.[33]

III

Much of the second generation's crisis of confidence, then, derived precisely from the centrality of the Great Migration in the lives of their parents. The rising generation could only suffer by comparison with their forebears, their collective identity defined in a negative fashion by their lack of such a heroic experience. No matter what their individual spiritual fates might be, no matter what personal agonies of the soul they might suffer, the founders could point to their voluntary emigration from a corrupt England as proof of their corporate piety. Even more compellingly, the events of their times testified that God had smiled on their endeavors. With only a few exceptions – notably the Pequot War and the Antinomian Controversy – the first generation had received little in the way of providential chastisement. As individual families, most of them achieved the modest prosperity that they understood to be a reward for their efforts. As a society, they had succeeded in creating congregations of visible saints and covenanted towns that justified their reputation as God's people.

These accomplishments in establishing the foundations of New England stood in sharp contrast to the troubles besetting the second generation – a contrast delineated in exquisite detail by the worried preachers of jeremiads but also hinted at by some of the founders who survived long enough to witness the passing of their peers. William Bradford, for instance, whose history of Plymouth Colony was no less a personal memoir than an official chronicle, interspersed his narrative with exclamations of concern for Plymouth's future once he and his fel-

---

[33] Mather, *A Serious Exhortation to the Present and Succeeding Generation in New England*, 17.

low founders were gone. Characteristically, Bradford explained that his account of the preparations for the *Mayflower*'s departure was exceptionally detailed so that it could reveal to the younger generation "what difficulties their fathers wrestled [with] in going through these things in their first beginnings; and how God brought them along, notwithstanding all their weaknesses and infirmities." This desire to preserve the story of the founders not just as a chronicle, but as a moral tale for the edification of their children, also informed Bradford's *Dialogue, or the Sum of a Conference between Some Young Men Born in New England and Sundry Ancient Men That Came out of Holland and Old England,* composed in 1648. Here Bradford recorded the questions "young men" posed to "ancient men" concerning the history of the Separatist faith practiced in Plymouth. Their elders had actually lived through the heady days of Separatism's beginnings, and the younger generation prevailed upon them to explain points of theology and "to tell us something of the persons and carriages of other eminent men about those times" before they too were gone from the scene.[34]

Bradford was typically gentle in his efforts to instruct posterity and instill in it an appreciation of the heroic era that the younger generation could only experience vicariously. In a more assertive vein, Edward Johnson composed his *Wonder-Working Providence of Sions Saviour in New England* (1654), the first published history of the Bay Colony. Though addressed to "my honoured Countrey-men" (evidently meaning those in England as well as in Massachusetts) and not specifically to colonial descendants, Johnson's account, with its millenarian overtones, linked New England's humble beginnings to the larger pageant of Christian history. In so doing, he chose (perhaps inevitably) to exalt the role of the founders. How would coming generations measure up to the "forerunners of Christs Army," whose efforts had been so regularly rewarded with "admirable

---

[34] Bradford, *Of Plymouth Plantation,* ed. Morison, 46; see also 62–3; "Gov. Bradford's Dialogue" in Alexander Young, ed., *Chronicles of The Pilgrim Fathers of the Colony of Plymouth, from 1602 to 1625,* 2nd ed. (Boston, 1844; reprinted Baltimore, 1974), 414–58; quote from 444.

Acts of Christs Providence"? Even before the first colonists arrived, according to Johnson, the Lord had cleared the land of its
native inhabitants so that His people might not encounter resis-
tance in their performance of His work. Once settled in New
England, the founding generation continued, by their strenuous efforts in establishing godly towns and churches, to please
the Lord: Thus economic prosperity, material comfort, and the
growth of trade all signified "the wonderful providence of the
most high God toward these his new-planted Churches, such
as was never heard of, since that Jacobs sons ceased to be a
people[.]"[35]
The urge to commemorate New England's origins and record the multiple instances of divine favor also inspired men
less eminent than Governor Bradford or Captain Johnson.
Near the end of his long life, Roger Clap, a Dorchester merchant, composed a memoir explicitly addressed to "his children and Childrens Children," whom he hoped would also
"serve the LORD in their Generations." Like Johnson, Clap
organized his memoirs around the theme of God's "Remarkable Providences." Difficult though the task of settlement had
been, the founders had never lacked for the blessings by
which "God manifest[ed] his Presence among us." In Clap's
version, the early days of the Bay Colony were remembered as
a halcyon era when the saints showed "great Love one to
another; [were] very ready to help each other; *not seeking their
own, but every one another's Wealth.*" In New England's beginnings, Clap continued, in a ringing admonition to posterity,
"Sin did not so openly abound among us[.]"[36]
In their various accounts, then, first-generation writers them-

---

[35] Edward Johnson, *Johnson's Wonder-Working Providence, 1628–1651*, ed. J.
Franklin Jameson, *Original Narratives of Early American History* (New York,
1910), 22, 60–1, 209, and passim.
[36] Roger Clap, "Memoirs of Roger Clap," Dorchester Antiquarian and Historical Society, *Collections* No. 1 (1844), 29. See also John Dane, "John Dane's
Narrative, 1682," *New England Historical and Genealogical Register*, VIII
(1854), 147–56. Dane's record of "remarkable providences" pertains more
to his own life than to New England history, but the implicit message
resembles that of Clap's memoir.

selves began the practice of celebrating the accomplishments of the founders, implicitly or explicitly to the disadvantage of the generations to follow. Yet their narratives differed in important ways from the histories produced by their immediate successors. Because Bradford, Johnson, and Clap in effect all wrote about themselves when they described the founders of New England, they scrupulously sought to avoid the sin of pride, and balanced accounts of their generation's triumphs with frequent acknowledgment of its frailties. Bradford's humility scarcely needs to be demonstrated, but even his less appealing contemporaries were hardly unreserved in their self-congratulation. Johnson, for instance, included detailed descriptions of the Antinomian and other "heresies" that had periodically erupted during New England's first decades. True, his vituperations against Anne Hutchinson (whom he could not even bring himself to mention by name) and Samuel Gorton were anything but eventempered, and he clearly reveled in their departures from the Bay Colony. But his lengthy discussion of their various errors admitted to the machinations of Satan even among the godly in New England, providing an instructive counterpoint to his litany of the "wonder-working providences" by which God blessed His new Israel. In a more personal vein, Roger Clap tempered his advice to posterity with an admission of his generation's fallibility. "And as you ought to follow and imitate good Examples in any godly Men or Women, so especially in your *Parents:* you ought to follow them as they followed Christ, and in nothing else," he wrote. But "Where you have seen them *missing* the Rule, as doubtless you have often done: let them be your *Warnings,* not your Patterns."[37]

This attempt to balance the celebration of the founders' accomplishments with an acknowledgment of their human frailties, however, all but disappeared in the histories of secondgeneration writers – even though these men often drew heavily upon their predecessors' narratives for information. For William

---

[37] Johnson, *Wonder-Working Providence,* ed. Jameson, 121–39, 152–3, 170–6, 222–5, 240–1; Clap, "Memoirs," 48.

Hubbard, New England's first decade constituted a "golden age," its luster scarcely dimmed by religious controversy or the Pequot War. And even as the ambiguity of the founders' legacy diminished, New England's second-generation spokesmen instructed their contemporaries more explicitly than ever in their debt to the first generation. As Nathaniel Morton reminded his readers in 1669, their "present Enjoyments of both outward and spirituall mercies" were the "fruits of their [parents'] Prayers, Tears, Travels and Labours."[38]

Like their predecessors, second-generation chroniclers also structured their narratives around the evidence of divine providence. But in carrying their stories into their own times, they remarked upon the ominous change in the character of that evidence. Whereas their parents had, with few exceptions, enjoyed a succession of blessings, the rising generation could not help but notice that their own days were overshadowed by an unrelieved series of bad tidings. Beginning with his summary for the year 1664, Nathaniel Morton recorded a depressing train of events. Over a period of just five years, New Englanders had witnessed the appearance of a portentous "Blazing-Star or Comet," had seen their wheat crops wither with "the Blast," had learned of the English defeat at the hands of the Catholic French at the island of St. Christopher, had suffered the loss through death of some of their preeminent political and religious leaders, and had seen their land afflicted by violent thunderstorms, drought, and visitations of smallpox. "Let not the familiarness or frequency of such Providences, cause them to be neglected by us," warned Morton, but let us "improve them as God would have us, to fear before him, and to turn from such iniquities especially as are most displeasing unto him." William Hubbard, who carried New England's history forward to 1682, likewise found little consolation in recent develop-

---

[38] Reverend William Hubbard, *A General History of New England, from the Discovery to MDCLXXX* (1682) (New York, 1972; reprinted from the Massachusetts Historical Society, *Collections*, 2nd ser., Vols. 5–6 [1815]), 247; Nathaniel Morton, *New-Englands Memoriall* (1669; reprinted Boston, 1903), from introduction (unpaginated).

ments. To Morton's depressing account he added more "memorable" and "sad" accidents, as well as the catastrophe of King Philip's War.[39]

In these later chronicles of New England the authors treated the deaths of prominent first-generation settlers in a new and telling way. Because so many of the founders had been born within the same decade or two, it was statistically inevitable that their deaths would cluster within a similarly short span of time; indeed, nearly half of the adult male emigrants died between 1670 and 1689.[40] And since over half of all first-generation males had died by 1675, it was precisely during the decade of the 1670s that the younger generation would have been particularly prone to notice the disappearance of their elders. Second-generation writers and preachers simply could not attribute this mortality to natural causes, for all of the other portentous events that coincided with it lent this demographic development a supernatural significance. Ministers began memorializing the lives of prominent founders in sermons, and Nathaniel Morton and William Hubbard scattered similar exemplary biographies throughout their histories. By the time this practice reached its apotheosis in Cotton Mather's *Magnalia Christi Americana*, it had long been embedded in New England's literary culture.

The second-generation writers exalted the lives and achievements of the founders to unprecedented heights, turning New England's founders, both civil and ecclesiastical, into something very much like "wonder-working providences" themselves. The providential character of their lives had two distinct phases. That God had directed such eminent men to settle in New England in the first place was one of many examples of the blessings that showered down in the region's early days.

---

[39] Morton, *New-Englands Memoriall*, 172–97; quotation on 179; Hubbard, *General History of New England*, 571–649.

[40] Of the 111 adult male emigrants (defined as born before 1620) for whom there is information, 50 (45.0 percent) died between 1670 and 1689, with a median date of death of 1674. As noted previously, women tended to die earlier than men; for the thirty-eight adult female emigrants for whom there is information, the median date of death was 1667.

Legacy

John Winthrop, who died in 1649, had, according to William Hubbard, "in those hard times of first planting the wilderness, endeavored to leave to others an unimitable pattern of temperance and frugality" that helped the infant colony to survive and prosper. Similarly, William Bradford was remembered as "the very prop and stay of [Plymouth] Colony during all the whole series of changes that passed over them."[41] Religious leaders were treated with even greater reverence. Morton included a touching anecdote of church elders gathering at the deathbed of the Reverend John Wilson, who had ministered to the Boston congregation for thirty-seven years. The elders sought Wilson's views of the dire events of the time (1667), because the minister had "been from the first a Pillar amongst them, and of much Experience in his observation of the state of things." His death was greeted with much "Lamentation" as the Boston congregation lost one of its few remaining links with the founding generation.[42]

But if the lives and works of eminent men provided irrefutable evidence of God's favor toward New England, the timing of their deaths supplied equally undeniable proof of divine displeasure. William Hubbard made quite plain the message he read in the disappearance of the founders. "The setting of so many bright stars (and some of them of the first magnitude,) in New England's firmament," he wrote, "seemed to presage a sad night of darkness and trouble not unlike ere long to ensue, which, in a great measure, hath since come to pass." Significantly, Hubbard made this observation in his chronicle of the events of 1666 to 1671 – exactly the time when many founders were dying with greater frequency – and appended a list of deceased ministers to buttress his point.[43] Nathaniel Morton

41 Hubbard, *General History of New England*, 519, 555.
42 Morton, *New-Englands Memoriall*, 183; see also 125–9, 131, 135–9, 153–5, 164–8, 181. On the memorialization of the founders, see also David M. Scobey, "Revising the Errand: New England's Ways and the Puritan Sense of the Past," *WMQ*, 3rd ser., XLI (1984), 22–4; Hambrick-Stowe, *Practice of Piety*, 246–56.
43 Hubbard, *General History of New England*, 603–7.

207

drew the same implications from the deaths of prominent pastors: "This Year [1668] it pleased God to visit *New-England* with the manifestation of his displeasure, by the death of three Eminent Instruments," the Reverends Samuel Shepard, Henry Flint, and Jonathan Mitchell.[44]

Colonists living through the generational transition of these decades likewise listened to sermons that expounded an idealized image of the founders. The Reverend Increase Mather described them as "in a degree, Martyrs of Jesus," or "*Davids, that is to say eminent Reformers.*" The Reverend William Hubbard declared that "Our Fore-Fathers . . . were made to see Gods Salvation" because of their persistence in hewing to godly ways. Though these sermons scarcely consigned the younger generation to damnation for its various failures, and did not overwhelm the ministers' regular Sabbath exhortations to renew their piety, the fact remains that the principal attempts to outline the providential history of New England during this period describe a sharp generational division that in fact existed in the society but that was interpreted in such a way as to minimize the godly exertions of the younger generation.[45]

---

[44] Morton, *New-Englands Memoriall*, 190. Shepard and Flint actually belonged to the second generation; nevertheless, Morton's preoccupation with the deaths of founders is evident in the fact that he simply mentioned those two men but included a lengthy biography and two elegiac poems dedicated to the memory of the first-generation minister Jonathan Mitchell; see 190–6.

[45] Increase Mather, *Pray for the Rising Generation, or a Sermone Wherein Godly Parents are Encouraged, to Pray and Believe for Their Children,* . . . (Cambridge, Mass., 1678), 18; Mather, *A Call from Heaven to the Present and Succeeding Generations,* 56; William Hubbard, *The Benefit of a Well-Ordered Conversation,* . . . (Boston, 1684), 93; see also Increase Mather, *The Life and Death of That Reverend Man of God, Mr. Richard Mather, Teacher of the Church in Dorchester in New England* (Cambridge, Mass., 1670). For a detailed explication of the sermons of this period, see also Elliott, *Power and the Pulpit,* 89–92, 99–105, 113–72. Harry Stout, in *New England Soul*, makes the important point that the jeremiads invoking the myth of the founders were almost exclusively occasional sermons, delivered much less frequently than the regular Sabbath sermons that dealt with themes of personal piety and salvation. Nevertheless, he also notes that the jeremiads constituted the ministers'

Legacy

So long as the hallmark of the first generation was its participation in the Great Migration and the founding of New England, its successors could only suffer by comparison. Even as the children of the founders inherited their farms and lived lives of modest comfort virtually indistinguishable from those of their parents, they were repeatedly chastised – on the one hand, for worldliness, and on the other, for failing to recognize that they owed their material comfort to the labors of their parents. Although the second generation of settlers had toiled on those farms themselves since childhood, the critical "foundation work" had been accomplished by their predecessors. It took no great leap of imagination for younger settlers listening to paeans describing the founders to understand that inimitable group to include not just eminent divines and political leaders but also their own parents. They too had emigrated and, by virtue of their creation of new towns and churches, they too had been founders of New England.

Similarly, although there was no significant decline in church attendance, the younger generation heard itself roundly criticized for a lack of piety. Much of this criticism was provoked by a decrease in the number of conversions and the corresponding reduction in the number of full church members – in other words, by the circumstances that had occasioned the Halfway Covenant. What contemporaries could not have recognized, because to them it seemed to be just one ominous trend among so many others, was that the decrease in conversions was in large part a temporary consequence of the region's distinctive demographic structure. Since most of the first-generation settlers had been born within the first two decades of the seventeenth century, most of their children were born roughly between 1630 and 1660. In the normal course of life, these second-generation colonists would mostly have sought membership themselves in their mid-twenties or early thirties – roughly during the period 1655 to 1685. Thus the fall-off in

principal efforts to describe the history of New England and account for recent troubled times; see 68–82.

209

conversions that precipitated the calling of the Halfway Synod of 1662 would probably have been reversed, at least in part, merely with the passage of time.[46]

Actual conversions did not, of course, follow a precise demographic timetable, since conversion was a spiritual experience and not simply a ritual attending the attainment of maturity.[47] Other factors intervened to affect the pace of each worshiper's spiritual progress toward full membership. Debates over the Halfway Covenant itself, for instance, and the variable timing of its acceptance by different congregations inevitably impinged upon rates of conversion. But none of this indicated that the root of the problem lay in the impiety of the younger generation, as contemporary commentators insisted. In fact, the opposite may have been true: In some congregations where the Halfway Covenant had been adopted, many younger settlers refused to avail themselves of its provisions, preferring instead to adhere to the old procedures, even though it meant postponing their children's entrance into the church.[48]

Excessive scrupulosity in examining their souls for evidence of the workings of grace may also have delayed second-generation believers' applications for full church membership. Those who had, in their youth, listened to their elders relate the circumstances of their own conversions could hardly help but recall how prominently the Great Migration had figured in their narratives. Emigrants often considered the decision to leave England as a watershed in their spiritual as well as secular lives, a testament to their striving after godliness. Ministers likewise described the believer's spiritual pilgrimage with reference to the first generation's actual experience of travel. If this was the narrative model that the succeeding generation tried to apply to their own experience, it is no wonder that their spiritual prog-

---

[46] For ages at conversion and a discussion of the cyclical changes in church membership, see Gerald F. Moran, "Religious Renewal, Puritan Tribalism, and the Family in Seventeenth-Century Milford, Connecticut," *WMQ*, 3rd ser., XXXVI (1979), 236–54; see also Pope, *The Half-Way Covenant*, Appendix.

[47] This is a point noted by Charles Cohen in *God's Caress*, 14–15.

[48] Pope, *The Half-Way Covenant*, 215–16, 226–8.

ress seemed stunted by comparison and wholly insufficient to qualify them for church membership.[49]

In the end, external crises – most notably King Philip's War and the disruptions accompanying the formation and dissolution of the Dominion of New England during the 1680s – may have served the same function for the second generation that the migration did for the first. These events sparked a collective spiritual crisis in New England, which in turn eventually contributed to a widespread adoption of the Halfway Covenant and a corresponding rise in the number of conversions.[50] The new generation had inevitably to reorient its attention and its sense of corporate identity with reference to New England. By the end of the century, the pressure of contemporary events, the disappearance of nearly all of the founders, and the younger generation's attenuated ties with the England that had loomed so large in their parents' lives all demanded such a change of focus.[51]

Even as English officials sought to tie New Englanders more closely to an imperial system through mercantilist legislation and administrative oversight of colonial affairs, most ordinary colonists were losing personal touch with the home country. Many of them maintained sporadic contact with their English relatives, but second-generation settlers counted most of their close kin among fellow inhabitants of New England. Their parents had often left brothers and sisters behind when they emigrated, but members of the younger generation had virtually all of their siblings nearby. And as these younger settlers married, they multiplied their ties within the New England population at the very time that their connections with English relatives

[49] Patricia Caldwell, *The Puritan Conversion Narrative: The Beginnings of American Expression* (Cambridge, 1983), 26–30, 119–34; Hambrick-Stowe, *Practice of Piety*, 69–72, 243.

[50] On the religious revival toward the end of the seventeenth century, see Pope, *The Half-Way Covenant*, 185–205, 271–5. The increase in conversions may also have partly been the result of the maturing of the second generation.

[51] Robert Middlekauff, *The Mathers: Three Generations of Puritan Intellectuals, 1596–1728* (New York, 1971), ch. 6; Hambrick-Stowe, *Practice of Piety*, ch. 8.

(whom they either had never met or could scarcely have remembered) diminished.[52]

Similarly, many colonists gradually relinquished family property located in England. If some early settlers had retained English land as a hedge against possible failure in the colonies, time and the achievement of competency evidently eased their minds. Some simply sold the property during their lifetimes, and others disposed of it in their wills. Comfort Starr and Walter Haynes, for example, conveyed such property to children who had stayed in England. Others bequeathed English land to New England descendants, less out of sentimental attachment to ancestral estates than from practical concerns: Their children (or, in several cases, their grandchildren) could use the rental income from it to supplement their colonial incomes. There was apparently no expectation that heirs would actually return to England to live on the land. Good intentions to the contrary notwithstanding, however, distance from England and difficulties of communication frequently undermined such prudent financial arrangements. Edward Johnson, for instance, directed that a portion of the income from his Kentish farm – £6 per year – go toward the support of his widow, Susannah. When she died eighteen years later, back rents amounting to £108 were due to the estate from English tenants who doubtless counted themselves lucky to have so distant a landlord. Such problems of collection were surely common knowledge and probably influenced Joseph Tilden's disposition of his father Nathaniel's English property. By virtue of his father's will, Joseph retained the right to sell Nathaniel's Kentish estate – and evidently did so, applying the proceeds to his agricultural and commercial activities in Scituate.[53]

[52] David Cressy describes the efforts of colonists to keep in touch with English relatives, noting that such contacts had inevitably decreased by the time the second generation reached maturity; see *Coming over: Migration and Communication between England and New England in the Seventeenth Century* (Cambridge, 1987), ch. 11.

[53] For evidence of colonists holding English property, see Cressy, *Coming over*, ch. 7; two of the settlers he mentions as having sold their English land

Legacy

The relinquishing of property that afforded them more problems than income, like the weakening of ties with relatives they barely knew, were parts of a larger process whereby second-generation settlers began to order their lives on their own terms, rather than on those dictated by the experience of their parents. Their ability to assess impartially their accomplishments as a generation, however, was sorely hampered by the powerful cultural dynamic that operated to diminish their efforts. That the creation of that dynamic was in large part fortuitous was of little consolation, for contemporaries could never have understood it as such. Examining the events of their time through the lens of providentialism, the culture's clerical spokesmen discerned a pattern that admitted of only one interpretation. That the crises of the second half of the seventeenth century proclaimed God's displeasure with His

fairly early – Augustine Clement and William Moulton – are emigrants included in the present study; see 186, 187. Walter Haynes left his Dorset property to his daughter and son-in-law, who were apparently living there; see Middlesex County Probate Records, docket no. 10939. In 1660 Comfort Starr divided his English property between two children then resident in England: his daughter Hannah, who was in New England two years later, and his son Comfort, Jr. The younger Comfort had emigrated with his parents in 1635, graduated from Harvard College in 1647, and returned to England in 1650 as a minister in Carlisle. Ejected from his living by the Act of Uniformity in 1662, he ended up as a dissenting preacher in Lewes, Sussex, where he died in 1711. The will of Comfort, Sr., is in the Suffolk County Probate Records, docket no. 233; genealogical information for the family is in Cornelia Bartow Williams, *Ancestry of Lawrence Williams* (Chicago, 1915), 273–5; John L. Sibley, *Biographical Sketches of Those Who Attended Harvard College*, 14 vols. (Cambridge, 1873–1968), I, 162. Those who retained English land for its rental income usually held property worth between £100 and £300. Edward Johnson's will is in the Middlesex County Probate Records, docket no. 12644; Susannah Johnson's inventory is docket no. 12763. Others who bequeathed rental income from English property include Thomas Besbeech (Middlesex County Probate Records, docket no. 1476), Peter Noyes (Middlesex County Probate Records, docket no. 16074), and Joseph Parker (Essex County Probate Records, docket no. 20520). Nathaniel Tilden's will is printed in *Mayflower Descendant*, vol. 3 (1901), 220–2. Joseph Tilden's will and inventory, which make no mention of English property, are in the Plymouth County Probate Records, Vol. 3, Pt. 1, 6–8.

New England Israel was a point beyond dispute; that they occurred so precisely when a new generation – more identifiable in New England than anywhere else in the world – was taking control left little doubt about who was to blame. Thus was the rhetoric of declension – expounded by a numerous ministry educated at a single institution and preserved in print in what was one of the most self-consciously literate societies of its time – embedded in New England culture. Created at a time when rhetoric and reality seemed to fit so closely together, it would endure – albeit in altered form – long after the conditions that had given it birth had passed from the scene.

IV

The final decade of the seventeenth century witnessed the unraveling of much of the fabric of the New England Way. In Massachusetts, the new charter of 1691 upset the careful balance of religious and social authority that Winthrop and his contemporaries had created. The Congregationalist faith of the founders lost its exclusive hold on the colony's spiritual life, and although their church would long retain preeminence as the province's establishment, Congregationalists found they had suddenly become members of just one of several Protestant sects (including the despised Quakers) whose adherents were permitted to worship freely. Church membership was no longer a prerequisite for exercising the franchise, and the welfare of the commonwealth was thus indiscriminately delivered into the hands of the unregenerate, provided only that they owned property. The governor of the Bay Colony ceased to function as the freely elected head of a godly magistracy, responsible for maintaining the people's special relationship with the Lord; rather than God's representative, he became the king's, and necessarily a man more attentive to royal preferment than to godliness. In both Connecticut (which managed to retain its elective governorship) and Massachusetts, the founders' plan of communal land distribution crumbled as a new set of leaders, anticipating English interference with colonial practice, began distributing land to individuals or groups of proprietors, who then sold, rather than granted, land in new towns to prospective inhabitants. And even as these sweeping changes altered the founders' arrangements in the Bay Colony and Connecticut, William Bradford's beloved Plymouth simply disappeared, absorbed by its larger and more influential neighbor to the north.[54]

Worldliness – a constant complaint in the jeremiads of the 1660s and 1670s – more accurately described the condition of many colonists in the 1690s and early 1700s than it did those of earlier decades. Changes in the land distribution system provided unprecedented opportunities for speculation, and disputes between proprietors and inhabitants without rights to undivided lands increased.[55] In Boston and Salem, prosperous merchants sought more than ever to live lives of high fashion, emulating the English gentry as best they could.[56] Moreover, New England's participation in King William's War, the first in a series of conflicts with France in the New World, forced colony leaders to raise taxes to unprecedented heights; ordinary colonists, whether they wanted to or not, were compelled to pay greater attention both to the state of the empire and to the state of their pocketbooks.[57]

[54] David S. Lovejoy, *The Glorious Revolution in America* (New York, 1972), 340–53; T. H. Breen, *The Character of the Good Ruler: Puritan Political Ideas in New England, 1630–1730* (New Haven, Conn., 1970), 181–202; Richard L. Bushman, *From Puritan to Yankee: Character and the Social Order in Connecticut, 1690–1765* (Cambridge, Mass., 1967), 40–53; John Frederick Martin, "Entrepreneurship and the Founding of New England Towns: The Seventeenth Century" (Ph.D. diss., Harvard University, 1985), 479–87. On the challenge posed by the events of the turn of the eighteenth century to New England's sense of identity, see also Bruce Tucker, "The Reinvention of New England, 1691–1770," *NEQ*, LIX (1986), esp. 317–22.

[55] Martin, "Entrepreneurship and the Founding of New England Towns," 485–93, 554–85; Bushman, *From Puritan to Yankee*, 47–53.

[56] Bernard Bailyn, *The New England Merchants in the Seventeenth Century* (Cambridge, 1955), 192–7; Paul Boyer and Stephen Nissenbaum, *Salem Possessed: The Social Origins of Witchcraft* (Cambridge, 1974), 86–9.

[57] T. H. Breen, *Puritans and Adventurers: Change and Persistence in Early America* (New York, 1980), ch. 5.

But these social and political changes provoked nothing like the cultural critique of previous years. Warnings about declension diminished in frequency and importance within a larger sermon literature invoking confidence in New England's survival through difficult times. Prominent ministers actually celebrated the new Massachusetts charter, in part because many had feared a worse outcome from the highly politicized deliberations in the English court. As they reached the ends of their lives, second-generation leaders at last emerged from the shadow of opprobrium cast by the jeremiads of an earlier era to be praised as faithful preservers of New England's culture.[58]

This more generous interpretation of New England's circumstances stemmed not from a growing indifference to the ideals of the founders, but from the changing context within which those ideals were understood. In part, the events of the Glorious Revolution and its aftermath – developments none of the founders could have anticipated – tied the colonies (especially Massachusetts) more closely to the imperial network and required pragmatic accommodation to such new political realities as religious toleration and royal governorship. Even more important, however, the precise conditions under which the earlier rhetoric of declension had been devised no longer obtained. True, New Englanders of 1700, no less than those of 1660, fell prey to the many sins of which humans will always be guilty. But the public and private evils of the time could no longer be harnessed effectively to create a compelling *generational* critique. Without this powerful and highly personalized organizing theme, so dominant in the jeremiads of an earlier period, subsequent attempts to employ the language of decline had more the character of incantation than of exhortation.

To a considerable extent, the weakening of the generational theme reflected an increasingly indistinct sense of generational identification in the population at large. Seventeenth-century generations could be defined according to two criteria: birth cohort and voluntary participation – or lack of it – in the Great

[58] Elliott, *Power and the Pulpit*, ch. 5; Stout, *New England Soul*, 115–23.

216

Migration. But by 1700, the second point was moot (since virtually all the original emigrants were dead) and the first nearly so, since rapid population growth had so expanded the range of the third-generation cohort as to include people born any time from around 1660 to the early eighteenth century. Such an extended temporal range for this and succeeding cohorts hampered efforts to find meaningful links between portentous contemporary events and the simultaneous transfer of authority from one generation to the next.

Once the Great Migration ceased to function as the critical event identifying New England's generations, its significance was subtly, powerfully transformed. New interpreters saw the Great Migration no longer as living experience but rather as the preeminent event in forming the region's collective historical identity. Building upon the rhetoric of their forebears, these commentators constructed a full-blown myth of the founding of New England. With their various accounts of the early "golden age," the second generation had begun the process, but their purpose had been more didactic than commemorative. By recording their own decline from the standards of the founders, second-generation spokesmen had hoped to spur their contemporaries to reverse the trend and regain New England's first purity. But by the early eighteenth century, a third generation of preachers, lacking personal acquaintance with the people about whom they were writing, recounted the glories of the founding era, not so much as a benchmark from which to measure subsequent decline, but as a shared myth of origins in which they could all take pride.

A century after the founding of New England, ministers who were the grandsons and great-grandsons of the eminent divines of the Migration emphasized the vitality of New England's historic covenant with the Lord and celebrated their connection with the founders who had first undertaken that solemn commitment. But because the founding era had grown so remote, and because they were compelled to adapt their cultural interpretations to a changed New England, preachers could – without any sense of irony – juxtapose praise of the founders and commendation of current political arrangements that had in fact dismantled much of the founders' work. Thus, in his sermon commemorating the centenary of Massachusetts's founding, the Reverend Thomas Prince included both their descent from "pious ancestors" and their present rule by "the illustrious House of Hanover" as "distinguishing advantages" of eighteenth-century New Englanders. Reverend Prince even suggested that "had there been then [in 1630] a succession of such indulgent princes and bishops in England as there have since the Prince of Orange ascended the throne" – a dynastic succession, it is worth remembering, that enforced toleration and subjected the Puritans' English brethren to a variety of legal disabilities for their beliefs – the founders would never have needed to leave England. Likewise, Prince and other preachers extolled the teamwork of first-generation ministers and magistrates in establishing pure churches and upholding God's holy ordinances, and exhorted their audiences to imitate their ancestors, even as the provisions of the new charter prevented the formation of such an alliance.[59]

Like their predecessors, these sermons celebrating the founders as paragons of piety invited comparisons to the present generation, and once again, ministers found evidence of declension in their own time. Their exhortations, however, seemed at most pale imitations of earlier jeremiads. Instead of reciting a litany of evil ways to focus his message, the Reverend Thomas Foxcroft, in a sermon commemorating the centenary of Boston's First Church, concluded with only a general complaint about "the Apostasies of this degenerate Day." Thomas Prince, in his centenary election sermon, also lamented "our great and dangerous declensions" but, instead of enlarging upon the

---

[59] Thomas Prince, *The People of New-England Put in Mind of the Righteous Acts of the Lord to Them and Their Fathers, and Reasoned with Concerning Them* (Boston, 1730), quotations from 35, 24; see also Thomas Foxcroft, *Observations Historical and Practical on the Rise and Primitive State of New-England, with a Special Reference to the Old or First Gathered Church in Boston* (Boston, 1730). For a general discussion of the context of third-generation preaching, see Stout, *New England Soul*, 127–81.

theme with specific reference to his own time, contented himself with citing jeremiads from second-generation ministers.
When his sermon was later published, he sought to strengthen
his case by including as an appendix not a list of current sins,
but an extract of William Stoughton's election sermon of 1668.
The theme of declension had become a requisite part of any
sermon dealing with New England's special history, but its gen-
eralized application severely reduced its potency as an instru-
ment of exhortation.[60]

Ministers such as Foxcroft and Prince could not have revived
the distinctive message of earlier jeremiads even if they had
wanted to. That message had been rooted in a particular time
and set of circumstances that had passed away. When second-
generation audiences were reminded of their backsliding, they
had direct knowledge of the people whose standards they were
failing to uphold. Accusations of worldliness and impiety had
for them a greater immediacy than they would carry for posterity because they had lived, if only as children, in the world their
parents (with the Lord's help) had made. And only they would
suffer the peculiar misfortune of assuming control, as an identifiable generational group, at precisely the time when virtually
every event seemed to challenge their efforts to claim and to
preserve their cultural inheritance.

The third generation thus tempered the theme of declension
even as they magnified the story of the Great Migration. It was
no longer a historic but rather an epic event: a foundation myth
that enabled them, as descendants of the founders, to celebrate
their forebears' achievements as prologue to their own special
(albeit attenuated) relationship to the God of their fathers. New
England thus became the only region of British North America
to fashion and to preserve an enduring myth of its own origins.
It succeeded in large part because the original migration, being
relatively short-lived, lent coherence to what in other colonies

[60] Foxcroft, *Observations Historical and Practical*, 39–42; Prince, *The People of
New-England*, 36–40, appendix. As Stout points out, in times of warfare,
the rhetoric of declension and divine judgment was revitalized; see *New
England Soul*, 144–7.

was a much more ungainly process of settlement. The religious sympathies of the bulk of the settlers likewise provided a unifying theme. But most important, only New England had, from its earliest days, a cadre of clerical spokesmen and a college dedicated to the production of their successors: men not only capable of interpreting the facts of history and current events within a compelling providentialist framework, but committed to instructing each rising generation in the story of its ancestors.

Like all enduring myths, that of New England's founding generation proved to be remarkably flexible. A century after Thomas Prince celebrated both the resemblance of the emigrants to the people of Israel and the blessings of George II's rule, another commentator would be able to discern in the founders a prototype of the revolutionary generation that threw off the oppressions of George III's tyranny.[61] Thus the region of British North America that accepted the smallest number of emigrants, that had, in the most literal sense, the least plausible claim to a "Great Migration," produced a disproportionately influential cultural legacy. Ironically, what allowed this founding myth to endure, even to the point of being absorbed into a national mythology that the founders could never have foreseen, was precisely that part of the story that it left out. Gone were the ordinary settlers – the pious Tildens, the industrious Emerys, the hapless Gaults, the unruly Nickersons –whose collective efforts at transplantation and survival provided the mundane foundation upon which the mythic story could be superimposed. The indispensable and unspectacular activities of average settlers wrestling with the decision to emigrate, enduring a frightening voyage, forming new towns and churches, and laboring for the competencies that would support their families created in England's least promising colonial region precisely the sort of stable, cohesive society capable of sustain-

---

[61] Prince, *The People of New-England*, 21; Edward Everett, *An Address Delivered on the 28th of June, 1830, the Anniversary of the Arrival of Governor Winthrop at Charlestown* (Boston, 1830), 34–5.

ing a myth about itself. Such settlers would scarcely have recognized their New England in the embellished accounts of their descendants. But they would doubtless have been gratified to know that their numerous posterity could perceive in their humble efforts a transcendent meaning.

Appendix

Table 1 *Distribution of ages of New England emigrants*

Age (in years)	N	%
0–10	98	23.7
11–20	102	24.7
21–30	102	24.7
31–40	71	17.2
41–50	29	7.0
51–60	10	2.5
61–70	1	0.2
Total	413	100.0

Table 2 *Age structure of the emigrant population and England's population in 1636*

	New England emigrants		English population, 1636
Age (in years)	N	%	%
0–4	48	11.62	12.40
5–14	81	19.61	19.73
15–24	108	26.15	17.72
25–59	172	41.65	42.03
60+	4	00.97	08.12
Total	413	100.00	100.00

Source for English figures: Wrigley and Schofield, *Population History of England*, Table A3.1, 528.

Table 3 *Sex ratio for New England emigrants*

	N	%
Male	386	56.8
Female	293	43.2
Total	679	100.0

Note: Sex ratio = 132.

Table 4 *The structure of household groups among New England emigrants*

Categories	Classes	Without servants	With servants	Total	%	No. of emigrants in each group category	
Solitaries	Widowed	2	0	2 ⎤	38.0	2	11.0%
	Single/unknown marital status	56	5	61 ⎦		73	
No family	Coresident siblings	3	0	3 ⎤	2.4	6	1.2%
	Coresident relatives of other kinds	1	0	1 ⎦		2	
Simple family households	Married couples, alone	4	6	10 ⎤		36	
	Married couples, with children	32	42	74	54.8	462	79.4%
	Husband with children	1	3	4		28	
	Wife with children	0	1	1		8	
	Widow with children	2	0	2 ⎦		6	
Extended family households	Extended laterally 1. Brothers	2	1	3 ⎤		18	
	2. Other kin	2	0	2		16	
	Combinations 1. Nuclear family and servant's family	0	1	1	4.8	7	8.4%
	2. Nuclear family with others of unknown relationship	1	0	1		10	
	3. Brothers and families with mother	0	1	1 ⎦		6	
Total number of groups				166	100.0	680	100.0% (Total number of emigrants in all groups)

Note: This table is modeled on that in Peter Laslett, *Family life and illicit love in earlier generations* (Cambridge, 1977), 96–7.

Appendix

Table 5 *Distribution of households in England and New England*

| No. of children | Groups with this no. of children | | No. of children in groups of this size | | |
| | New England | | New England | | Sample of 100 English parishes |
	N	%	N	%	%
1	14	16.1	14	5.2	11.2
2	25	28.7	50	18.7	18.4
3	17	19.5	51	19.0	23.1
4	13	14.9	52	19.4	18.1
5	12	13.8	60	22.4	13.4
6	2	2.3	12	4.5	7.7
7+	4	4.7	29	10.8	7.2
Total	87	100.0	268	100.0	99.1

Source for English figures: Laslett, "Mean household size," in Laslett and Wall, eds., *Household and Family in Past Time*, 148.

Table 6 *Occupational distribution of adult male emigrants*

Category	N	%
Agriculture	47	33.8
Cloth trades	35	25.2
Other artisans	46	33.1
Trade	3	2.2
Maritime	3	2.2
Professional	5	3.6
Total	139	100.1

Appendix

Table 7 Timing of ship departures for New England

	Winthrop		Banks	
	N	%	N	%
January–February	0	0	1	1
March–April	20	65	49	56
May–June	4	13	24	28
July–August	5	16	9	10
September–October	1	3	3	3
November–December	1	3	1	1
Total	31	100	87	99

Sources: Winthrop, History of New England, ed. Savage, passim; Banks, Planters of the Commonwealth, passim.

Table 8 Ages at death of adult emigrants to New England

	Men			Women		
Age (in years)	N	%	Cum. %	N	%	Cum. %
30–39	1	1.2	1.2	2	5.9	5.9
40–49	5	5.9	7.1	4	11.8	17.7
50–59	15	17.6	24.7	7	20.6	38.3
60–69	13	15.3	40.0	7	20.6	58.9
70–79	31	36.5	76.5	8	23.5	82.4
80–89	20	23.5	100.0	5	14.7	97.1
90–99	0	0.0	100.0	1	2.9	100.0
Total	85			34		

Median: 71 years   Median: 67 years

Appendix

Table 9 *Relation of age at migration to age at death*

Age at migration (in years)	Men Avg. age at death		Women Avg. age at death	
	N	(in years)	N	(in years)
10–19	1	63.0	0	–
20–29	26	68.9	9	62.7
30–39	29	71.0	16	61.1
40–49	19	71.0	5	75.6
50–59	9	66.8	4	71.5
60–69	1	64.0	0	–
Total	85		34	

Table 10 *Completed family sizes of men who emigrated as household heads*

Number of children	No. of families with this no. of children	Percent of families with this no. of children
3	2	5.1
4	2	5.1
5	5	12.8
6	4	10.3
7	8	20.5
8	5	12.8
9	4	10.3
10	2	5.1
11	3	7.7
12	2	5.1
13	0	0.0
14	1	2.6
15	0	0.0
16	1	2.6
Total	39	100.0

Note: This table includes only those families in which the same husband and wife survived for the duration of the wife's reproductive years.

Index

Index

Cooper, Elizabeth, 62, 64
coopers, 145, 147
Corwin, George, 170
Cottle, William, 155
Cotton, John, 86–7
covenants, 95, 128, 190, 195, 197, 199, 217
Cromwell, Philip, 170
currency, scarcity of, 131, 145, 164–5
Curtis, Zacheus, 106, 118

Dane, John, 41–2
death, of founders, 179–81, 182, 191, 198, 205, 206, 207–8, 225, 226
declension, rhetoric of, 178–9, 195–9, 204–8, 216, 218–19; see also New England, generational crisis
Dedham (Mass.), 97–8, 140, 147, 185
deeds of gift, 186–7
Dickerson, Philemon, 113–14, 142n
diet
  on voyage, 55–7
  in New England, 152, 156n, 164
dissidents, religious, 118–22, 190, 192; see also Quakers
Dix, Samuel, 33n
Dixson, Rachel, 21
Doggett, Thomas, 111n, 118
Dominion of New England, 211
Dorchester (Mass.), 97, 111, 186, 203
Dover (N. H.), 119
Dow, Henry, 51, 104, 154
Downing, Emmanuel, 38, 43
Dudley, Thomas, 37, 38, 44, 196
Duxbury (Mass.), 113, 119, 147

Eden, Alice, 101
Emery, Alice, 13
Emery, Anthony, 13, 119, 122
Emery, Frances, 13
Emery, John, 13, 42, 52, 144, 146, 186
Emery, Jonathan, 186
emigrants, to New England, 4, 6–8, 9, 17, 18–36
  demographic profile, 19–21, 222, 223
  economic status, in England, 33–4
  English origins, 5, 28–31
  family groups, 21–3, 223, 224
  motivation, 8, 18, 26–7, 34–7, 37–46
  occupational profile, 31–2, 224
  servants, 24–5
  social homogeneity, 34–5

emigrants, to other British colonies, 15, 19
emigration
  cost of, 33–4
  timing of, 5
entrepreneurialism, in New England, 94–5, 152–4
estates, in New England
  contents, 162–5, 167–8, 170, 171
  size and value, 162, 162n, 169, 170, 171
Ewell, Henry, 24
exports, from New England, 132–3, 152, 154

families, 72, 183, 190
  among emigrants, 21–3, 26, 42, 223
  size of, 22–3, 182–3, 182n, 224, 226
  and land distribution, 95–7, 98
  migration within New England, 107–8
  and competency, 124–5, 147–8, 190–1
  and labor, 157–8, 171, 187–90
  see also inheritance; kinship; patriarchalism
farmers, 30, 32, 140, 141, 146, 149–60; see also agriculture
Felmingham, Francis, 62
flax, 135–6
Flint, Henry, 208
Foxcroft, Thomas, 218, 219
franchise, 172–3, 214
freeholdership, in New England, 93–4, 96, 124, 125, 172

Gault, Mary, 170
Gault, William, 15, 52, 115, 169, 171, 175
Gedney, John, 33n, 115, 139, 170
General Court (Mass.), 91, 93, 102, 132, 134, 136, 143, 144, 146, 157, 177
General Court (Plymouth), 126–7
generation
  demographic definition, 199–200, 206, 209–10, 216–17
  meaning of, in New England, 179, 198–203, 208, 214, 216–17, 219
gentlemen, 125
Glorious Revolution, 216
Gloucester (Mass.), 106
Goodenow, Ursula, 22
Goodens, Adam, 41, 101, 107
Gorton, Samuel, 118, 204
grandparents, 21, 184

228

Index

Index

life expectancy
  in England, 12, 12n, 181n
  in New England, 180–2, 181n
Lincoln, Samuel, 22
Lincoln, Stephen, 22
Lincoln, Thomas, 22
Little Neptune (ship), 58–9
livestock, 30, 63, 135, 150, 151–2, 154–6, 158, 162, 165; *see also* cattle; sheep
London, 27, 29n, 66, 141, 192
longevity
  of founders, 11, 180–1, 183
  of second generation, 181–2
Ludkin, William, 33n, 52, 141

Maine, 119
maize, 150–1, 153, 156
market exchange, in New England, 152–5, 165
market towns, 28–9
Marlborough (Wilts.), 104
Mary Anne (ship), 4n, 33n, 62, 67, 104n, 116, 142n, 170
Mason, Emme, 170–1, 175
Massachusetts Bay Colony, 7, 40, 121, 172, 214–15, 216, 218
Massachusetts Bay Company, 56, 60, 61, 66, 90
Mather, Cotton, 206
Mather, Eleazer, 196, 198–9, 200
Mather, Increase, 180, 182, 198, 199, 208
Mather, Richard, 57, 65, 74, 78, 79, 80, 82, 83–4, 86
Mayflower (ship), 202
Medfield, 148, 185
merchants, 115, 129, 132, 164, 166, 167, 168–9, 176, 203, 215
Metcalf, Elizabeth, 185
Metcalf, Jane, 185
Metcalf, Michael, 29n, 33n, 40, 140, 174, 184, 185
migration
  marital, 184–5
  within England, 26–8
  within New England, 8, 9, 92–3, 99–100, 103, 103n, 104–7, 107n, 108–14, 117–22, 124–8, 129–30
ministers, 18, 18n, 86, 119–20, 177–9, 180, 193–4, 195–9, 201, 206, 210, 216, 217n, 219, 220
Mitchell, Jonathan, 208

mobility; *see* migration
Monomoit, 118, 126–7
Morse, Anthony, 52, 104, 112–13, 186
Morse, Benjamin, 186
Morse, William, 104, 112–13
mortality
  at sea, 47, 57–8, 76
  childhood, 12, 182
Morton, Nathaniel, 205–6, 207–8
Moulton, Anne, 72n, 100–2, 104, 107
Moulton, Henry, 107–8
Moulton, John, 51, 72n, 100–3, 104, 107
Moulton, John, Jr., 72n, 108
Moulton, William, 213n
Muddy River, 116

Nantucket, 135
Neave, Margaret, 21, 41
New England, 1–4, 190–1
  descriptions of, 35–6, 43–4
  economy of, 131–3, 145–9, 152–6, 160
  founding myth, 11, 201–10, 217–21
  generational crisis, 179, 191–211, 213–14, 216, 219
  population growth, 132, 181–3, 217
New Hampshire, 7
New Haven, 7, 104, 113, 172
New Jersey, 155
New York, 155
Newbury (Mass.), 101–2, 104, 113, 119, 122n, 125, 146, 147, 154, 165, 186
Nickerson, Anne, 13–14, 42
Nickerson, Robert, 14
Nickerson, William, 14, 33n, 118, 126–7
Norwich, 13, 27, 28, 29, 29n, 40, 41, 51, 116, 117, 139, 140
Nowell, Increase, 67
Noyes, Peter, 41, 49, 50, 51, 51n, 125, 213n

occupations
  adaptation in New England, 144–9, 149–60
  change from English, 10, 115, 133, 137–42
  continuation of English, 142–4, 149
  in England, 31–2
  see also artisans; farmers; *specific trades*
Oliver, Mary, 41
Oliver, Thomas, 33n, 41

230

Index

Index